The Illustrated Atlas of the World's

GREAT
BUILDINGS

A History of World Architecture
From the Classical Perfection of the Parthenon to the
Breathtaking Grandeur of the Skyscraper

The Illustrated Atlas of the World's

GREAT BUILDINGS

A History of World Architecture
From the Classical Perfection of the Parthenon to the
Breathtaking Grandeur of the Skyscraper

Philip Bagenal and Jonathan Meades

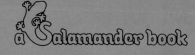

a Salamander book

Published by Salamander Books Limited
LONDON

A Salamander Book

Published by Salamander Books Ltd,
Salamander House
27 Old Gloucester Street
London WC1N 3AF
United Kingdom

© Salamander Books Ltd 1980

ISBN 0 86101 059 0

Distributed in the United Kingdom by New English Library Ltd

All correspondence concerning the content of this volume should be addressed to Salamander Books Ltd

Credits

Editor:
Martin Schultz

Designer:
Mark Holt

Picture Research:
Irene Reed

Editorial Research:
Helen Hill

Line Drawings:
Terry Allen Designs Ltd.
© Salamander Books Ltd

Maps:
Alan Hollingberry
© Salamander Books Ltd

Filmset:
Modern Text Typesetting Ltd,
England

Colour and monochrome reproduction:
Bantam Litho Ltd,
Colour Craftsmen Ltd,
Tenreck Ltd, England.

Printed in Belgium:
Henri Proost et Cie, Turnhout.

Contents

Master Time Chart of World Architecture

During the past 5,000 years of architectural history, a great number of building styles have appeared. Some have had a lasting influence, and individual examples of a particular style may abound. Others have vanished from sight, with only a single structure or two to remind us they ever existed. In the Master Time Chart of World Architecture (*below*) we have attempted to give some impression of both the vast periods we are dealing with and the variety of styles that have evolved since

the building of the pyramids by the Ancient Egyptians. No less important are the relationships between different styles at various points in time, and the influence they have had on each other and on future architectural periods. The Master Time Chart brings together the reference data and illustrated examples of every architectural style dealt with in the 30 chapters of this book, beginning with the monumental civilizations and ending with Post-War Recent.

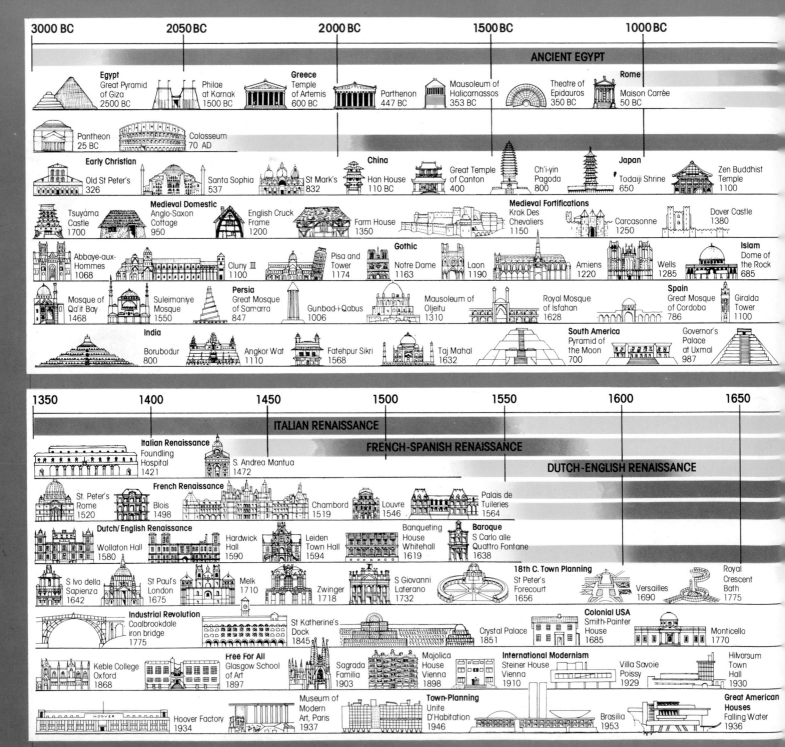

The Long, the Short and the Tall

So as to gain some impression of the true scale or height of the various building referred to in the *Illustrated Atlas of the World's Great Buildings,* we have taken the height of one of the most renowned structures of modern times—the Arc de Triumph—and made that the standard by which we have compared the heights of buildings selected from other architectural styles and periods. Each chapter in the book covers a single building style and there is a corresponding scale drawing.

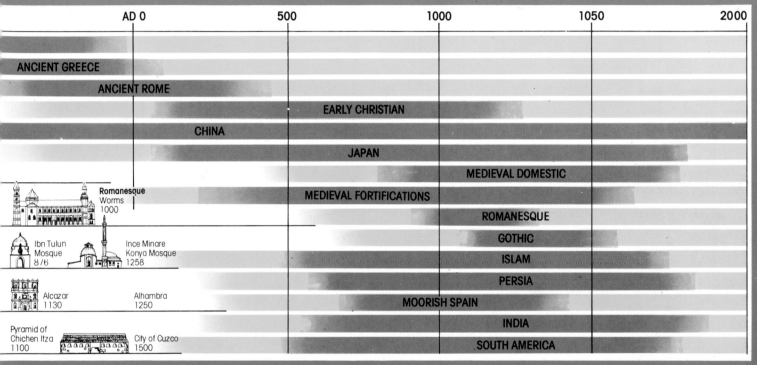

AD 0 — 500 — 1000 — 1050 — 2000

ANCIENT GREECE
ANCIENT ROME
EARLY CHRISTIAN
CHINA
JAPAN
MEDIEVAL DOMESTIC
Romanesque Worms 1000
MEDIEVAL FORTIFICATIONS
ROMANESQUE
Ibn Tulun Mosque 876 — Ince Minare Konya Mosque 1258
GOTHIC
ISLAM
PERSIA
Alcazar 1130 — Alhambra 1250
MOORISH SPAIN
Pyramid of Chichen Itza 1100 — City of Cuzco 1500
INDIA
SOUTH AMERICA

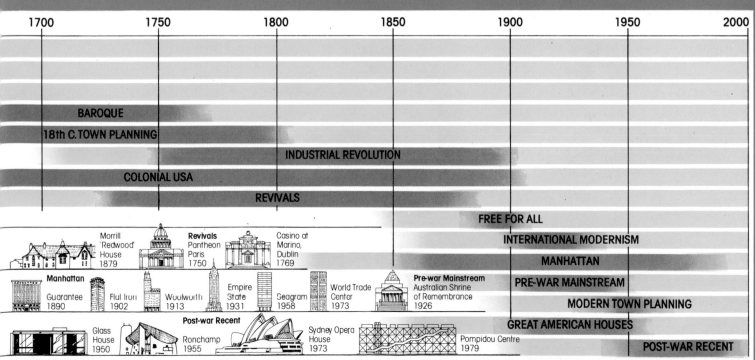

1700 — 1750 — 1800 — 1850 — 1900 — 1950 — 2000

BAROQUE
18th C. TOWN PLANNING
INDUSTRIAL REVOLUTION
COLONIAL USA
REVIVALS
FREE FOR ALL
Morrill 'Redwood' House 1879 — Revivals Pantheon Paris 1750 — Casino at Marino, Dublin 1769
INTERNATIONAL MODERNISM
MANHATTAN
Manhattan — Guarantee 1890 — Flat Iron 1902 — Woolworth 1913 — Empire State 1931 — Seagram 1958 — World Trade Center 1973 — Pre-war Mainstream Australian Shrine of Remembrance 1926
PRE-WAR MAINSTREAM
MODERN TOWN PLANNING
GREAT AMERICAN HOUSES
Post-war Recent — Glass House 1950 — Ronchamp 1955 — Sydney Opera House 1973 — Pompidou Centre 1979
POST-WAR RECENT

Monuments in Stone
Egypt-Land of the Dead

Mediterranean
Giza• •Cairo
Saqqara•
E G Y P T
Nile   Red Sea
Thebes• •Karnak
•Luxor
Edfu•

Architectural Importance:
Earliest use of stone in the construction of monumental buildings. The invention of the capital, cornice and the pediment; technical features that were directly translated from one building material (ie wood) to another (stone). The Egyptians were responsible for the construction of the pyramids, giant piles of stones used initially to protect the remains of the pharaoh. The pyramids also formed part of a larger architectural complex— a necropolis, or city of the dead, which included temples and tombs.

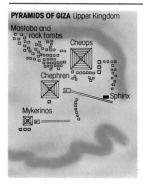

PYRAMIDS OF GIZA Upper Kingdom
Mastaba and
rock tombs
Cheops
Chephren
Sphinx
Mykerinos

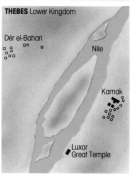

THEBES Lower Kingdom
Dér el-Bahari
Nile
Karnak
Luxor
Great Temple

Nearly five thousand years ago, King Zoser commanded his architect, Imhotep, to build a vast complex of stone structures at Saqqara, on the River Nile. Here, the Pharaoh decreed, would lie the embalmed remains of his body, to be safeguarded for eternity by the priests of the God, Ammon. The edifice itself would glorify his name, for evermore a monument to the illustrious king.

As his reign advanced, a strange city arose in the desert. This necropolis, with its elegant funerary temples, colonnaded entrance-ways and high stone wall, was of imposing scale and grandeur. Yet, nearby a colossal edifice was forming that would dwarf even this structure. For Zoser had commanded that the central feature of the Saqqara necropolis was to be a huge sepulchre.

Known throughout the ages as the Step Pyramid, this imposing structure is the most

Stylistic Essentials: Heavy column and beam construction. Massive bulk forms. Inward sloping walls (battered). Generally, Egyptian masons worked to a high standard and their construction of

the early pyramids and funerary temples followed an exacting level of precision – in the case of the Giza pyramid, it is impossible to fit the blade of a knife between the various, massive limestone blocks.

Primary Building Materials: The most widely-used material for the monuments was a combination of limestone and granite. Many of the pyramids were covered with polished limestone

blocks. Domestic buildings made use of mud brick, and vegetative materials such as bundled reeds and, occasionally, wood.

Spread of Influence: Egypt was largely isolated at first, but later it had a marked influence on Greek architecture and, to a lesser extent on the development of Roman architecture.

ancient edifice of hewn stone yet discovered. The first of a succession that would immortalize the architecture of ancient Egypt, the Step Pyramid dominated the desert landscape. The only other man-made structures in the vicinity were crude mud and brick constructions that had barely changed in appearance since Egypt's distant Neolithic past. Obsession with the after-life had inspired an architectural revolution. Death had changed the face of the desert.

Indeed, death was the concern of all classes of society in ancient Egypt. Within the nobility, a pre-occupation with the after-life was only subordinate to one's obligatory duty to the pharaoh. Those with sufficient means and power constructed a 'House of Eternity' to accommodate their mummified remains. If the flesh could be protected from decay and desecration, sustained by the food and equipment provided in the tomb, then the soul could survive in perpetuity.

Barely one hundred years after Zoser's death, Pharaoh Cheops built the greatest tomb in history — a meticulously stacked pile of more than two million gravestones that has kept scholars arguing ever since.

The Cheops Pyramid, first of the three Great Pyramids of Giza, is man's most indestructable artefact. A spectacular display of accurate engineering, it was undertaken by a society whose only building technology was fire, the lever, copper hand tools, and human muscle power. Sophisticated modern surveying equipment has confirmed the extraordinary precision of construction; exactly how this was achieved, we may never know. Even now, there are some who believe that the mathematical proportions of the pyramid contain a codified message from a civilization far superior to our own.

Visually, Egyptian architecture is neither subtle nor sophisticated; the epic scale and dramatic setting

provide the impact. And yet, it was the Egyptian architect, Imhotep, who invented the column, capital, and cornice, recreating in stone the characteristic features of brick, reed, and mud constructions. These stone building components were later transformed and refined by the Greeks to generate the 'classical' style, the basis of almost all great architecture up to the 20th century.

Imhotep's revolutionary concept did not go unrecognized. His successors made him a god, an honour bestowed upon no other architect. His masterpiece, at Saqqara, built 2,700 years before the birth of Christ, is now a ravaged stone ruin. In its nascent glory, with its polished limestone walls gleaming in the desert sun, it must have been awesome. One can only imagine its colourfully decorated temples, thronged with thousands of people celebrating a royal festival or a funerary rite.

Below: The Step Pyramid of Zoser at Saqqara. Built in 2778 BC, in the form of a mastaba, it was subsequently enlarged. **Above:** The first cut-stone (ashlar) wall in the world; the joints of the wall surrounding Zoser's necropolis.

For nearly three thousand years the ancient Egyptian civilization persisted, only to decline with the disintegration of the Hellenistic Empire. An isolated culture, it was ruled for the most part by a highly conservative, authoritarian priesthood and monarchy, whose beliefs and customs are preserved in elaborate bas-relief carvings that decorate many of the existing tombs. Though we may criticize the Egyptians for a legacy which includes taxation and bureaucracy, few would disagree that their sense of occasion and scale helped to generate the world's first recognizable style of construction.

River of History

Without the River Nile there would have been no Egypt as we know it. As Herodotus, the Greek historian, wrote: 'Egypt is the gift of the river.' Circumvented by

arid desert and a perpetually blue sky, the 960 kilometer (600 mile) narrow valley of fertile land that follows the Nile to the Mediterranean has been continuously settled for more than ten thousand years. In 300 BC, the priest, Manetho, compiled a record of Egyptian history, fragments of which still exist. He codified the dynasties into three convenient groups: the 'Ancient Kingdom', the 'Middle Kingdom' and the 'New Empire', with an interregnum between each.

The capital of the Ancient Kingdom was established at Memphis by Menes, the first pharaoh, chiefly remembered for his skill in unifying upper and lower Egypt into one kingdom. It was also during the first dynasty that the system of writing known as hieroglyphic evolved. By the third dynasty, the fundamental elements of Egyptian architecture were established with Zoser's necropolis at Saqqara, followed a century later by the Great Pyramids. The zenith reached by Egyptian culture during the first six dynasties was never surpassed.

Then followed a period of social upheaval, when the arts were despised and monuments defaced and pillaged. Not till 2130 BC (11th dynasty), was political stability re-established. During the next 350 years, the arts recovered; great works of surveying, construction, and irrigation were carried out, and an effective administrative system evolved. During this, the Middle Kingdom, the great cult temples were founded, and the first obelisks erected. After a further period of anarchy, the nomad Hyksos using large numbers of horse-drawn chariots, overran the Delta.

In 1570 BC, Ahmose I routed the Hyksos, established Thebes as the capital, and inaugurated the New Empire. With the colonization of Palestine and Sinai there

Below: Examples of lotus leaf capitals atop 'engaged' columns attached to the wall of Zoser's necropolis. At this time, cut stone was very much a revolutionary building material and the confidence with which the architect Imhotep's masons handled it is astonishing. These columns represent the beginnings of classical architecture; the Greeks derived their Doric system from Egyptian prototypes.

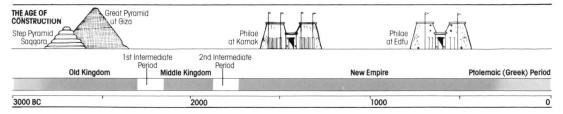

THE AGE OF CONSTRUCTION

	1st Intermediate Period	2nd Intermediate Period		
Old Kingdom	Middle Kingdom		New Empire	Ptolemaic (Greek) Period

3000 BC   2000   1000   0

followed an age of expansion and imperialism. Famous pharaohs of the New Kingdom include Hatshepsat ('Queen Elizabeth I' of Egypt, who sent expeditions to Nubia and Arabia for ivory, gold and myrrh); Tutenkhamen (whose richly furnished tomb was discovered in 1922); and Ramses I (who was responsible for the Hypostyle Hall at Karnak).

In time, the priesthood gained in power and prestige, and began to challenge the rule of the monarchy, contributing to a slow decline until the Persian invasion by Cambyses in 525 BC. Alexander the Great liberated the Egyptians from the Persians in 332 BC, entrusting Egypt to his general, Ptolemy, the next year. Greek and Egyptian cultures merged in the 'Ptolemaic' period (during which the temples of Philae and Edfu were built) until the coming of the Roman legions in AD 30.

The Nile was the life-blood of Egyptian civilization — providing irrigation, transport, building materials, and even an accurate calender. Flooding with precise timing every year, it deposited a rich, black mud that was easily cultivated. One quickly-grown crop per year was enough to sustain the population, leaving plenty of time free for the construction of great monuments for the ruling elite.

The Roots of a Style

The origins of Egyptian architecture can be traced to the reed huts and boat cabins of Neolithic times. Originally oval, the huts became square as mud was used to plaster reed frames, with inward sloping or 'battered' walls and thick bases to resist the annual inundation.

Dynastic Egyptian domestic buildings were all constructed of sun-dried, mud brick. The palaces of the rich were decorated with brightly painted stucco panels, glazed tiles, and woven mats.

Above: The colossi of Memnon, at western Thebes. Whenever there is a desert storm, a strange wailing sound is heard coming from these statues. This apparently formed the basis for a number of Greek myths about the Egyptians.

Doors were made of cedar wood, imported at great expense from the Lebanon; internal columns were richly carved and inlaid with gold or electrum (a silver-gold alloy).

The decorative, vertical and horizontal 'bundling' of reeds used in early building styles probably inspired the invention of the capital and cornice. Such visual details of domestic architecture were later transferred, in vestigial form, to stone construction. This can be seen clearly at Saqqara, with its many examples of fluted columns, capitals with double fluted leaves, and heavy stone roofs made of beams, rounded beneath, imitative of thick logs.

A Tomb Transformed

The earliest tombs specifically built for the pharaohs of Egypt were called 'mastabas', i.e. 'benches', by the ancient Egyptians. These developed from Neolithic burial pits, and took the form of rectangular, flat-topped

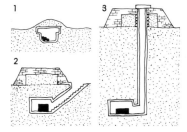

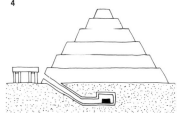

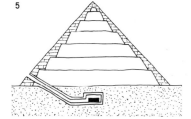

Left and Below: The evolution of the pyramid. 1. Neolithic pit-tomb. 2. Early mastaba. 3. Fully developed mastaba with granite-lined burial pit deep below ground. 4. Step Pyramid. 5. True pyramid with layer of facing stones.

Above: A fine example of an Egyptian bas-relief carving outside a rock tomb at Aswan. Although the figures are rather stylized, they nevertheless reveal a deeply-felt humanity associated with the relaxed atmosphere of the New Empire.

mounds, with walls made from mud bricks. They were about 3 metres (12 feet) deep. Inside was a group of chambers, usually arranged to resemble an Egyptian house, containing all the furnishings and equipment necessary for life after death — chairs, boats, farming tools, and even a latrine. After burial, access to this 'House of Eternity' was sealed.

The external walls had recessed panels of brick, imitating a technique in palace walls, but using slabs of wood. This is an early example of the translation of construction details, for decorative purposes, from one material and application to another.

For King Zoser, Imhotep planned the building of a huge mastaba. During the construction, however, he decided to enlarge it even further, both upwards and outwards. This resulted in the development of the first pyramid, a massive, six-tiered structure over 60 metres (200 feet) high.

The small, granite-lined burial chamber is at the bottom of a pit, 92 metres (300 feet) below ground level, sealed after burial with a huge stone 'plug'. Fanning out from the pit bottom is a labyrinth of corridors, with false stone doors delicately carved in bas-

relief with scenes from the King's reign. Zoser's family members were buried at the bottom of eleven adjacent separate pits, 100 metres (327 feet) deep.

The pyramid was completely surrounded by a large, walled, enclosure, which contained a number of ceremonial courts, temples, and various ancillary buildings. The outer wall was finished in white limestone. Slightly 'battered', it had a number of recessed panels, in the style of earlier mastabas.

This astonishing architectural achievement demonstrates the remarkable confidence displayed by the newly-established culture of the Old Kingdom, particularly in its fearless experimentation with new ideas and materials. Building in stone was still a novel idea. Its innovative use can be seen in the short roof-spans and the fact that the columns are constructed attached to the walls; the architects of the first dynasty were not yet so bold that they would risk supporting roofs on free-standing columns.

Domestic architecture played a vital role in the evolution of the great stone monuments that assured ancient Egypt a place in history. Many decorative features are derived from structural components that had been incorporated into primitive buildings for thousands of years before Zoser ascended the throne. The roof of the 'Hall of Pillars', for example, is carved to resemble the half-round palm logs used in mud-brick houses, the fluted or 'reeded' (vertically grooved) columns imitate bundles of reeds, and the now-famous stone capitals derive from papyrus or mud-bonded leaves. These 'vegetative' origins and domestic characteristics provided the House of Eternity with a human scale, yet the use of stone gave a sense of permanence, in keeping with the ancient Egyptians' attitude towards immortality.

By the onset of the fourth dynasty, the pyramid concept had been considerably refined. During Seneferu's reign, the first true pyramid, and the curious 'Bent' pyramid (it changes angle halfway up) were completed. His son, Cheops, built the first and largest of the three Great Pyramids of Giza.

Art and architecture at this time had reached a solid, monumental, if somewhat austere maturity. Delight in experimentation had been replaced by confident and skillful engineering. To assemble a pile of two million stones weighing two and a half tons each (several weighing 70 tons each) would be an achievement in any era. But to construct this pile with extreme accuracy in 20 years, using only levers, ropes, and wedges as mechanical plant, and human muscle as motive power—is a triumph of engineering unequalled to this day.

During construction Cheops altered the plans for his tomb chamber three times; the original subterranean chamber and inter-

Right: Fluted columns at the tomb of Queen Hatshepsut at Thebes; a short step to the Doric column. **Far right:** The mighty columns of the Temple of Karnak, in this example crowned with a 'bell' capital.

Papyrus column Bell column Palm column Lotus column

Above: Various types of capital, showing the vegetable origins of the ornament.

Above: The lotus-bud columns at the Temple of Ammon at Luxor, built around 1400 BC. By now, the priests were as powerful as the pharaohs.

Below: The mortuary temple of Queen Hatshepsut, carved into the solid rock of the Theban mountains. The Queen's body was hidden in a deep cave.

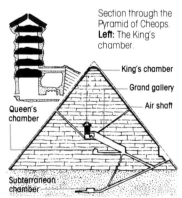

Section through the Pyramid of Cheops. **Left:** The King's chamber.

- King's chamber
- Grand gallery
- Air shaft
- Queen's chamber
- Subterranean chamber

mediate Queen's chamber were abandoned and replaced by the King's chamber, lined in polished pink granite. Here lies the sarcophagus (a massive granite coffin), though there is no conclusive proof that the pharaoh's body was actually placed in it. A tall, narrow passage (the 'Grand Gallery') leads up to the chamber which was sealed by three massive granite port-cullises. Cheops buried his three queens in adjacent miniature pyramids. Little remains of the attendant buildings or the enclosing wall. In 1954, well-preserved wooden boats were discovered buried in pits on the

south side of the pyramid—provided, perhaps, for transport in the after-life.

Pharaohs Chephren and Mykerinos, who followed Cheops, built two smaller pyramids, with Chephren's being guarded by a sphinx, a representation of the pharaoh himself as occult protector of the necropolis. With the decline of the Old Kingdom, pyramids became more modest. The maintenance of the legion of priests who tended the temples and served the pharaohs and their pyramids had become prohibitively costly and contributed to the drain on Egypt's economy.

Indeed, as repositories for the embalmed remains of pharaohs and their queens, the pyramids declined even more rapidly. This was as much the result of changing attitudes as of the perpetual concern over tomb robbers.

Tomb robbery had been a persistent worry for the priests almost from the beginning of the pyramid building age. The tomb of Cheop's mother was plundered during his lifetime, precipitating a national crisis. In a desperate move designed to outmanoeuvre the thieves, the attendant priests decided to secretly move their charges to a location beyond the

clutches of the tomb robbers.

Various sites were investigated, including the now-famous Valley of the Tombs of the Kings and Queens at Thebes. It was decided by the kings of the New Kingdom that, while their mortuary temples would be built in full view of the valley, their burial chambers would be concealed in deep cliff-side caves. Here, a large number of kings, queens, princes, and other nobles were buried, together with all their riches and household belongings.

Each tomb consisted of a long corridor (in the case of Queen Hatshepsut's, the entranceway to the burial chamber is 213 metres— 700 feet deep), opening out into a columned hall containing wall paintings depicting ceremonial and funerary events.

In time, the pyramids and their accompanying temples were abandoned to the looters and the sand. Their gleaming façades were stripped away to be used on later buildings. The temples were left deserted when the state found it could no longer maintain the enormous numbers of priests and attendants needed to guard them; their treasures were stolen, their sculptures were smashed and their columns were slowly covered by the relentless drift of the desert.

Places of Worship

Temples of the Old Kingdom fall into two main groups: those dedicated to the worship of the dead pharaohs and those dedicated to the worship of the gods. The earliest cult temples were probably not unlike contemporary dwellings, simple cabins, where the god 'resided' in the form of a sculpture. Only the priesthood was allowed contact with the deity. Three times a day the image of the god (seated in its sacred boat or 'barque') was washed, dressed, annointed with oil, and offered food, incense, and prayers. Public participation was restricted to festivals outside the precincts of the temple.

The temple of Ammon at Karnak, the grandest of the cult temples, started as a small shrine early in the Middle Kingdom. Successive dynasties added their own cult edifices to the basic

structure, until in its final form, it boasted six huge entry pylons, and was surrounded by a vast, walled enclosure containing a sacred lake, nine subsidiary temples, obelisks, and the Hypostyle Hall. The entire complex occupied some 25 hectares (43 acres) of land, a short distance from the east bank of the Nile. An avenue of sphinxes connected the complex to the temple at Luxor.

The Hypostyle Hall illustrates the way Egyptian architecture manipulated interior space. The main processional route in the centre is flanked by 14 massive pillars, 23 metres (78 feet) high, with capitals sculpted in the form of papyrus buds, supporting a massive slab-stone roof. On either side, light filters through from the high stone screens. The lower roof on each side recedes into darkness, supported by a forest of columns that give the illusion of unlimited extent. The columns, walls, and architraves are covered with carved inscriptions and coloured reliefs that praise the kings who built the temple and the gods to whom it was dedicated.

When the pharaohs resorted to hidden, rock-cut, tombs, the mortuary temple became the focus of architectural display. They developed from the funerary chapels that flanked the mastabas and pyramids of the Old Kingdom.

Queen Hatshepsut had her mortuary temple constructed at the foot of steep cliffs in the Theban mountains, adjacent to that of Mennhotep, built 500 years earlier. It was connected to the valley below by an avenue of sphinxes, leading to a three-tiered terrace (approached by massive ramps) which mirrors the three essential components of the landscape: the flat expanse of sand, the great rock projections, and the steep backdrop of the cliff. The third tier led to the chief sanctuary, cut into the cliff face itself, and approached through a walled court lined with a double row of columns. To the left is the queen's mortuary chapel,

and to the right, a temple devoted to the Sun God, Ra. The wall reliefs of this monument are exceptionally fine, depicting various events in the queen's life.

The later temples of the Ptolemaic period followed the basic layout of those of the New Empire, with the same progression of darkness and gloom leading to the inner sanctum. The temple of Horus-Edfu is quite probably the best preserved example.

Miracle of Precision

Stone for the pyramids and other temples was cut in quarries by pounding and carving a groove around the block and inserting wooden wedges that were swelled with water to cause a crack along the grain. In the case of granite, the

Right: A cut-away section of the Temple of Khons as it looked originally and (**below**) the ruined temple today. When completed, it was arranged as a series of spaces that became progressively smaller and darker as the inner and most sacred temple sanctuary was approached by the priests.

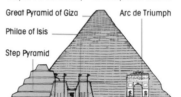

Great Pyramid of Giza — Arc de Triumph

Philae of Isis —

Step Pyramid —

cracks may have been made with heat, by laying a fire in the groove. The blocks were numbered by the quarrymen and loaded on to barges towed by rowing boats. (According to one account, 30 rowing boats of 900 oars were

needed.) Delivery to the site was by canal or, during the annual inundation, by flood water.

The pyramids were constructed layer by layer, with the stones slightly tilting inwards to add stability. The blocks were dragged into place up earthen ramps, on hard acacia-wood sledges, lubricated by wetting the earth just ahead of the front wheels. After the blocks were manoeuvred into position with levers and ropes, the ramps were dismantled.

The pyramid at Maydum was built in 17 years, requiring 600,000 two-ton blocks; this meant that 100 blocks a day had to be hauled into position by at least 200 men, in teams working without a break. When the (local) limestone core was finished, the outside was cased with highly polished limestone from the quarries at Turra, in the Mokattam hills, a short distance south of modern Cairo. Over 8 hectares (20 acres) of this polished stone was used to case the Great Pyramid of Cheops, all of it cut with extreme accuracy. Inside there are mortar joints over two metres (6 feet) long that are less than 2 millimetres (one fifteenth of an inch) thick, through which it is impossible for a knife blade to pass.

Controversy still exists over the methods of transport and erection of the great stone obelisks. These tall granite slabs, carved with hieroglyphs, were installed at temple entrances. One theory is that they were dragged up earthen ramps and then the bottom end was slowly lowered by removing the earth beneath, until the slab was nearly vertical, requiring less force to pull it into its final position. The largest, originally from the temple at Karnak, was removed to Rome and is 33 metres (107 feet) high.

During construction, the Hypostyle Hall at Karnak was probably filled with earth, to provide firm support while manoeuvring the blocks and column 'drums' into position.

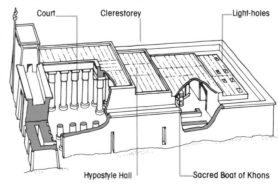

Court — Clerestorey — Light-holes

Hypostyle Hall — Sacred Boat of Khons

Perfection of Form
Greece-The Pursuit of the Ideal

Architectural Importance:
The perfection of the most widely-used decorative elements of European architecture the Doric, Ionic and Corinthian orders. The Greeks endeavoured to discover the sacred rules governing the harmony of form, and they consequently sought to endow their buildings with a sense of balance and proportion. Extreme conservatism of form and structure. Having set the limits of their style, they thereafter sought simply to refine the design and then pass it on to succeeding generations of architects.

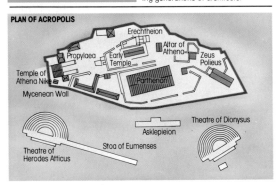

In 480 BC, Persian forces, advancing in strength through the region of Attica, poured almost unopposed into Athens and razed the city. The inhabitants, compelled to flee to the nearby island of Salamis, watched with horror as flames engulfed the sacred temple atop the mighty rock of the Acropolis.

Despite this humiliation, the Athenian commander, Themistocles, rallied his demoralized naval forces and inflicted a shattering defeat on the Persian fleet. Within a year, the Greeks had banished the Persians from the mainland.

This victory, won against all odds, inspired a renewed confidence in the vigour of Greek culture, which was celebrated in the erection of the supreme architectural achievement of the ancient world, the Parthenon.

From the day of its completion, the Parthenon commanded the admiration of the

Stylistic Essentials: Simple post and beam construction. Exteriors considered more important than interiors. Building as sculpture, and thus intended to be subservient to the surrounding landscape.

Classical Greek architecture is characterized by its austerity and grace: lines are rigid and free of ornate carving. Greek architecture was a 'kit of parts' handed down through generations.

Primary Building Materials: Stone (limestone and marble). Highest standards of masonry and carving. Sophisticated optical corrections (entasis). Marble was rarely used in solid form.

Spread of Influence: Western civilization owes an enormous debt to ancient Greece, and this is shown particularly clearly in the development of architecture. The elements of Greek building practice and the Greek theory of proportion has had a continuing influence on building styles for the last 2,000 years.

world. It was a miracle of balanced composition and elegant harmony. In this Doric temple, with its shimmering colour and gleaming marble, the Greeks approached perfection with a systematic method of constructing buildings in stone.

The evolution of the Doric temple represents a relentless pursuit of the ideal, a quest for perfection rather than for originality. The Parthenon is the quintessence of this search. No expense or labour did the architects spare to realize their ideal. The result was the most perfectly proportioned building in the ancient world, and perhaps the greatest temple ever known.

To the Greeks, the celebration of beauty was an act of sacred devotion; such beauty could only be achieved by an understanding of the science of proportion, the dynamic relationship of the parts to the whole.

The Greek temple was a very simple type of building. It was no more than a room or 'cella' housing the image of the god, approached by an entrance porch, and surrounded by a row of columns. Purely formal in concept, the Greek temple was more a perfectly proportioned sculpture that glorified the visible or external environment than a functional building designed for human activity. Thus the siting of temples was of great importance: not only because the location itself must be sanctified ground, but also because of the juxtaposition of sharply defined geometric shapes with the rough, natural landscape. Each complemented and ennobled the other.

The Greek architects who established the design criteria for their temples were little concerned with change or evolution in the basic form of the building. Not interested in structural gymnastics, their sole motive was the fastidious refinement of the sacrosanct 'kit of parts' inherited from their fore-fathers.

The Parthenon was built by Athens at the peak of its glory, during the 'Periclean Age'. This was the civilization that gave to the world the concepts of politics, philosophy and justice, and even laid the foundation for the study of science and medicine.

Exactly how this small band of people achieved so much in such a short time remains a mystery.

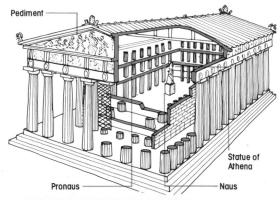

Pediment

Statue of Athena

Pronaus

Naus

But one thing is certainly true: the Greeks of this period struck a subtle balance between hardship and prosperity in a manner that was never subsequently repeated. Their concern with these twin poles of existence affected everything with which they came into contact. When material wealth and stability increased (with the conquests of Alexander and the Macedonian empire) the Hellenic culture suffered a decline from which it never recovered.

The sacred aspects of Doric and Ionic temple design were subsequently transferred to secular building, and used more as a style of decoration than as an integral and self-sufficient technique of construction. The Romans who eventually grew impatient with the limitations of 'post and beam' construction, took this process a stage further. In order to create large, open, internal spaces, unencumbered by columns, they developed the arch, the vault and the dome, borrowing the Greek orders purely for various decorative purposes.

Today, one can buy plastic Doric and Ionic columns from hardware stores to embellish a front porch or frame a four-poster bed. Doubtless, the architects of the Parthenon would be horrified at this corruption of their sacred system. Yet they

Left: A cut-away view of the Parthenon as it looked when first built. It was an 'octastyle' temple, which means that it had eight columns at either end of the building.

Below: The Grand Staircase of the Minoan Royal Palace, at Knossos, in Crete, showing the 'inverted' columns, perhaps derived originally from upturned tree trunks.

might equally be proud of the fact that the unique system of construction evolved in ancient Greece, with its sense of proportion and clarity, provided the most important architectural decorative elements right up to the early 20th century.

Evolving in Isolation

The landscape of the Greek mainland is mountainous and rocky, with a jagged coastline which provides many natural harbours. Good agricultural land is scarce and is mainly confined to narrow strips along coastal valleys. The difficulties of inland travel in this uncompromising environment stimulated the formation of isolated, independent settlements.

Like the Minoan and Mycenean civilizations that preceded them, the ancient Greeks were seafarers. The sea provided them with a means of transport and trade, and was invaluable in the movement and handling of large blocks of stone for the building industry. In contrast, the movement of stone by land was both time-consuming and labour-intensive, adding very considerably to construction costs.

During the formative years of Greek civilization, religion played a dominant role in the life of a citizen. It was a healthy pantheism, quite unlike the sinister, gloomy mysticism of the Egyptians, and fit perfectly with the Greek love of the outdoor life. Most of the religious festivals (and many social activities) were held in the open, or in open-sided shelters. Greek pantheism held the physical environment in veneration, treating it not merely as a scenic backdrop, but as a vital, sacred force that contained, in every tree and rock, the beauty and power of the gods themselves. Every Greek consequently gloried in the beauty of the visible world; and it fol-

Temple of Artemis · Temple of Zeus, Olympia · Parthenon, Athens · Theseion · Mausoleum of Halicarnassos · Theatre of Epidauros · Temple of Athena Pelius, Priene · Stoa of Attalos 11, Athens

Hellenic Period · Hellenistic Period

650 BC · 500 · 350 · 200 · 50

lowed that the primary task of the architect was to find a focus for this piety. The result was the Doric temple.

The important sanctuaries at Delphi, Olympia and Delos evolved independently of the major cities, but the majority of Greek temples were attached to city-states, often located in the position with the best natural defenses. The Acropolis at Athens is a prime example: a complex of temples perched atop a vast limestone crag, accessible from only one direction, dominating the city below. It was the spiritual centre of the city, while the Forum was the political focus.

The Greeks were continually founding new communities or city-states either in Italy, Asia Minor or North Africa. The defense of these colonies and of the home towns, as well, required vast fortifications absorbing much of their building energy.

Initially, Greek cities developed in a fairly chaotic way, expanding by absorbing whatever buildings lay in their paths. Later cities were laid out in an orderly arrangement, often conforming to a 'grid-iron' street plan. Tradition has it that the father of Greek town-planning was Hippodamus of Miletus, who laid out the Athenian satellite towns of Piraeus and Thuru. The buildings were grouped according to

type and function, and arranged according to their relative status.

If the geography of the Greek landscape favoured the evolution of the Poleis or city-state, the independence and love of freedom of the Greek mind confirmed the principle of self-sufficient communities, small and intimate enough to allow each citizen active participation in the affairs of state, culture and sport — and an ideal environment for the flowering of art and architecture.

Origins Shrouded in Mystery

In the Aegean, two civilizations preceded the classical Greek or 'Hellenic' culture: the Minoans and Myceneans. The Minoans were the first great sea-power of the Mediterranean, establishing trading links with Egypt, Asia Minor, Syria, Palestine and Libya that were subsequently taken over by the colonists who founded classical Greece.

Based on the island of Crete, the Minoans produced some beautiful pottery, jewellery, and metalwork, but their building skills were comparatively primitive. The three great palaces of Knossos, Malha and Phantis are chaotic mazes consisting of small chambers connected by rambling corridors, the result of repeated alterations and ad-hoc additions with no apparent logic to their layout.

The Minoans' seafaring prowess and the natural defenses of the island obviated any need for fortifications. The architecture is

Mausoleum of Halicarnassos · Theatre of Epidauros (plan) · Parthenon · Arc de Triumph

Above: The size of the Greek challenge. Shown here are the heights of various Greek buildings in comparison with the Arc de Triumph. Unlike the Egyptians the Greeks did not practice architectural gigantism. Instead they designed buildings according to the laws of proportion.

almost entirely domestic. We can only guess what the palaces actually looked like, since the foundations and lower walls alone remain. The structures may have had two, three or even four stories, with upper walls constructed of a wooden framework filled in with rubble and mud brick, plastered and decorated, perhaps, with glazed tiles and painted panels. Internal wooden columns tapered downwards, as though the architects had taken tree trunks and inverted them, providing a wide capital or platform at the top to support the heavy roof beams.

The Mycenean civilization that coincided with, and eventually superceded, the Minoans, was more militaristic. The Myceneans were skilled in the art of working stone, hence domestic buildings were heavily fortified. The city of Mycenae itself was a naturally impregnable citadel, guarding the port that was the

basis of its economy. The famous lion gate exemplifies the massive style: a huge stone beam, 4.8 metres (16 feet) long, 1 metre (three and a half feet) high, and 2.43 metres (eight feet) deep, spans the gateway that led to the palace of Tiryus. Above this lintel is a thin stone slab carved with two lions 'rampant', facing a central column.

The palace was surrounded by huge walls, and in time of war included accommodation for villagers and their sheep and goats. There was a bathroom with a floor made from one huge slab of black stone, 3.96 metres × 3.35 metres (13 feet × 11 feet).

The Burial Complex

Several forms of tomb architecture were adopted by the peoples of the Aegean, including the chamber or rock-cut tomb, and the 'tholos' type. The Treasury of Atreus at Mycenae, the famous 'Tomb of Agamemnon' is the finest example of the 'tholos' or beehive tomb. It is made of 34 rings of masonry, capped with a stone-domed vault buried below an earth mound. The inside of the dome was lined with metal (possibly gold) rosettes.

The only clue to the origins of classical Greek architecture and the Doric temple is the Mycenean 'megaron' or chieftain's house, a

Below: The Treasury of Atreus, also known as the 'Tomb of Agamemnon,' is one of the finest surviving examples of Mycenean stonework. Behind the doorway is a circular vault, the 'tholos'.

Below: The Lion gate entrance to the fortified citadel at the Greek city of Mycenae. The massive lintel above the doorway is well over 4 metres (16 feet) long. It is capped by two stone lions.

17

simple, rectangular building, little more than a hall with a pitched roof and a front porch.

The Mycenean culture faded with the Doric invasions of the 11th century. Few buildings survive from the following four centuries—the so-called 'dark ages'—before the explosion of classical Greek architecture.

Reaching for Perfection

The earliest classical Greek temples were constructed from mud brick and reinforced by a timber frame with rubble or crude stone foundations. Simply a room with an entrance porch, its roof was probably thatched and therefore pitched (or sloping), thus breaking with the traditions of Mycenean megarons and most early Asiatic buildings, which generally used flat mud roofs.

During the seventh century BC, the Greeks began making roof tiles of terracotta, a far more satisfactory and permanent roofing material than thatch, but considerably heavier. This extra weight (and the influence of Egyptian architecture which resulted from trading contacts), prompted the change to carved stone as the primary building material for temples. Amazingly, though, few details of layout or construction were drastically altered by the use of the new material: the wooden building system was simply recreated in stone. If the scale was increased and the span widened, the Greeks thickened the posts and made the beam or architrave larger; hence the vast solidity and heavy grandeur of the early Doric temples in Sicily and on the mainland.

The earliest stone Doric temples were probably the Temple of Artemis at Corfu and the Temple of Hera at Olympia. The Temple of Artemis was subsequently demolished; only scattered blocks of weathered limestone remain, though enough of the pediment exists to deduce that a high relief carving of an enormous gorgon, flanked by two leopards and smaller figures representing the battle between the gods and the giants, originally covered the wall. Some of the mouldings were sheathed in terracotta, while other parts of the stone work were painted in various patterns.

The Temple of Hera reveals, rather startlingly, the transition from wood to stone. It was rebuilt many times: the stylobate or stone platform base and lower walls of the naus or sanctuary remain, together with some stone columns. The columns were made of wood, later to be replaced by stone. According to a tourist's guide book written by the Roman, Pausanias, in AD 173, a wooden column was still standing in the arch. The walls of the naus were of limestone up to a height of one metre (three and a half feet), then continued in sun-dried brick.

By the end of the sixth century BC, the set of rules governing

Left: An exaggerated view of how the Parthenon would appear without optical correction. **Below:** An exaggerated version with optical corrections. **Right:** The Parthenon as it appears to the eye.

Above: Detail of the Doric columns of the Parthenon. Even in the days of Pericles, the Parthenon was a costly building project. Many of the circular stone drums came from a previous temple.

temple design had been firmly established, and the relative proportions of the component parts were fixed. The system reached its glorious perfection in the Parthenon, shortly after the middle of the fifth century.

The key component of the system is the column and its capital. The diameter of the column base was the unit used to fix the proportions of the rest of the parts and, thus, of the whole. By a gradual process of trial and error, the Greek architects discovered the most visually satisfying ratios between column width, spacing and height; the ratio of temple length to width, and the ratio of column height to depth of 'entablature' (the decorated beam that the columns support).

As in many great art forms, perfection was obtained by minute 'bending' of the rules to achieve complete harmony. For the same reason that the ear requires mathematically pure musical intervals to be adjusted very slightly in order to sound 'true', the Greeks evolved the concept of 'entasis'; subtle 'refinements' to tune their system, and thereby compensate for two-dimensional tricks played by the eye.

The first 'refinement' was made to the columns. Because a column with perfectly straight sides would appear thinner in the middle when seen against the sky, the upward taper is very

slightly curved outwards. As a result of this modification, the curve not only counteracts this optical illusion, it also prevents the taper from leading the eye upwards too strongly. The column appears to have more vitality and elasticity. Absolutely pure geometrical forms would seem static and heavy; the slight curves bring a sensuality that makes the stone come alive.

The stylobate, or platform base, has a convex curve, with the highest point at the centre of the temple and the lowest at the corners. All the columns lean inwards very slightly, while the four corner ones are spaced a little closer to their adjacent companions (if you projected the vertical axes of the corner columns of the Parthenon, they would meet about 1.6 kilometers [one mile] above). In fact, very few parts of most classical Greek temples are actually straight, perpendicular or horizontal. Yet while each distortion is too small to be easily noticed in itself, their sum effect gives these temples their marvellously peaceful sense of balance and repose.

A Temple without Equal

The supreme embodiment of the principles of Doric temple design is the Parthenon, the inspiration of the Athenian leader, Pericles. During the planning stage of the

Parthenon, it was decided to use a scale large enough to accommodate an enormous statue of Athena Parthenes—carved by Phidias, the most famous of all Greek sculptors. Consequently, the ratio of 4 : 9 was applied to the more important dimensions, including the ratio of column base diameter to column spacing.

The temple was built eight columns' wide by 17 long, conforming to the rule that the sides should have double the number at the ends, plus one. The ratio of overall width to length is again 4 : 9, taking into account the fact that the four corner columns are spaced slightly closer to their neighbours. The height of the columns is 5.48 times the column diameter, and the column height, plus the depth of entablature above, is in the ratio of 4 : 9 to the width of the temple.

The main entrance was placed on the eastern side: an antechamber called the pronaos led through huge wooden doors to the naus itself, 19 metres (63 feet) wide by 29 metres (98 feet) long. At the far end of this chamber was Phidias' enormous sculpture of the virgin Athena, 12 metres (42 feet) high including its pedestal. It was 'chryselephantine', meaning carved from gold and ivory: the drapery, armour and accessories over the wooden core were removable should the temple be threatened in war. The face, hands and feet were ivory, and the eyes glittered with various precious stones.

Beyond the naus was another room—the 'Parthenon' or virgins' chamber—from which the temple took its name. This was entered from the western end via another antechamber, the 'opisthodomus'. The pronaos and opisthodomus were used as treasuries, with hefty metal grills fitted between the columns for security.

Outside the temple, the triangular pediments at either end framed more sculptures by Phidias, representing the birth of Athena and the contest between Athena and the god Poseidon for

Above: The vast semi-circular auditorium of the theatre at Epidauros, built in 350 BC by the justly renowned Greek architect, Polycleitos.

Above: The caryatid porch of the Erechtheion; on the Acropolis in Athens, built of solid, pentelic marble between the years 421 and 405 BC.

the land on which Athens was built. Along the top of the naus was a marvellous frieze representing a great procession of men, maidens and animals—the Panatheic Frieze.

In the fifth century AD, the Parthenon was converted into a Byzantine church, and in 1458 it became a Turkish mosque. The Venetians caused much damage when they shelled part of the temple being used as a gunpowder store. As with other monuments on the Acropolis, the Parthenon is now suffering from disintegration of the marble, due to atmospheric pollution from modern Athens.

The New Orders Emerge

The Ionic order is thought to have originated in Asia Minor, but it was later used throughout classical Greece and reached its perfection, as with the Doric order, in Athens. Ionic capitals were derived from wooden prototypes, influenced by Egyptian and Asian decorative motifs. It is a more richly decorated system than Doric, with thinner columns about nine times the width of the base. The distinctive feature is the spiral scroll or 'volute' at the top of the capital that spreads the load of the beam. This may have been derived from the curl of rams' horns or the leaves of the lotus flower.

The Ionic order was first used on the Greek mainland for small buildings, such as treasuries, until the second half of the fifth century BC, when several important temples used the order—notably the temple of Nike Apteros, and the Erechtheion, both in Athens.

The design of the Erechtheion, built between 421 and 405 BC, was something of a compromise, since in its planning it was necessary to incorporate part of an earlier temple that had survived the Persian desecration.

The Corinthian order first appeared in the fifth century as a decorative variant of the Ionic. Vilomius, the Roman architectural historian, tells the story that it was the inspiration of the Corinthian bronze-worker, Callimaclius, who saw a basket (covered with a tile) that had been placed over an acanthus plant on the grave of a Corinthian maiden.

The Corinthian order contains many of the same components as the Ionic, but differs in the design of the capitals, which are less abstract and more elaborate. It was originally used merely for internal supports, where slender and more decorative columns were required, though it later became the favourite order of the Romans, who were strongly attracted by its rich decoration.

The Challenge of Marble

Marble is unquestionably the best material for carving fine detail. Its subtle grain allows extremely accurate, sharp edges to be obtained, and, when polished, it produces in strong sunlight a wonderful luminous sheen. It goes without saying that if the Greeks had not discovered a supply of excellent marble, they would not have been able to indulge in the 'refinements' or optical corrections which make their Doric temples such masterpieces of elegance. Indeed, no other stone is capable of accepting the precision of cutting necessary to produce a curve of one in 750 in the stylobate or base of the Parthenon, though it should be realized that such accuracy was of course very costly and time-consuming. The marble used in the Parthenon came from the famous quarries of Mount Pentelikon, near Athens.

The first temple to be constructed entirely of marble was the Athenian treasury at Delphi, dated at about 490 BC. Thereafter, it was the preferred material, when financial resources were sufficient. When funds were short, marble would either be used for the parts requiring finer carving, or in powdered form to be made into stucco (plaster), as a surface treatment.

The Greeks achieved a very high standard of stone masonry, perhaps unequalled to this day. They used no mortar, and in their best work blocks were cut to fit with extraordinary accuracy. Employing a technique invented by the Egyptians and copied by the Myceneans, known as 'anathyrosis', they concentrated on achieving smooth contact between just two planes of a block. This was obtained only along the edges, with the centre being rough cut. Wherever possible, this time-saving measure was used though if large loads were to be borne, it was restricted to vertical joints. Lateral movement was restrained with the use of iron or bronze clamps, soldered in place with lead, and column drums were sometimes secured vertically with metal dowels. This use of metal resulted in some vandalism during Medieval times. The high value of metals and their shortage made demolition an attractive alternative to mining and smelting. Temple roofs had a timber structure, supporting terracotta tiles. The Greeks did not discover the principle of the timber roof truss until the second century BC; before this spans were kept short by frequent internal supports, such as in the use of the solid walls of the cella itself and the two-tiered row of columns within.

Although it is the temples that have had the main impact on western architecture, the Greeks devoted almost as much of their energy to building fortifications. (The city-states were constantly at war either amongst themselves or defending colonies from barbarian intrusion.) These massive constructions used no mortar and relied entirely on sheer size and weight to resist the seige equipment of their attackers.

Below: The three Greek orders 1 Doric, 2 Ionic and 3 Corinthian. **Left:** An Ionic capital from Delphi. It has been suggested that the spiral 'volutes' are derived from ram's horns.

Acanthus leaf (Corinthian)

Doric   Ionic   Corinthian

Conquest of Space
Rome-Imperial City of Concrete

Architectural Importance:
First architects to create and manipulate large interior spaces. Perfection of concrete led to the invention of a system of vaulting. Highly sophisticated engineering skills. Roman architecture strongly influenced by classical Greece, and many of the architects of Imperial Rome were themselves Greek. Roman architecture generally adopted an imposing scale to reflect the grandeur of the empire, thus buildings were mostly large, very solid and very impressive. But Romans less concerned with form than were the Greeks.

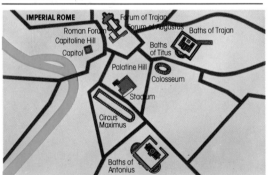

The Roman Emperor Augustus boasted that he had found Rome a city of brick and left it a city of marble. Actually, he left it a city of concrete: a material less glamorous, perhaps, but more versatile—essential for the construction of vast, imposing, arches, vaults, and domes needed to ennoble the great buildings of Imperial Rome. In contrast with the philistine attitudes of the earlier republican period, the first emperors had been determined to beautify and embellish the city with the splendid monuments that a world capital deserved and, in the process, to preserve their deeds for posterity.

The Forum Romanum, once the centre of political life in republican times, subsequently represented an orgy of architectural extravagance. Begun by Julius Caesar in 46 BC, the Forum was completed with monumental panache by the Emperor Trajan, who built a vast complex that included a basilica, a temple and two libraries—one Greek and one Latin.

Below: The Colosseum, a triumph of engineering and possibly the most impressive monument of Roman architecture. Construction was begun in AD 70, and completed 12 years later. There was room for 50,000 seated spectators. The arena in the foreground could be flooded for aquatic or naval displays.

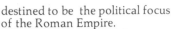

Stylistic Essentials: Deliberate separation of structure and decoration. Elaborate ornamentation derived from, among others. Hellenistic sources. Generally austere exteriors, and increasingly lavish interiors. Formal axial planning. Communities and towns constructed on a grid plan.

Primary Building Materials: Concrete used for structures; stone (marble, granite, alabaster); brick mosaics, stucco applied for decoration. Pioneered most forms of vaulting. Sophisticated building services (plumbing, heating, water supply), public baths, aqueducts.

Spread of Influence: Strong affect on early Christian building styles, with a marked influence on the later tradition of Romanesque, Gothic and Renaissance building. Revival of interest in classical styles.

Much of the inspiration for the design and decorative treatment of Roman architecture came from classical Greece. The Roman architect Vitruvius, who dedicated his famous 'Treatise on Architecture' to Augustus, implies that many of the architects of Imperial Rome were themselves Greek. But the Doric, Ionic and Corinthian orders were borrowed entirely for ornament, and later adapted, perverted and embellished in ways that would certainly have horrified the fastidious classical Greeks.

Although reproductions of Greek sculpture were fashionable in well-to-do Roman households — and real ones avidly collected by the elite — in general, the Romans felt contempt for the purely formal, sculptural themes of Greek architecture. Romans were proud of their own spectacular feats of engineering and were not ashamed to devote those skills to utilitarian ends. Whilst Greek architects were obsessed with the perfection of external proportions and the emotional interaction of building and landscape, the Romans discovered the excitement of huge, open spaces created by dramatic vaults and domes. Often, interiors were as important as exteriors, sometimes more so, for the Romans were the first to appreciate the aesthetic possibilities of manipulating internal space.

The most famous monuments of ancient Rome, the Colosseum and the Pantheon, are supreme examples of Roman engineering: outwardly simple buildings that incorporate sophisticated solutions to extremely complex structural problems. For hundreds of years the dome of the Pantheon was the largest in the world, and was intended to represent the vault of heaven. With such a massive construction, the architects took no chances and provided for every conceivable stress to which the building might be subjected. And, yet, by piercing the 21-foot walls with eight niches, an illusion of lightness is created, as if the dome merely rests on slender columns. The interior space has no obvious limitations, and the eye is led to prolong the space to infinity.

It is this dazzling engineering virtuosity, coupled with powerful manipulation of space, mass and volume, that is the greatest achievement of Roman architecture.

From Village to Capital

Before 700 BC, Rome was a confederation of villages perched on small hills above a marshy plain, adjacent to the River Tiber. During the seventh century the marshes were partially drained, and one of the hills, the Forum, became a cultural centre. It was

Below: Remains of the Forum in Rome. On the right is the Arch of Septimus Severus. On the left is the Temple of Saturn, which dominates the west end of the Forum.

destined to be the political focus of the Roman Empire.

In the early years, there was little to distinguish Rome from the hundreds of other small towns on the Italian peninsula — all self-contained communities, though much less aggressively independent than the Greek city-states, and intermittently united in political and military leagues. The population of Italy was a mixture of several racial groups, some of them recent immigrants from Greece and Asia Minor. One group, the Etruscans, gradually became dominant during the seventh century BC and, during the sixth century, actually controlled Rome itself.

The Etruscans were great builders, and many of their methods were adopted by the Romans. Indeed, they were the first people in Europe to fully exploit the arch, a method of spanning openings completely ignored by the Greeks. The Etruscans were also responsible for organizing large-scale engineering works, such as building city walls, canals and sewers, as well as draining marshes and controlling floods.

The Romans expelled the Etruscans in 509 BC, and founded a republic. Subsequently, their power declined, and in 474 BC the Etruscans were defeated by the Greek colonists of Syracuse. The initiative then passed to the Romans, who gradually embarked on a policy of conquest throughout the south of Italy, and confronted the Carthaginians (from North Africa) in the Punic wars. After an epic and bitter struggle with Hannibal, the Carthaginians were defeated (in 146 BC); Greece and Macedonia were conquered and the empire expanded to North Africa, Spain, and the Middle East. Julius Caesar's campaign (58-49 BC) extended the northern border to the Rhine and the English Channel; by the middle of the first century AD the Roman Empire, territorially, had reached its fullest extent.

Fusion of Opposites

The Romans' first contribution to architectural progress was to combine the column and beam system of classical Greece with the arch and vault system developed by the Etruscans. Their second great discovery was that it was far cheaper to build with small stones and rubble held together with mortar than with large cut blocks, laid dry. The Romans may not have actually invented concrete (perhaps the credit for that should go to the Carthaginians), but they were certainly the first to exploit its full potential.

Roman mortar was made from lime and 'pozzolana' — a fine volcanic earth. Similar to sand, it is found in many parts of Italy. First used extensively in the third century BC, mortar was invaluable in binding large rectangular blocks of stone. Often, the stone

THE AGE OF CONSTRUCTION

Maison Carree   Colosseum   Pantheon   Baths of Caracalla

Roman Republic   Roman Empire

400 BC   300   200   100   0   100   200   300   400

was simply a facing material, while the core of the wall would be filled with concrete: layers of broken brick, rubble and mortar. Skilled craftsmen would construct the facing, and supervise the filling of the core which was then accomplished by slaves or soldiers.

As confidence in concrete increased, so the facing stones became thinner and smaller, eventually ceasing to have any structural significance at all. Later, facing stones were cut square (about 100mm, 4in) and laid in a diagonal pattern. This was further developed by the use of specially shaped bricks, instead of stone.

Roman architects soon applied concrete walling methods to the construction of arches and vaults. Here was a material that matched the aspirations of empire-builders. The greatest Roman vaults had spans unequalled until the construction of 19th century steel buildings; even Gothic cathedral vaults dwindle by comparison, rarely more than 12 metres (40 feet) across, compared to the 27 metres (90 feet) or more of the Roman spans.

The advantage of concrete was that vaults could be moulded to fit complex room shapes, without recourse to laborious stone-cutting procedures. It was also cheap,

required fewer skilled craftsmen, and increased the possibilities for elaborate modelling of interior spaces. Thus, curves could be substituted for straight lines in both plan and elevation, leading to the flowing lines of later 'baroque' Roman styles.

Inherently not a decorative material, concrete was usually sheathed with painted plaster stucco, and, in luxurious developments, with thin veneers of col-

Below: Roman concrete techniques. First stones then

Opus incertum

Opus testaceum   Opus reticulatum

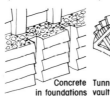

Concrete in foundations   Tunnel or barrel vault

bricks were used to provide a framework to hold the concrete while it set. The walls were built slightly in advance of the concrete core.

oured marble, glued to the walls with plaster and secured with bronze clamps. Sometimes, painted stucco was used to imitate coloured marble, and in private houses, fine, smooth, stucco walls were painted with elaborately designed frescoes.

The wide range of construction problems and building techniques successfully treated by Roman architects remained unsurpassed for some 1600 years. They developed an extensive variety of specialized building materials: glass and marble mosaic; special bricks, plasters, stuccos, and mortars; light-weight aggregates; bronze sheathing and gilding. They also anticipated the main types of vaults and buttresses used in Medieval architecture.

Imposing Order on Nature

The engineering skill of the Romans, as well as their brilliant inventiveness with concrete enabled them to remodel the landscape, where the Greeks had been subservient to it. There was a strong desire to impose order and a militaristic, rectilinear control over natural, organic phenomena. The town of Pracneste (Palestrina) was carved out of a great spur of rock, with symmetrical ramps and stairways leading to terraces containing squares and colonnades. At the summit of this complex was a theatre, carved into the solid rock.

New towns and colonies were laid out according to rectangular grid plans, and buildings arranged in a logical hierarchy based on their function and relative importance. Old towns were sometimes ripped apart to achieve this regularity: the Greek city at Marseilles, for example, was completely pulled down and rebuilt. Despite several attempts, Rome itself was never replanned on a larger scale, although several piecemeal developments by successive emperors managed to provide pockets of grandiose planning amongst the chaotic urban sprawl.

Roman architects applied the same ruthless logic of town planning to the construction of

buildings. Their well-ordered hierarchy of disparate spaces and activities contained within a formal structure or plan is analogous to the political organization of the Roman Empire itself: a degree of freedom within a defined set of rules or laws. In such vast complexes as the baths of Caraculla or the palace of Diocletian, Roman architects skillfully accommodated a wide variety of activities and needs—manipulating and controlling the spaces to contain them in a way that was both functional and symbolic. This kind of planning has provided much of the inspiration for today's architects and town-planners.

The thermae or public baths were a central feature of everyday Roman life. Even smaller towns could boast some sort of bathing emporium, but the largest and most luxurious were in Rome and Pompeii—palatial buildings provided by the ruling elite for the relaxation and entertainment of a pleasure-loving populace.

Besides baths, there were libraries, lecture halls, and private rooms for philosophers, poets and statesmen. A large, elaborately-landscaped open space provided an area for gymnastic and athletic displays with seating for spectators. Above all, these institutions were a meeting place for the exchange of gossip and news (and political intrigues).

The baths of Caracalla and Diocletian in Rome are the two most splendid examples. Their scale is difficult to comprehend: Caracalla's baths provided for 1600 bathers, and the central building block covered an area 228 metres by 115 metres (750 feet × 380 feet), set in a sumptuous park of 12 hectares (32 acres). Diocletian's was even larger. These leisure centres catered to every conceivable sensual activity, until the early Christian emperors finally banned the most decadent pastimes in the fourth century.

The bathing pools of the thermae of Caracalla were raised on a platform 6 metres (20 feet) high, 321 metres (352 yards) square, beneath which were the furnaces, hot air ducts and hypo-

Left: An arch from the Baths of Caracalla, built between AD 211 and AD 217 for the use of all citizens.

Right: An aerial reconstruction of the Baths of Caracalla. There were facilities for 1600 bathers, with hot, tepid and cold pools raised on a high platform.

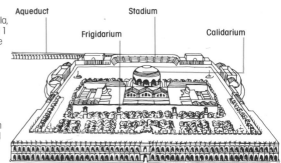

Aqueduct   Stadium   Frigidarium   Calidarium

causts for heating the building. A two-storey colonnade along the entrance-side contained shops and small private baths. The main entrance led into the formal landscaped park (laid out for wrestling, gymnastics and athletics), with the lecture halls and libraries on either side.

A huge vaulted reservoir on the far side stored water, supplied by the Marcian aqueduct and distributed by lead piping throughout the complex. Dominating the building block in the middle of the park, was a vast hall with a roof of intersecting semicircular vaults, 32 metres (108 feet) high. The calidarium (hot bath) was circular, covered by a dome similar to the Pantheon, with walls heated by concealed hot-air ducts. The frigidarium or cold pool was open to the sky, a welcome antidote to the sultry summer sun of Rome. Interiors were lavishly decorated with richly-veined, coloured marbles and painted stucco. Marble, polished granite, alabaster and other luxurious stones were used for columns, capitals and much of the carvings, while the dome and vaults were modelled with painted stucco. In the great halls were housed some of the finest figure sculptures of antiquity, many of them brought from Greece. Such elaborately decorated interiors offered a strong contrast with their austere, plain exteriors—a complete reversal of the priorities of Greek architecture.

Politically, the baths of Rome and provincial cities played a vital part in imperial social policy: all members of the community (even slaves) could enjoy many of the same luxuries as the nobility. The enormous expenditure on building and water supply helped to buy public support, necessary perhaps even in the most unimaginative totalitarian regimes.

Architecturally, the thermae provided a model for many later building types, and discoveries were applied to the great basilicas of Maxentius and Constantine;

the domed or vaulted Christian churches of the eastern empire (such as Santa Sophia); and even the vaulted cathedrals that appeared in Medieval Europe.

Stones with a Bloody Past

The Romans copied Greek theatres, at first by making use of natural hollows in the ground, and later by building concentric rows of tiered seats, supported by vaults and arches. The central area at ground level became part of the auditorium, providing seats for the most important spectators. Perhaps the best-preserved example of this is the theatre at Orange, in the south of France.

It might be supposed from a reading of the history of the Games, that the Romans were more interested in real-life entertainment than in the stylized posturing of literary drama, for certainly the Roman government sponsored gruesome displays of mortal combat to amuse their citizens and to distract them from political activities.

Architects constructed vast amphitheatres for these spectacles, of which the Colosseum is the most famous. (Curiously, the word 'arena', used for the central performing space, was derived from the Latin for 'sand', spread on the ground to absorb the blood of the victims.)

Started by Vespian in AD 70, the Colosseum was finished 12 years later by Domitian. It is an eclipse 188 metres (620 feet) long. Four tiers of seats for 50,000 people were supported by a rigid, honeycomb of vaults and arches, disguised by a simple and elegant, curved façade. Two fundamental architectural concepts are featured in this monument: firstly, the separation of structure and applied decoration, and secondly, the use of all three Greek orders (Doric, Ionic and Corinthian) in one building, attached or engaged to the façade, and constructed in tiers above one another.

In the Greek temple, structure

is simple and self-evident—expressed by the building's decorative components. The structure of the Colosseum is extremely complex, involving arches that curve in all directions, spanning openings that taper both upwards and inwards. Many different materials were used for the concrete: lava for foundation, tufa and brick for walls, and to reduce weight, pumice for vaults.

Although the structure seems open, the combined cross-sectional area of the supporting piers adds up to about one-sixth of the total ground-floor area, distributing the load from above. On the façade, these massive piers were surfaced with travertine (limestone) slabs, their bulk disguised by slender white marble columns, capitals and a continuous flowing entablature (horizontal decorative moulding supported by the columns). The corridors or arcades between the piers formed an effective pedestrian circulation system, with access to the tiered seating via tunnels and steps that emerge into the auditorium at regular intervals.

The Colosseum could be roofed with canvas, stretched across

ropes hung from masts attached to the top outside edge. For naval and aquatic spectacles, the arena could also be flooded. Gladiators, Christians, wild beasts and other victims for slaughter were held in chambers on the inner ground floor and in corridors beneath the arena.

Even in ruins the Colosseum is an awesome monument. It was used as a model for amphitheatres throughout the empire—yet another example of the way architects and engineers from the capital influenced building in the provinces. Two early attempts at amphitheatres, at Arles and Nîmes, have survived. Well-preserved, they are built entirely of stone, antedating the flowering of concrete technology.

Triumph of the Curve

During the expansion of the Roman Empire, a long procession of pagan cults appeared and disappeared, victims either of fashion or of official disapproval. Generally, the Romans were much less religious than were the Greeks or the Egyptians.

Early Roman temples combined

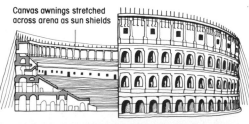

Right: The Colosseum, a cut-away section showing the massive concrete vaulting that was employed.

Below: The façade of the Colosseum as it is today.

Canvas awnings stretched across arena as sun shields

features from both Greek and Etruscan prototypes. Somewhat shorter than the Greek model, the typical Roman temple was raised on a high podium and approached by broad steps. Side columns were engaged or attached to the walls, and the front entrance was formed by a portico, flanked with sculptures. The Masion Carrée at Nîmes, in France, is one of the best-preserved examples of the Roman temple architecture.

The Maison Carrée exhibits the restrained, almost severe, classicism associated with Augustan architecture, as propagated by the rules of the architect, Vitruvius. Like the earlier Greek temple, from which it was derived,

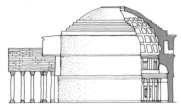

Above: Section of the Pantheon, showing the vault; lighter materials such as pumice were used to reduce weight. **Below:** The interior as it looks today, still a magnificent structure.

Maison Carrée was built to be externally impressive. Thus, the architect strove more for a sculptural than an architectural effect; in particular, the Corinthian capitals used throughout the temple have provided architects, from the Renaissance to the late 19th century, with excellent models.

The Pantheon provides a contrast to the Nîmes temple. The principal visual attraction of the Pantheon is the vast space that fills the interior, enclosed by the gargantuan dome. This temple, unique among the imperial buildings of Rome in having best survived the ravages of time, represents the antithesis of the Greek temple. In fact, it has more in common with the great thermae or bathing establishments.

Despite the many additions, removals and restorations, the Pantheon is sufficiently well preserved for the visitor to stand beneath the dome and imagine the building's original magnificence during the rule of Hadrian. Partly, it was conceived as an architectural celebration of the triumph of the curve over the straight line. First came the replacement of the conventional beam by the Etruscan arch. By the time it was completed, however, the Pantheon had the appearance of the Roman baroque style, generally associated with the grandiose flourishes of the late period of the empire.

The dome itself is the supreme masterpiece of Roman engineering. Resting on a massive cylindrical drum supported by 6 metre (21 foot) thick walls, the dome grows thinner and lighter nearer the summit. To reduce the overall weight, the rubble used to make the concrete changes from tufa and travertine limestone at the base, and tufa and brick for the lower part of the dome, to pumice for the highest section. Additional easing of the weight is achieved by 'coffers', or moulded, decorative, rectangular hollows, arranged in five layers and subtly foreshortened for optical effect. The entire space is dramatically lit by the 8 metres (27 feet) wide 'eye' or opening at the top. This provides the sole source of light.

The thrust of the dome is collected and spread by a sophisticated system of buttresses, disguised within the walls. The lower wall is hollowed out by eight giant niches, each slotted between buttresses that structurally connect inner and outer walls. These once contained colossal statues of the Roman Emperor Augustus. Slender Corinthian columns in front of each niche create the illusion of supporting the drum and dome, thereby visually 'reducing' the apparent weight of the dome. One of these niches was designed to form the entrance.

The Pantheon was erected on the site of a temple built in 25 BC by Agrippa, son-in-law of Augustus; this structure had been severely damaged by fire at the end of the first century AD. By

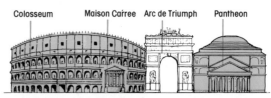

Colosseum   Maison Carrée   Arc de Triumph   Pantheon

Above: The Pont du Gard, in the south of France, built to supply water to the city of Nîmes; it was erected almost without using mortar. It is made up of three separate tiers of arches.

incorporating the portico of Agrippa's temple, Hadrian was able to reduce the number of columns from ten to eight. Originally, the dome gleamed with a sheathing of gilded brass plates, but these were removed to Constantinople in AD 655. The massive bronze relief portraying the battle between the Titans and the gods on the portico and the white marble facing on the outer walls are now lost.

Dwellings of the Wealthy

Sightseers in Rome at the height of the empire would visit a rude hut preserved on the Palatine Hill. This was the reputed home of Romulus. By contrast, the classic Roman 'atrium' house was a model of sophistication. It represented a succession of spaces leading from the accessible public areas to the strictly private, family rooms which were arranged in an axial plan.

The visitor entered the house through the middle of the façade, into a vestibule or ante room, which led to the atrium. Beyond this was the 'tablinum', where the head of the household received his guests. The atrium was roofed over, but a gap was left in the centre to admit light; a vessel was usually placed beneath to collect rainwater.

Pompeii, a provincial town, was buried by the sudden eruption of Vesuvius in AD 79, miraculously preserving the houses and streets, and thereby leaving a vivid impression of life in the first century AD.

The house of Pansa is a typical Pompeiian family dwelling. The structure occupies a single, large block, 34m by 97m (112ft by 319ft). Around the perimeter of

the building were a variety of shops, smaller dwellings and a bakery. The main house itself was entered via a passage at one end; all the rooms faced inwards, with the exception of kitchens and service quarters requiring direct access to the street. The central feature was a completely private courtyard (open to the sky), planted with flowers and adorned with statues, fountains and water basins.

Water played an important part in both landscaping and in interior design. During the first century BC, an aqueduct was constructed to divert water to Pompeii, enabling generous supplies of fresh water to be provided through leaden pipes, for street fountains and water basins. There were domestic taps in most houses, and many of the larger houses had their own private bathroom suits and pools.

The high density and land values of Rome itself prompted the evolution of multi-storey buildings: the so-called 'insulae', or apartment blocks—four, five or even six stories high. These were the world's first tenements. For the wealthy, there were richly-endowed country villas; in some cases built entirely for pleasure.

The Spalato palace (in what is now Split, in Yugoslavia) was a grand, fortified mansion built in AD 300 by the Emperor Diocletian for his retirement. A masterpiece of formal, axial planning, it covers 3 hectares (8 acres) facing the sea on the south. The principal entry is from the north, between two octagonal towers. A route lined with trees leads through the barracks and workshops of the garrison to the magnificent state apartments. Within the rigid rectangle of the plan, a range of widely differing functional units are accommodated—creating spatial variety, logically controlled by an axial grid—an expression of the power of a ruthless emperor.

Faith Veiled in Mystery
Constantinople - City of Gold

Architectural Importance:
The early Christian basilica became the prototype for Medieval churches and cathedrals throughout western Europe. Byzantine architecture was the first to exploit the articulation of interior spaces and to create a unified whole. Santa Sophia, an unrivalled masterpiece of daring engineering, and sophisticated spatial effects. Byzantine style exported to Russia, Armenia, Greece, Venice and Ravenna. The architectural style of Byzantium also had a strong affect on Arab building designs.

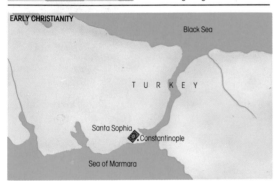

By the fourth century AD, the Roman Empire began to disintegrate, threatened externally by barbarian hordes advancing both from the Germanic territories and from the north, and internally by a combination of excessive taxation, rampant inflation and worsening food shortages.

To stave off complete collapse, the Emperor Diocletian divided the empire into two spheres in the hope of making it more manageable. His successor, Constantine, continued this process by transferring the political centre from the western part to the strategically and economically more valuable east. The site chosen for the new capital was a city that had been sacked and rebuilt many times before coming under the domination of Rome.

In AD 330, New Rome was officially inaugurated—an act of immense historical importance. Constantinople was destined to become one of the world's most renowned

Below: Hagia Sophia, the greatest of all Byzantine churches. Its engineering virtuosity and spectacular interior decoration had a profound effect on Western architecture. Sadly much of its original interior was destroyed when the Ottomans captured the church and converted it into a mosque.

Stylistic Essentials:
Early Christian churches; simple rectangular plan, nave with two aisles either side, longitudinal/horizontal emphasis. Byzantine: Centralized plan involving circular or polygonal Greek cross. Flat, unmoulded surfaces covered with rich mosaics and frescoes. Much use of dome.

Primary Building Materials:
With early Christian, stone or brick, with wooden roof or stone barrel vault. Byzantine: brick, used with mortar joints to develop light, strong arches and domes. External covering of plaster, internal covering of thin marble veneers and rich mosaics. Columns strengthened with metal rings or amulets.

Spread of Influence: Until the appearance of the secular culture of the Renaissance, European architects devoted their skills and energies to the construction of churches and cathedrals, all based, to a lesser or greater extent, on early Christian models.

capitals: a city of tremendous wealth and the political, religious and cultural focus of Europe for 700 years.

The decision to move the capital from Rome had a lasting effect upon the classical world; foremost by preserving the legacy of the dying empire and, equally if not more importantly, by encouraging the first fusion of Oriental and western art.

Under the aegis of the first Christian emperor of Rome, Constantinople rapidly grew in size and importance. Here the caravans from Persia and China unloaded their silks, carpets, procelains, and precious stones. Here, too, flocked travellers and traders, princes and painters from the dark and troubled lands of Europe and the mysterious cultures of the East.

Constantine had been a Christian convert for some years before he founded the capital of New Rome, but it was not until the inauguration of the city that he proclaimed Christianity the official religion of the eastern empire. With his ruthless support, it rapidly evolved from a small, curious sect to a glorious and powerful institution. Ritual and worship became much more elaborate, requiring a more ostentatious architecture to match this new importance. Barely 200 years later, the Emperor Justinian, witnessing the consecration of the Hagia Sophia ('Holy Wisdom' in Greek), uttered his famous words: 'Solomon, I have surpassed thee.'

Then the most incredible church in Christendom, the Hagia Sophia can be considered the outstanding achievement of the Byzantine era.

In its fierce boldness Santa Sophia represents the antithesis of the logic of Roman architecture and of the fastidious perfectionism of the classical Greek style. It is an example of architecture intended, not to impress and overwhelm, but to stir one's deepest religious sentiments.

St Augustine wrote that: 'Beauty cannot be beheld in any bodily matter.' Notwithstanding the fact that Santa Sophia appears physically beautiful, this principal Byzantine church seems to radiate an ethereal beauty that would undoubtedly qualify her even for Augustine's spiritual definition.

An Empire Disintegrates

The early history of Christianity is a saga of official persecution, indifference, toleration and finally acceptance. Before the promulgation of the Edict of Milan in AD 313, when Christianity was made publicly 'acceptable', adherents generally refrained from public displays of their faith. The process of accommodating religion with state-held beliefs was a gradual one, though persecutions of Christians often erupted whenever imperial authority felt threatened by the sheer weight and numbers of converts, or their accession to high office.

The early Christians tended to congregate discreetly, usually meeting in one another's houses. It was not until 300 years after the birth of Christ that worship and religious administration had both reached such a level of complexity that they required special types of buildings in which to conduct the Church's affairs.

During Constantine's reign, the seeds of a deep doctrinal schism between East and West were sown, and state protection on both sides brought this rivalry into the open. In the East, there developed a penchant for mystery; rituals were performed by priests separated from the congregation by screens, effectively shrouding the service in darkness. In the West, worship took a more open, ceremonial form, involving the active participation of the congregation. The difference of approach was just one aspect of the dogmatic schism which was made permanent in AD 800.

The division of the Church had an inevitable effect on the development of early Christian architecture. The result was the appearance of two different forms of building: one rectangular and the other circular. Initially, they were equally favoured in both East and West, but the requirements of congregational worship in the West led to a preference for the rectangular basilica, forerunner of the cruciform plan of Romanesque and Gothic cathedrals. The East adopted the circular form, which culminated in the construction of Santa Sophia.

Holy Designs

One important aspect of Christianity that differentiated it from earlier religions was that Christians worshipped together, generally inside a building. Greek and Roman temples were built to contain god-images, not people, their pagan associations too strong for them to be used as models for Christian architecture.

The Roman type of building most popular for non-religious public activities was the basilica. Although the great basilicas in Roman Fora were principally intended for use by magistrates and tribunals, others were used as money exchanges, shops and special law courts. In many instances, large reception rooms in wealthy houses were also referred to as basilicas, so it seems that the word itself simply meant 'meeting place' and was applied to a wide range of architectural forms. Since Christian worship involved a meeting of the faithful, it seemed natural to use the word basilica to describe the first churches.

Official encouragement of Christianity brought with it the need to invent a Christian church architecture. Gradually, the wide range of plans narrowed, until the term basilica came to mean very much what it does today: (the 'nave'); a long rectangular space (the 'apse'), with a semicircular niche at the east end, and two 'aisles' on either side of the nave separated by a row of columns or piers. Sometimes there would also be a 'narthex' or ante-room at the western end. The roof was usually of timber.

Perhaps the most famous early Christian basilica was Old St. Peter's in Rome, built by Constantine near the site of the martyrdom of St. Peter in Nero's Circus. Pulled down in 1505 to make way for the present cathedral, originally St. Peter's was large enough to accommodate the huge crowds that came to venerate this very popular saint; it later became the religious focus of the Western (Catholic) Church.

The other important early building form was round, with a central nave and surrounding 'ambulatory' (a circular aisle). First used for tombs and funeral chapels, a circular plan was subsequently preferred to the rectangular basilica for the Eastern (Orthodox) churches of the Byzantine Empire. Domes have always been a traditional feature of Eastern architecture—perhaps circular or curving forms appeal to the Eastern mind because they appear infinite.

Circular floor plans give rise to practical organizational difficulties, and so Byzantine architecture was forced to invent a satisfactory way of joining a circle (the dome) to a rectangular plan (the Romans only used domes above circular or polygonal structures). The solution to this problem was the pendentive. The creator remains unknown, but the pendentive was an architectural breakthrough equal to the discovery of the arch or the vault.

The pendentive is a curved

Below: The Church of S. Maria Maggiore, in Rome. A typical basilican plan, this church is very close to its model in classical architecture. It has solid marble columns and fine ceiling mosaics.

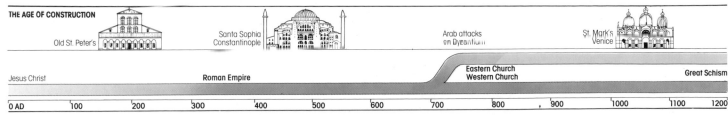

THE AGE OF CONSTRUCTION

Old St. Peter's   Santa Sophia Constantinople   Arab attacks on Byzantium   St. Mark's Venice

Jesus Christ   Roman Empire   Eastern Church Western Church   Great Schism

0 AD   100   200   300   400   500   600   700   800   900   1000   1100   1200

triangular vault that allows a natural transition from rectangular forms to circular ones, leading the eye continuously upwards without interruption by beams, plinths or intermediate supports. Thus the horizontal emphasis of the basilica—columns marching towards the altar; strong horizontals of a flat roof or barrel vault—melts away, and internal

Above: The problem of building a dome over a square plan. 1 Early domes over round plans. 2

Forming an octagon. 3 Using several over-hanging beams. 4 The pendentive, a perfect solution.

space rises smoothly and inevitably to the dome above. Byzantine architecture was essentially centripetal, whereas Western Christian architecture created long vistas down a narrow nave—the visual climax being the sanctuary at the far end.

Christianity forbade the worship of idols, and the Orthodox hierarchy took steps to ban the representation of Christ and the saints in three-dimensional (sculptured) form. To overcome this restriction, artists resorted to the use of mosaics and frescoes to illustrate the lives of the saints, martyrs and apostles. The possibilities this gave to painters and decorators were practically endless, and in time icons, frescoes and mosaics in the most vivid combinations of colours adorned every available internal surface.

Jewel of the East

In 527, Justinian ascended the throne of the Eastern Empire. A

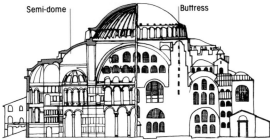

Semi-dome   Buttress

devout Christian and a great organizer, his 40 years of autocratic rule had a profound effect on Byzantine culture. He saw himself as divinely appointed, both to lead the Christian Church and to re-assemble and revive the old Roman Empire, with Ravenna as the Western sub-capital and Constantinople as the New Rome, a 'daughter more ravishing than the mother'.

Justinian reformed and unified the law (the 'Corpus Luvis' or Justinian Code), recaptured North Africa, Italy and Dalmatia from barbarian rule, made a truce with

the Persians, tried to unify the various Christian factions, and initiated an ambitious building programme that included the jewel of Byzantine architecture, the Church of Santa Sophia.

Justinian allocated enormous sums for this project. His official historian (Procopius) devoted a whole book to his building programme. Justinian's reign marks the adoption of the centrally planned, domed church as the main building form in the East, and the rejection of the basilica (as retained by the West). It is the start of Byzantine architecture.

Above: Santa Sophia, the interior, still a magnificent space although now denuded of its glorious Byzantine decoration.

Left: A cut-away section, showing how the subsidiary domes distribute the thrusts of the main dome.

Faith Veiled in Mystery

This project took barely five years to complete, a remarkable tribute to the organizational skills of the early Christian builders. The overall plan is based on the square. Four massive piers form a square, rising to four arches 21 metres (70 feet) high that are linked by pendentives. These in turn form a circle that supports the dome 32 metres (107 feet) across. Two hemispherical domes, connected to the arches on either side, create a rectangular space (nave), which is given a strong central emphasis by the higher central dome. On the sides of the nave are subsidiary spaces (aisles) and above galleries with separate access for the women. Originally the church was entered through a large atrium (which was destroyed) that led, via a great triple door, into the outer narthex, the (higher) inner narthex and thence to the nave itself.

The basic geometry of the space is bold and simple, an impression reinforced by the overall structural system. Generally the feeling is one of vast domed space, yet the intricacy of decoration and graduation of smaller spaces that soar upwards to the dome itself suggest a much greater complexity of structure than is immediately apparent. Before it was covered with paint and plaster during Moslem occupation, the rich decoration of gold, mosaic, coloured marble and intricate carving would have emphasized the impression of interior lightness. The almost infinite voids of the aisles and the flooding of the galleries with light from the windows high in the nave and around the dome help to reinforce the sense of airiness.

The basic planning of the church suited the liturgical form of worship popular at the time: a magnificent, 'heavenly' space at the centre, where patriarch, priests and emperor performed their rituals with ancillary spaces for the passive congregation which was granted a mere glimpse of the proceedings and a restricted view of the central nave. The architecture is symbolic of a circular, theocratic approach to religion: the all-powerful union of emperor and priesthood at the focal point with the common people hidden in semi-darkness about the circumference. Physically, the hierarchy of spaces, rising to the heavenly dome in the middle, mirrors the rigid Orthodox Church hierarchy of divinity in the centre, with light radiating through the apostles, angles, saints, patriarch, clergy, emperor, and thence to the common people.

Santa Sophia is constructed mainly of brick (solid ashlar stone is used only for the eight main piers). Each brick was about 50mm (two inches) thick, and 600mm (24 inches) square, laid with a 50mm (two inch) bed of immensely strong mortar made from differing combinations of lime, sand and crushed pottery,

Above: St. Mark's, Venice, an architectural showpiece celebrating the wealth and confidence of the Venetian republic of the 1100s.

Right: A scene from the famous mosaic of the 6th century Church of S. Apollinare Nuova in Ravenna, depicting the wanderings of the Three Wise Men.

tiles, or bricks. The bricks in the dome were laid practically horizontally, rather than radiating to the centre of the hemisphere. This was done in order to diminish the thrust. In fact, the dome collapsed in 558, 21 years after it had been finished.

Architecturally, Santa Sophia represented a complete departure from the basilica type of church favoured by the early Christians. Its origins are closer to the great central halls of the public baths of Rome, the huge vaulted basilica of Constantine, and the vaulting techniques of Mesopotamia. Although the structural principle of using rigid lightweight vaults made from brick embedded in thick mortar was fashionable in the Greek cities of Asia Minor during the fourth and fifth centuries, no other structure remotely compared in scale to that of Santa Sophia. The extreme lightness of the vaulting of Santa Sophia allowed a much bolder skeletal structure requiring few internal supports but wide spans — in contrast to the monolithic, weighty concrete of Roman times.

Gradually, the techniques of spatial organization and thin-shell vaulting pioneered in Santa Sophia were applied to later buildings, though in a more conservative manner. Once again in the hands of the master builders, rather than bold innovators, church building returned to less imaginative, but sounder and more sober principles. Santa Sophia remains a unique and isolated architectural event, yet always a glorious source of inspiration to architects from both hemispheres.

A Blend of Opposites

In its early days, the merchant republic of Venice depended

Right: Scale comparison of the great Byzantine churches with the Arc de Triumph. Dominating the group is Santa Sophia of Constantinople.

Old St. Peter's   Santa Sophia   Arc de Triumph   St. Mark's

heavily for its survival on trade with Constantinople, where Venetian diplomats and businessmen formed an immensely strong colony. Thus, it is not particularly surprising to find that this fast-growing Adriatic republic should have so fully absorbed the influence of Byzantine architecture. One of the greatest examples of this is St Marks, first built in AD 830 to house the relics of the Evangelist (Patron of the Sea), removed from Alexandria by Venetian traders.

In 1063, the Venetians made plans to replace the old church with another, grander building that was not to be completely finished for another five centuries. It became a rather gaudy repository for the considerable spoils of war and commercial wizardry of the Venetian merchants, the bulk of which came from the sacking of Constantinople by the armies of the crusaders.

The core of St. Marks looks much the way it did in the 11th century. It has a cruciform plan, with four domes above each arm, and a higher dome above the central bay. This basic arrangement was copied from Justinian's

Church of the Holy Apostles in Constantinople, but in Venice the domes are raised higher, on drums, giving the church its oriental fairy-tale flavour. The mosaics which decorate the interior are the most elaborate of the Byzantine era, and as such perhaps lack the direct simplicity and charm of those in other Italianate-Byzantine churches.

Architecturally, St. Marks is a florid blend of Byzantine, Gothic and Renaissance styles; a symphony of coloured marbles and glittering gold set against the azure Venetian sky and reflected in the shimmering waters of the Adriatic.

Unity of Style

The Romans had used Ravenna as a naval base ever since the era of Augustus Caesar. In AD 402, Honarius (who had inherited the western half of the Roman Empire) moved his capital here, having left Rome because it was more difficult to defend from the attacking Goths, and was plagued with malaria from the surrounding marshes. Honarius was succeeded by his sister, Galia Placidia, whose mausoleum was one of the earliest

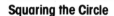

Squaring the Circle

The two greatest achievements in building technology of the Byzantine era are: firstly, the invention of the pendentive, and secondly, the perfection of thin shell vaulting using light-weight brick work. While the dome of the Pantheon in Rome is structurally sophisticated, it is much heavier than the shells used in the dome of Santa Sophia, even though pumice was used by the Romans as a light-weight concrete material. To cope with the enormous thrusts encountered, the Romans built great thick walls and buttresses which were then visually disguised with niches and superimposed columns, etc. In contrast, the light brick shells of Byzantine vaulting produced far lower thrusts, requiring many fewer and less powerful supports.

The triangular pendentive not only solved the problem of visually connecting a square structure to a circular dome, but also provided an elegant way of structurally spreading the load. The two hemispherical side domes absorb the thrusts of the central dome, and together with the four central arches and the eight main piers form a rigid, structurally-independent system. The subsidiary spaces (aisles, galleries, narthices, etc) are independent of the central structure, which forms a light honey-comb of brick vaults. The brick-work carcass was built first, and allowed to settle before internal sheathings of marble and mosaic were attached. The decorative patterns produced by brickwork coursing were used to break up the surfaces. Byzantine vaults and domes were probably constructed without 'centering' or temporary support: the large flat bricks could be built up so that each layer extended a bit farther, until the dome was complete, a technique that may have originated in Mesopotamia.

examples of the 'cruciform' (cross-shaped) church plan. According to legend her embalmed body could be seen through a peephole in the sarcophagus, that is until a small boy pushed a taper through the hole to get a better view and consequently reduced the contents to ashes.

For its intended purpose, the mausoleum of Galia Placidia is tiny, only 10 metres (33 feet) by 11 metres (37 feet), yet the space seems bigger, an illusion created by the glittering mosaics that cover the walls and vaults. Against a strong blue ground, figures of St. Lawrence and the apostles placidly gaze down from the flat bays between the archers, while upon the dome shine the stars of the galaxy.

Barely decades after Galia Placide's mausoleum had been built, Theodoric the Ostrogoth captured Ravenna and was proclaimed King of Italy. Though a barbarian, he was, nevertheless, a man of culture who strove to bring order and harmony to his kingdom. During his reign, Theodoric ordered the construction of two fine Byzantine churches. At his death, in 526, he was buried in a remarkable mausoleum that still exists in Ravenna.

One of Italy's most impressive early churches is S. Apollinare Nuova, built by Theodoric around AD 520. It is a classic basilican church, with a high, wide, central nave. In between the windows, high up in the walls of the nave,

are the original mosaics dating from Theodoric's reign. Bold, yet simple, they contrast strongly with the dazzling mosaic pagent of martyrs, virgins and saints below, applied later by Justinian. Leading from the Virgin enthroned at one end to Christ at the other is a repetitive pattern of a procession of figures marching in step with the columns and arches emphasizing the length of the nave. The aim was to reinforce the unity of the whole—art and architecture integral in the service of religion.

When Justinian reclaimed Italy for the Byzantine Empire in AD 540, Ravenna became the second most important city of the empire. For 200 years to come, Byzantine architecture flourished here.

The finest church of the Justinian period is San Vitale, built on the basis of a centralized plan composed of two concentric octagons surrounded by aisles and vaulted galleries. The central space is crowned with a feather-light dome made from hollow clay pots (covered with a tiled, wooden roof) light enough to be supported by the arches alone, without need of additional buttresses.

The church was planned just prior to the building of Santa Sophia, and financed by the wealthy banker, Julianus. Byzantine can be seen in every aspect of

Right: The Church of San Vitale, Ravenna (6th century). Typical of the plain, austere, exteriors associated with church architecture which appeared in the Byzantine era.

the building, from the type of brick used to the octagonal planning, and the intricate decor. There is a unity of design and a flowing graduation of space that is suggestive of Santa Sophia.

The vaults of the sanctuary in San Vitale are lined with luxurious mosaics depicting the reign of Justinian and the lives of the saints. A full-size figure of the Emperor Justinian, attired in purple and gold and crowned with jewels, surrounded by priests and soldiers, stares across the apse at his equally resplendent wife, Theodora (a legendary beauty, she was said to have been an actress—a euphemism for a 'lady of pleasure'.

Centre of the Universe
Peking-Palaces within Palaces

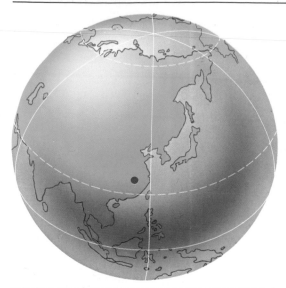

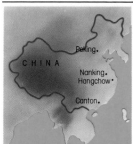

Architectural Importance:
Strong influence on Japanese architecture but apart from fashion for Chinese landscape-design in 18th and 19th century England, it was largely isolated, little or no influence on world architecture. Structural concept unique to Chinese development. Closely integrated with philosophical concepts as exposed by Confucious very great reliance on traditional methods of construction, and the widespread use of vegetable products such as wood, straw and reeds, which by their nature do not make for architectural permanence.

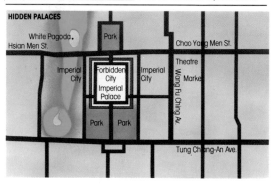

HIDDEN PALACES

White Pagoda.
Hsian Men St.
Park
Chao Yang Men St.
Imperial City
Forbidden City Imperial Palace
Imperial City
Theatre
Market
Wang Fu Ching Av.
Park
Park
Tung Chiang-An Ave.

In China, architectural conceptions radically differ from any encountered so far in this book. While other ancient cultures have left visual records of their arts, often in the form of monuments, our knowledge of dynastic Chinese artistic achievements is largely derived from the fragments of written evidence which have survived.

Very little material evidence remains inside the country. Indeed, the earliest large-scale building in China still standing dates only from the sixth century AD. Our knowledge of earlier buildings comes from later reconstructions, from stylistic imitations in other countries and from designs incorporated into paintings and onto pottery.

The fact that few early Chinese buildings have survived is not entirely the result of accident. A great part of the reason was the Chinese attitude towards time. They were not concerned with such vague concepts as

Below: The Hall of
Supreme Harmony, in
the Forbidden City in
Peking. Built in the
17th century, it is
the largest hall of the
Imperial Palace, and
was used for important
state ceremonies.
The podium in the
foreground is made
of marble, and the
ornate balustrades
are typical of Ming
architecture. The roof
is of glazed tiles.

Stylistic Essentials:
Generally single storey, post and beam, construction based on modular rectangular bays, large curved roofs, with overhanging eaves supported by intricately-carved timber beam and brackets. Enclosed, rectilinear courts arranged on strong north/south axis. Chinese roof construction not based on triangular tied frames, a traditional method in the West.

Primary Building Materials:
Timber considered the most fitting material for structure, both functionally and philosophically. Chinese timber truss system allowed multiple roof shapes; in particular, concave curves. Stone and brick used for foundations, fortifications and pagodas. Some use of ceramic materials; palace design became elaborate, with heavy use of ornamentation. Great emphasis on 'naturalistic' features, such as gardens, water courses, orchards rocks, etc.

eternity or, indeed to any great extent, with the future. Taoism and Buddhism taught their adherents to concern themselves with the present, the here and now, and to endeavour thus to be in harmony with nature. Such values imply a delicate balancing of opposing forces, an equilibrium liable to undergo change from one moment to the next.

Chinese architecture sought to reflect this striving for balance, this attempt at continuity within a changing universe. The Chinese did not build their palaces and pagodas to last forever—they built them to reflect their society's preoccupation with the balance of forces within their world.

A corollary of this was the extensive reliance on traditional methods of construction and the widespread use of wood and other organic products, materials that do not survive well the passage of time.

Imperial Chinese buildings were transitory, almost ephemeral. Every generation rebuilt according to its particular needs and desires. Thus what mattered most was the symbolic value of the buildings and their relationship to each other, to the landscape and ultimately to the universe. Architecture, in its practical sense, was a minor art. Architecture, as a physical expression of the harmony between man and nature, emperor and subject, individual and family, was a matter of supreme importance.

A Country without Equal

China is a land of superlatives. It is the third largest country in the world; the largest in Asia. It is twice the size of Europe, has one-quarter of the global population and possesses the world's highest mountain, the largest plateau and the world's sixth longest river.

It is also a land of extremes. Arctic winters alternate with sweltering summers; ice-covered mountain passes, often hidden behind dense fog, give way to vast, flat plains periodically subject to monsoon flooding or ferocious droughts. Not infrequently, cyclones and earthquakes wreak their destruction upon the country.

It is a land of demographic and linguistic extremes, as well. While the Han make up the bulk of the population, there are 53 minority groups spread over 60 percent of the country, each group speaking its own language. Once a predominantly agricultural land, China now boasts no fewer than 22 cities each with populations of more than one million.

The extreme variations of climate, terrain and dialect have had a predictably dramatic effect upon the history of China, with the pattern of development seeming more like a ragged jigsaw puzzle than a linear path moving clearly towards modernity.

Below: The massive gateway into Peking. Little else remains of the fortifications that once encircled the royal domain of the Chinese emperors.

The true origins of the Chinese people are buried in the bedrock of antiquity; but discounting the tales of sages set down in the few ancient books still in existence, it seems 2,000 BC is the date most historians tentatively put forward as the rude beginning of Chinese civilization.

Until 221 BC, when China first became a politically unified nation, the picture is confused: warlords struggling to assert themselves against local rivals, emerging kingdom-states defending their hard-won territories only to lose them again, periods of anarchy and civil war.

With the emergence of the Ch'in empire came an era of stability and progress and, in time, the state became rich and powerful. The first Ch'in emperor, Shih Huang Ti, abolished the feudal system established by his predecessors and ruled the country directly, through appointed inspectors. This system of centralized state bureaucracy lasted more or less intact for some 2,000 years, until the collapse of the Manchu dynasty in 1912.

Centre of the Universe

The ancient pseudo-science of 'fengshui' was essential in Chinese construction. Before even a single stone was turned, it was imperative to consult a geomancer, who could ascertain whether the chosen site would favour the good spirits while keeping the evil ones at bay. Fengshui is literally translated as 'wind and water'. The relationship of trees, water and rocks to the lay of the land was analyzed in great detail, and if the diagnosis was favourable, the architect could begin. Fengshui is just one example of the many restrictions that governed the design of buildings in Imperial China. It reflects a characteristic duality between practical and spiritual needs—a balance between intellect and emotion.

Chinese society was more hierarchical and autocratic than any other culture yet discovered. The emperor was effectively the centre of the universe; all power and control radiated from him. This compulsive desire to create order out of chaos can be seen in every aspect of Chinese architecture and town-planning.

The centre of the Roman city was the forum, where citizens met to engage in business and politics. The Chinese people were subjects, not citizens, and the centre of the Chinese city was the walled enclosure of the ruler's palace. Cities were laid out according to a rigid rectangular grid, on a powerful north-south axis. Each building or activity was allotted its place in the system, according to its function and status—from markets to pleasure parks, temples to administrative offices, palaces to the humblest dwellings.

The organization of individual buildings themselves expresses the same logic and clarity of thought. Chinese architecture used several discrete buildings where Europeans used one large mass. Instead of a single dramatic vista, leading to a single climax (as with the Renaissance palace), the Imperial Palace in Peking is a succession of visual climaxes. One delightful surprise follows another with the tension being heightened at critical points by some event such as a flowing stream, a marble bridge or an ornate balustrade. In place of one building, there are hundreds, connected by courtyards, separate yet integrated, linked to the city as a whole by its all-powerful axial grid.

The simple 'post and beam' structural system of Chinese architecture reflects the same clear logic. The structure is a timber lattice framework, made up of rectangular bays—a modular system in which the final size of the building depends on the number of identical units or bays. (The size of dwellings was strictly controlled according to rank: the more senior the occupant, the more bays in his house.) The foundation or floor is a rectangular terrace or raised podium, the roof a tiled 'hat' that sits astride the lattice. Walls are made from lightweight panels fixed between the pillars, though sometimes this space is left void, to allow free movement.

Thus Chinese architecture is like a number of concentric systems—independent, discrete units ordered and contained within a rigid framework of rules. The house is like a miniature city; the city like a huge house. The overlapping relationships and hierarchies of individual, family, city, state, and universe are mirrored by the symbolic organization of architectural elements: pillar, lattice framework, pavilion, palace and city.

The podium or terrace symbolizes the earth, hence made of earthly materials—rock, stone, brick. The walls were timber—the trees between earth and sky. The roof is a reflection of heaven.

Great Wall · Han House · Great Temple of Canton · Ch'i-yin Pagoda · Gateway to Peking · Temple of Heaven

New Stone Age	Shang-An-yang	Chou	Han	T'ang	Sung	Ming	Ching

| 2000 BC | 1500 | 1000 | 500 | 0 AD | 500 | 1000 | 1500 |

Left: The Temple of Heaven, Peking. To add a natural touch, tree trunks were used as supports.

Above: Entrance to Altar of Heaven. This is one of the most sacred of all Chinese temples.

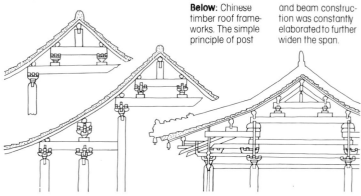

Below: Chinese timber roof frameworks. The simple principle of post and beam construction was constantly elaborated to further widen the span.

The most characteristic feature of Chinese architecture was the roof. The Chinese roof truss or support system allowed a wide range of types, varying according to climatic conditions or local building traditions. In the Ming and Ching dynasties there was a rigid hierarchy of roof shapes, reflecting the status of the building and its occupants. The Chinese roof truss was made up from a number of horizontal beams stacked on top of each other, becoming shorter towards the apex. Unlike the Western truss (which is like a rigid triangle) the Chinese system allowed shallow curves, multiple gabled roofs stacked one above another, hip and half-hip roofs, and all manner of variations. These multiple beams, the decorative brackets and the complex systems of supports that held up the roof hung over the edge from an elaborate interlocking web of timber tracery — an ornamental feature that was also functional.

The main limitation of 'port and beam' construction is the span, restricted by the length of beam that can be made from one piece of wood. The so-called 'ang' or 'lever arm' increased the effective span somewhat, by balancing the weight of overhanging eves with the load of the beam using a lever — supported in the middle by a pillar. The high point of timber roof design was perhaps during the Sung dynasty, when the system was both structurally elegant and decorative without being ostentatious.

Palaces of Supreme Harmony

Chinese palaces were like cities within cities, and thus differed fundamentally from the large, homogeneous palaces found in Europe. The Chinese palace was made up of a collection of single-storey pavilions, grouped according to their specific functions or activities.

This is known from extant documents, for little remains of their former glory, save for a few rammed earth terraces or mounds. Until the sixth century BC, royal palaces in China remained rather diminuitive, a reflection, perhaps, of the uncertain status of their resident owners. But from that time on, imperial edifices gradually became larger, grander and more luxurious as the power and prestige of the government gradually increased.

The emperors of the T'ang dynasty built several vast palace complexes, the grandest of which was the Danning Gong at Changan. Its construction was financed largely by levying a special tax on the population and withholding a month's salary from all officials. The Changan palace covered an area of 200 hectares (500 acres), divided into two sections; one, official, and the other, private. It was comprised of 24 halls, including a throne-room and a banqueting suite, the latter 77 by 130 metres (255 x 427 feet). The private apartments were surrounded by beautiful gardens. Around the outside was a vast number of towers, pavilions and kiosks for use as government offices, meditation chambers or pleasure halls.

The Imperial palace in Peking was built by the Mongol invaders to celebrate their conquest of China. Individual units in the complex were connected by a series of long galleries. The emperor conducted his private affairs in the halls of state, while audiences were held in an outer court. An inner court contained administrative buildings, and beyond this was the Palace City, or emperor's residence, where access was limited solely to members of the imperial family. Begun in 1406, the present palace was built on the site of the original Mongol edifice. Although the basic layout has remained unchanged, several buildings have been renovated or replaced.

The Forbidden City is a huge walled rectangle, 1005 metres by 758 metres (1,100 × 830 yards), surrounded by a moat. There are two main gates, leading to the official part of the palace which is aligned on the central north-south axis. This same axis extends beyond the walls of the Forbidden City, and forms the principal axis of Peking itself. The south entrance to the Forbidden City is guarded by the great Wu Min or Meridian Gate—a large central pavilion, 60 metres (200 feet) long, flanked by two square pavilions, and raised on a tremendous marble platform 15 metres (50 feet) high.

The effect is one of overpowering majesty, a feeling enhanced by the massive solidity of the dark red (plastered) podium, the ornate horizontals of the balustrade, the intricate timber roof supports, and the gracefully floating curves of the roofs, which were covered with golden glazed tiles (a colour reserved for the emperor alone).

The Meridian Gate leads into an inner courtyard, through which flows the 'River of Golden Water', crossed by five marble bridges. The emperor alone used the central bridge. At the far end is the 'Gate of Supreme Harmony', approached by three marble stairways. Beyond is the largest courtyard, with three ceremonial halls, standing upon a vast three-tiered marble podium: the 'Hall of Supreme Harmony' (containing the throne), the 'Hall of Central Harmony' and the 'Hall of Preservation of Harmony'.

The 'Hall of Supreme Harmony' is the largest of the three and was

35

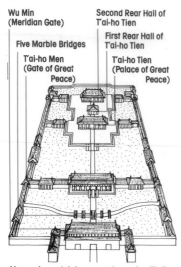

Wu Min
(Meridian Gate)

Second Rear Hall of
T'ai-ho Tien

Five Marble Bridges

First Rear Hall of
T'ai-ho Tien

T'ai-ho Men
(Gate of Great
Peace)

T'ai-ho Tien
(Palace of Great
Peace)

Above: An aerial view of the Imperial Palace. It is laid out as a series of court- yards, each with its own gateway and separate architec- tural climax.

used for important ceremonies such as coronations, court homage on the emperor's birthday or special proclamations. It is eleven 'bays' long and five bays deep, so that the interior is divided by four rows of eight pillars.

Beyond the great ceremonial halls are the private apartments of the emperor, which are more intimate in scale, but still alligned on the same north/south axis. Here are located three great palaces set in a magnificent garden, dotted with pavilions.

The Forbidden City is at the very heart of old Peking. It represents a progression of spaces, each with its own visual connection, order and climax. Whereas the planning of large Renaissance palaces depended on long, dramatic vistas leading to a single, dominating climax, the Chinese conception is more subtle and complex. It comprises a whole series of architectural experiences, each revealing only partial clues to the next event.

The colossal scale, the axial symmetry and the tremendous sweep of the great roofs all combine to create at the heart of the Forbidden City a symbol of imperial power that has never been surpassed.

Five Jewels of Paradise

Confucianism and Taoism evolved during the sixth century BC. Confucianism was more than just a religion; it was a code of social conduct and a way of life. Among the imperial Chinese elite, its appeal was immense, and it affected the life and attitudes of adherents of Taoism and Buddhism.

Buddhism was introduced from India some time around the first century AD, and it spread rapidly thereafter. By the end of the sixth century, as many as 40,000 Buddhist monasteries and shrines had been established. In outward appearance, the temples of all three religions show little difference and, like Chinese palaces, they consist of pavilions arranged along an axial plan.

A typical Buddhist temple had a gate house facing south (protected from evil spirits by a screen wall) beyond which were three or more pavilions: an entrance hall (containing the statues of the guardians of the gate), a Hall of the four Heavenly Kings (guarding the four cardinal points), and the central hall (containing the main altar with the statue of the Buddha). Farther north, there may have been a library/hall of meditation. Subsidiary buildings, located on either side of the main axis, included dormitories, granaries, kitchens, a sick bay, etc.

The main innovation introduced by the Buddhists was the pagoda. Chinese pagodas can be traced to two sources: the Indian Buddhist 'Stupa' and the Chinese 'Lou' (a multi-storey monument, erected by special authority as a memorial to a distinguished person).

During the Sui and T'ang dynasties, it was customary for two pagodas to be erected at important monasteries. These were symmetrically placed on either side of the main axis.

Pagodas were shrines, and one of their principal functions was to be a repository for holy relics. The earliest examples became focuses for pious devotion, but later pagodas were built primarily to celebrate military victories or to bestow good fortune upon the builder. Architecturally, the pagoda represented the one strong vertical element in a complex that was otherwise composed of horizontal planes.

Pagodas initially were made of wood, but, from the sixth century onwards, brick or stone became the primary building material. Indeed, the skillful use of masonry was one of the main contributions of Buddhism to Chinese architecture. A fascinating example of a stone pagoda is the one attached to the Sung Tuan Temple in Honan. Dating from AD 523, it is actually the oldest surviving building in China.

Built of brick, the Honan Pagoda has a 12-sided polygonal plan and is 27 metres (90 feet) high. Each of the 15 false stories had its own elaborately-decorated roof, covered with coloured, glazed tiles.

While the Honan Pagoda is the oldest, the most famous is the Porcelain Pagoda, near Peking. Its design was based on the Porcelain Pagoda in Nanking, which was destroyed by the Taiping rebels in 1854. It is a brick structure with multiple, projecting roofs covered with porcelain tiles glazed in a combination of five vivid colours, said to be in imitation of the five jewels of Buddhist paradise.

The Power of Tradition

For 5,000 years, age has been given precedence over youth in China, the elderly expecting and receiving the veneration of their children. This accords with the rigid social hierarchy and exten-

ded family order as espoused by Confucious. The Chinese family maintained (and continues to do so) extremely close ties. The head of the household (whether male or female) expected unmarried children, and married sons and their wives and families all to live in one complex of buildings. Daughters were the exception: they left as soon as they married, going off to join their husband's family group.

Traditionally, the Chinese house is arranged round an enclosed courtyard, with the main room facing south and inferior or subordinate rooms or buildings lying on the east and west sides. The house was the first refuge from the outside world, an

Below: Pagoda of Nanking. Originally, pagodas were built for religious pur- poses, for example to house holy relics or sacred books or works of art.

ordered, humanized enclave that contrasted with the wild, untamed nature of the busy metropolis outside. In some respects, this compares with the Roman 'atrium' house. Larger and more important Chinese households often had more than one courtyard, with the main hall or reception rooms always facing south.

The siting of houses was governed by the rules of the fengshui, 'geomancers' employed to determine the suitability of a location according to psychic forces. Before the house was built, sacrifices had to be offered. If everything was favourable, the ground was leveled and compacted, foundations were laid with stone or brick and built up 300 mm (12 inches) or so. The pillars were erected, followed by the roof, with the walls being filled in last.

The size and form of the dwelling were rigidly controlled by laws of state, devized to preserve the social hierarchy on which Chinese society was based. The number of bays, degree of ornamentation, size of reception rooms, building height, and even front door size, were graded according to the status of the head of the household, based on a system of seven grades from kings and dukes through the civil service ranks down to the common people.

Refuge from the Outside World

Whereas the Chinese house represented an enclosed oasis of man-made symmetry, order and hierarchy, the Chinese garden came to symbolize a mystical, irregular, curvilinear experience— a delightful and charming refuge from the autocracy of a rigidly-controlled society. The garden was not intended to imitate nature, so much as to distil its essence, to create a poetic, deeply spiritual composition delicately suggestive of the macrocosm— earth, water, rocks, sand, trees, flowers and moss. Perhaps the contrast between house and garden is analogous to the differences between Confucian and Taoist philosophies—the one clear, lyrical, hierarchical, the other, mystical and original.

The Han dynasty was the first to give gardens a naturalistic appearance. These quickly became meditation retreats for poets, philosophers, painters and Buddhist monks. Some of the grander gardens were laid out by the aristocracy, both for pleasure purposes, or as locations for the display of rare plants and exotic rocks. By the time of the Sung dynasty, the small urban garden had become a flourishing past time, more modest than the formal gardens of the nobility, it is true, but still an essential foil to the hard symmetry of the town house. The most fabulous private gardens of all were neither the Han nor the Sung ones, but those of the Ming dynasty in Peking, Nanchow and Hangchow.

Water is the most important element in Chinese landscape design, and the choice of sites was often dictated by its availability. By the movement of streams, the shimmering reflections, the interplay of light and shadow, water provided a garden with a dynamic element. Slow-moving streams and softly-shaped lakes were thought essential in any garden of size.

Next in importance came rocks. At first, stones were simply (and crudely) piled high, presumably to represesnt mountains, but in time this effect was given a more subtle quality by using a single monumental rock. In the words of a 12th-century writer: 'The objects that constitute the purest quintessence of Heaven and Earth are incorporated in rocks'.

Unusual-shaped rocks were avidly collected, and a particularly rare sample could change hands for an astronomical sum, or even become the focal point of an entire treatise on gardening. Great care was taken with the siting of such a rock in order to show it off to its best advantage. Thus, it might be placed against the background of a white wall, or in the middle of a lake. The plum tree was the most popular arboreal choice for gardens, other favourites were the gnarled and knobbly pine, and the delicate bamboo.

The layout of a Chinese garden was carefully contrived to create a sequence of visual 'events'. No single all-embracing vista, there was instead a series of delightful miniature 'views' unfolding as each new tree or bush was approached. Bridges, galleries, decorative balustrades, and pavilions, too, each man-made object was delicately interwoven into the natural composition.

Wall of Death

The Great Wall, the most famous construction in China, is the only artifact visible with the naked eye from the moon. It was conceived by Emperor Qin Shi Huang Di, the founder of the Chin Empire, though sections had already been built by several states to keep out raiders from the north. To link the various individual sections together, hundreds of thousands of convicts and conscripted workmen were drafted on to the project.

The building of the Great Wall of China caused untold misery. So many people were thought to have died on the job (and in later improvement works), that in time the wall became proverbially known as the 'longest cemetery in the world'. As first constructed, the wall was merely a rampart of heavily tramped earth and rubble, reinforced in some places with stone blocks. During the Sui dynasty, in AD 580, 150,000 men were employed in building the main stone bulwarks and in strengthening the wall.

Once they drove out the Mongols, the Ming emperors were anxious to keep them out, and they accordingly set about improving long sections of the Great Wall. Work was begun in 1368 and completed around 1500. In places, for additional protection, several walls were positioned one behind the other. The new wall was nearly 2720 kilometers (1700 miles) long, rising from 2 metres (eight feet) below sea level at its lowest point to 3000 metres (10,000 feet) above sea level at its highest. The eastern section, which begins north of Peking, has an average height of 7 metres (23 feet), with 1.5 metres (five feet) battlements on the outer face. The top, which is generally wide enough for five horses abreast, is paved with brick, bonded to keep water out. The walls are faced with ashlar. In the Ming period, there were some 20,000 watch-towers along the Wall, each rising about 3.6 metres (12 feet) above the rampart.

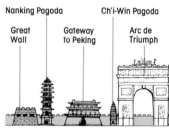

Below: A scale comparison of Chinese buildings. Only pagodas were built tall; most other buildings extended to only one or two storeys.

Nanking Pagoda   Ch'i-Win Pagoda

Great Wall   Gateway to Peking   Arc de Triumph

Left: A Pai-Lons or monumental entrance to a Ming tomb, near Peking.

Below: The Great Wall of China. It is nearly 2720 kilometers long.

The Poetry of Structure
Japan-In Harmony with Nature

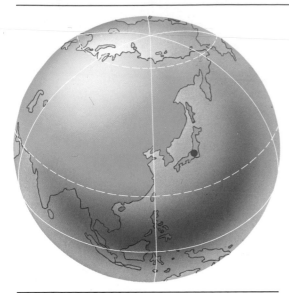

Architectural Importance:
Although much influenced by Chinese architecture, Japanese styles of building have their own unique vitality and abstract purity. A higher standard of carpentry evolved in Japan than in China, and it provided a rich source of inspiration for modern architects, such as the American, Frank Lloyd Wright. The Japanese take a deep, spiritual delight in their architecture. They expect their shrines, palaces and even domestic buildings to follow certain, prescribed rules of siting, construction and composition.

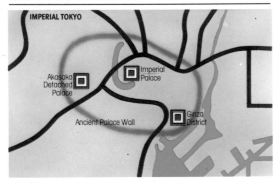

The most startling characteristic of traditional Japanese architecture is the deliberate juxtaposition of opposites to create an exciting effect—fragile materials used on a monumental scale, for example; light-hearted humour linked with deep, philosophical symbolism; ornamental exuberance contrasted with frugal modesty.

The Phoenix Hall of the Byodo-in Temple, built in 1053, perfectly exemplifies this desire for contrasting effect: the exterior is an enchanting spectacle of curving roofs, intricate shapes, rich ornamentation and striking, even vivid, colours—delicately reflected in the temple lake. The building seems alive, as though it were a reincarnation of the Buddha himself. In complete contrast, the interior is marked by its austerity; in its simplicity and lack of decoration, it demands humility and quietness. The interior is as impoverished as the exterior is rich, the

Below: The Golden Pavilion and temple of Kinkakuja, in Kyoto. An early 14th century building, it was originally constructed as a villa for a retiring patron of the arts, but on his death it was converted into a Buddhist temple. Kinkakuja is a typical building of the Kamakura dynastic period.

The Poetry of Structure

Stylistic Essentials:
Religious architecture derived from Chinese Buddhist influences. Formal, axial planning, though more delicate and less repetitive than Chinese temple designs. Domestic architecture was very flexibly planned. Light screens divide interior space, simplicity of design, skillful balance of decoration and plain materials. Modular layout and construction. Extremely conservative approach to building methods.

Primary Building Materials:
Wood is the primary building material. Japanese carpenters became highly skilled in its use, with each craftsman designing and perfecting his own type of joints. Paper used for screens and walls, which were thus extremely light and easily movable. Use, too, of various vegetative materials, such as reed and straw, for floor coverings and simple roofs, etc.

one quiet, the other loud, the one demure, the other brash. These contrasts reveal something of the double identity which tends to characterize the whole of Japanese culture.

The Katsura Detached Palace in Kyoto, built in 1647 and the Toshogu Mausoleum in Nikko show a very different kind of contrast. Katsura was built as a country house for a noble family, just south of Kyoto; its simple, timber-framed system and exposed, natural surfaces represent a powerful expression of the Japanese tradition of using materials in the most honest, simple, and direct manner possible. Paper, timber and rice straw are used in such an unaffected and open manner that one realizes it is the qualities of the materials themselves, just as much as the way they are used, that compel our admiration.

Toshogu, built at approximately the same time, was a mausoleum for the first and third Tokugawa Shoguns (emperors), and some 780,000 craftsmen and labourers were engaged in the building work. It is a wild extravaganza of decoration. One's senses are assaulted both by the density of buildings inside the compound and by an even greater density of decoration. Not the minutest area of space is left untouched. The well-known gate of Yomeimon is perhaps the most gorgeously embellished edifice; it is a riot of Buddhist mythological creatures and scenes adorning the structure all the way up to the roof-line. Yet once again, there is deliberate contrast: the shrine is set against a bleak and isolated mountain background—providing a perfect foil for the architectural pyrotechnics of the man-made construction.

Another aspect of this polarization of attitudes in Japanese architecture is the tradition of dividing the method of construction into two categories—one is based on the use of lightweight screens to distinguish various types of rooms, and the other is centred on heavyweight gravity systems. The building type best known outside Japan involves the separation of the exterior and interior of the building by sliding paper doors, with the various rooms divided by free-standing screens and curtains. This type of construction caught the imagination of Western architects and was influential in the evolution of building design in the early 20th century.

Alongside this, there has always been a complementary tradition of solid construction: thick-walled buildings used for store houses, treasury buildings and other structures, many of which have gone largely unnoticed in the West.

Nation of 1,000 Islands

The Japanese archipelago faces the Pacific Ocean and the eastern edge of the Eurasian continent. It is composed of four main islands: Hokkaido, Honshu, Shikoku and Kyushu, and a chain of more than 1,000 smaller ones that stretch for some 1280 kilometers (800 miles) from north to south. The land is predominantly mountainous, subject to volcanic eruptions and earthquakes, while the climate ranges from the subtropical south of Okinawa to the almost arctic conditions of northernmost Hokkaido, where coastal waters freeze during the winter months. Ethnic origins are multifarious—the Tungus, the Mongolians, the Malayans and the Ainus—each have migrated to the Japanese archipelago. The seventh-century Ise Shrine, the premier Shinto sanctuary, has some affinity with primitive hut styles in the South Sea Islands, and the possibility of migrations from these Pacific Islands to Japan cannot be eliminated.

The Jomon period is the time of Neolithic culture in Japan (10,000 BC to 300 BC), followed by the Yayoi period (300 BC-300 AD), when the more prosperous lived in pit-dwellings and agricultural tools were made of iron. The Kofun era (300-500), inaugurated the development of the imperial system. During the Asuka and Hakuko periods (550-700) the major sanctuary at Ise was established for the animistic Shinto cults; at the same time, Buddhism was introduced from China, and the first Buddhist temples were constructed at Asuka-dera (588) and Jorjuji in the eighth century.

The Nara and Heian periods (700-1200) witnessed the blossoming of urban communities in which city layouts were modelled

Right: The Toshogu Shrine in Nikko. A mausoleum for the first and third Tokugawa shoguns (emperors), it reveals the extreme decorative tendencies of the late Edo era.

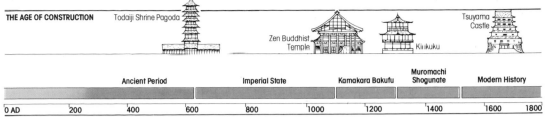

| | Todaiji Shrine Pagoda | | | Zen Buddhist Temple | Kinkuku | | Tsuyama Castle |

| Ancient Period | Imperial State | Kamakara Bakufu | Muromachi Shogunate | Modern History |

| 0 AD | 200 | 400 | 600 | 800 | 1000 | 1200 | 1400 | 1600 | 1800 |

closely on Chinese precedent. In the Kamakura period (1200-1400) shrine and temple layouts were further elaborated, with important examples at Eiheiji (1244) and Daitokuji (1324). The Muromachi period (1400-1600) saw the establishment of quasi-autonomous regional governors (bakufu) who built castles to protect their interests: Himeji castle (1580) and Osaka castle (1584) are the most famous examples in the Tokugawa period (1600-1858); during this era, the capital was switched from Kyoto to Tokyo and the prosperity brought by the merchant class's success in trading provided a foundation for a brilliant urban culture, colourfully depicted in the evocative prints of Hokujai. The Meiji Reformation in 1858

Below: A scale comparison of Japanese buildings. Unlike the Chinese, Japanese architects were not afraid to build high if they felt it to be desirable or necessary.

Yakushiji Temple / Great Buddha Hall, Todai-ji / Arc de Triumph

re-introduced Western ideas and institutions to Japan, sowing the seeds for the economic miracle of 20th century Japan.

Mobile Capital

The modern Japanese word for capital city, 'miyako', meant originally the location of the imperial palace. It was customary to erect a new palace when a new emperor was enthroned. One emperor moved his palace several times during his reign following rather extraordinary events, both good and bad. In 646, the institution of an imperial capital was introduced from China, but the old idea of a transient political centre did not entirely disappear—over a dozen magnificent capitals were built at great cost and herculean effort, only to be abandoned on the accession of a new emperor. Heian-Kyo (Kyoto) was the last imperial capital and

continued to be the seat of imperial aristocracy for over ten centuries, until the Emperor Meiji moved to Tokyo in 1869. The form of these capitals—a gridded, orthogonal layout—was determined by two factors; the existing gridiron layout of the surrounding paddy-fields and the type of capital city in China at that time—represented best by Chang 'an.

Imperial palace life during the period it was located in Kyoto was characterized by a courtly aestheticism—poetry-reading parties, moon-viewing trips and cherry blossom festivals were the order of the day. Ladies of the court sat ensconced behind screens, while suitors declaimed their love from the gardens.

In contrast to the refined aristocratic pomp and ritual of the Imperial palace, life in the castles of the Muromachi era was a more rigorous and worldly affair. Built by the bakufus or

regional administrators, these castles were perched on hill tops, dominating the towns below; conspicuous emblems of defence with their concentric rings of fortifications. Himeji castle is one of the most spectacular of these fortresses. It exploited its site in a very picturesque way: despite the very extensive nature of the ramparts and defence-works, the lightness of touch in the main building itself has earned the appellation of 'Heron Castle' suggestive of its airy qualities.

Pious Conception

The early Japanese venerated the spirits of the sky, the earth, the rocks, and the first places of veneration were natural features that had some special sacred significance; in time, those features came to be enclosed within a fence (himorogi), and surrounded by sacred ropes from which offerings were hung. The fences came to be further elaborated into building types when Shinto emerged as the one coherent voice harmonizing the previous web of animistic beliefs.

The first major Shinto shrines at Izuma and Sumiyoshi date from the seventh century. In 685, Ise Shrine was constructed, enshrining the sun goddess, and, in

Left: Todaiji, the temple of the Imperial family. The main structure is supported on 40 tall pillars.

Below: Himeji castle, at once extremely picturesque and, with its massive ramparts, rather forbidding.

859, the Iwashimizu Hachiman Shrine was founded. All of these structures were of timber and were renewed regularly; the form of the Ise Shrine has been preserved to this day by being rebuilt every 20 years in the exact manner of the original.

The Buddhist religion was imported from China via Korea, in the sixth century, and it came equipped with temple styles that had already been evolved on the mainland. The Buddhist temples in Japan were elaborate and hierarchical; they did not go through the simple stages of evolution associated with the history of the Shinto shrines. The temple of Asuka-dera was raised in 588, and Shittenoji Temple in 593 — both feature covered walkways surrounding a pagoda and other central buildings. Horyuji, Todaiji, Daigo, Ishiyama-dera illustrate the tremendous advances made in Buddhist architectural organization. Different types of temple came into being to serve the demands of both the different sects and distinct types of location — one favourite type was the mountain-top monastery (Mt. Hiei, Mt. Koyal).

Traditional Forms

The three main stages in the evolution of the traditional house are the Neolithic pit-dwelling, the village house and the urban house. The pit-dwelling had a single entrance, and it comprised a single-room space for all household activities. The village house in its most simple form has an arrangement of four rooms, separated by sliding screens — there are no corridors — movement within the house entailing movement from room to room. The town house is long and narrow, with a corridor

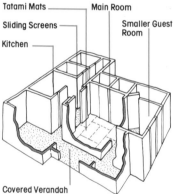

Above: Horyuji, a Buddhist temple containing the world's oldest wooden buildings.

Right: Reconstruction of a traditional Japanese family house in an open-air museum.

Tatami Mats
Sliding Screens
Kitchen
Main Room
Smaller Guest Room
Covered Verandah

Above: A cut-away view of a typical Japanese house. It shows the arrangement of various rooms separated from each other by movable screens. The main floor area is of rammed earth.

leading from the street deep into the heart of the dwelling's interior.

A typical element of the traditional house is the hearth, around which the family sit in a prescribed order. A mechanism suspended above the hearth enabled a kettle to be warmed over the fire — it is normally decorated with a fish to protect the house from fire. The 'tokonoma' is an alcove reserved for seasonal and festive displays, and the tea house (chasitsu) is the place reserved in more aristocratic residences for the tea-ceremony. The roof is often very much exaggerated and, when thatched, gives the impression of a nest.

The entrance hall floor is usually of rammed earth and this is a characteristic of most archaic Japanese houses. To move from the entrance hall into the interior of the house entails the visitor in first removing his shoes.

The layout of all houses and their gardens, from the backwoods' hut to a Kyoto palace, had to obey certain geomantic laws, imported from China, which laid down what shape of site and which directions were auspicious for any given location. The north-east was generally considered unfavourable, for it was believed to be the direction from which demons entered the ordinary world. The interior layout of rooms and furnishings, particularly the household shrines and temples, had to obey these same conditions.

Universal Symbol

The pagoda was a typical Buddhist structure normally located within the precincts of a temple. Its purpose was to contain a sacred relic of a Buddhist saint. Only the seven-storey type

(and there were many others) was considered truly holy, since it was intended to represent the magic Mount Meru, the mythical mountain at the centre of the Buddhist universe, which was composed of seven levels.

In Japan, however, five was considered a more auspicious number for it represented the five directions, the four cardinal points and the centre. Five also represents the five elements: earth, water, fire, wind and sky. The pagoda has no intrinsic function; it is a representation of the universe: the square platform it rests on symbolizing the earth, and the central pillar which runs through the entire structure symbolizing the world axis uniting earth and heaven. It is crowned by a square shape with an inverted bowl on top representing the palace of the gods, and by nine umbrellas, one set above the

other, a symbol of the kingship of the Buddha as the ruler of the universe. At the very top is an ornament in the shape of a flaming bauble which represents the precious jewel of Buddhist truth, shining through the world. The pagoda as a whole reveals the supremacy of Buddhist law, functioning in the same way as a church tower. Similar symbolic meanings are attached to the main elements of most forms of traditional Japanese architecture.

Transcient Beauty

Mono-no-aware is a term used to describe the 'ah-ness of things' — a feeling for natural loveliness tinged with sadness at its transience. In a country which uses primarily timber construction for its buildings and which is highly vulnerable to earthquakes and volcanic activity, the sentiments expressed by mono-no-aware are particularly apt.

Sabi is a concept that overlaps with mono-no-aware, and is a poetic quality best felt and understood in solitude — 'loneliness in the sense of Buddhist detachment, of seeing all things as happening'. The mingling of the aesthetic and the melancholic is an essential feature of Japanese architecture, in particular the design of the teahouse. Both sabi and mono-no-aware depict the contemplative, solitary side of the Japanese architectural sensibility.

Wabi expresses something more by way of instant enlightenment — the sudden glimpse of a temple building after a long approach route, or the unexpected view of a castle from within the town. Yugen also expresses the unanticipated — it is the 'poetic shock' of seeing moss growing on a roof, or seeing the gateway to the shrine at Itsukushima bay, normally up to its plinth in water, at low tide.

Perhaps a more comprehensive model of the delight the Japanese take in their architecture, its spaces and material qualities, can be found in the term 'ma', which literally means 'between', but in fact is a very general term summarizing a person's attitudes towards the sense of place. It is really seen in the harmonic union of man and nature, part and whole, route and temple, space and time. Ma is suggested by the movement through a gateway into a temple or shrine complex; it is suggested by the act of entering, crossing thresholds, 'arrival'. One of the most succinct expressions of it can be found in the Fushimi Inari shrine, just north of Kyoto. Here, there is a custom that people can have a torii (shrine gateway) erected by way of an offering. So many people have had these built that they stretch for an immense distance over the twisting and turning mountain paths leading to the main shrine. In climbing to the top, one must follow what amounts to a tunnel of sacred gateways — an elaborate expression of the Japanese sense of place, a celebration of the moment of arrival and the transition between outside and inside.

A Natural Appearance

Nearly all building materials were vegetable in origin. Owing to the temperate climate, more than 90 per cent of Japanese land was covered with forests, but due to indiscriminate felling for building purposes, the forest coverage had decreased by one-tenth by the start of this century. Now it is around 60 per cent. The principal timbers used for structural purposes are the conifers, such as cedar, pine, cypress and fir, and such deciduous trees as oak and chestnut for furniture and fixtures. Paper made from the mulberry tree was used for the sliding paper screens (shoji) and bamboo was used for the wall lathing. This was coated with a mixture of clay, sand and straw fibres and sometimes tiny fragments of iron were mixed in, for their rust-coloured stain was considered highly aesthetic. The 'tatami' mat, the principal floor covering, was made of beaten rice straw coloured with a tightly woven mat of rush.

Except for the castle ramparts, stone was used in architecture only as the base for posts and pillars. Clay was used extensively, not only for the wall (from the core to its final coating), but also for producing roof tiles. 'Hongawara' was the kind of tile most widely employed prior to the 17th century — after that, a type called 'sangawara' gained popularity, since it was lighter.

Since Japanese structures were mainly of timber, it should be no surprise that they were built primarily by carpenters (daiku-san) — even today, most buildings are designed and erected by carpenters; the architect tends to be employed for larger-scale projects and the occasional small house. Many traditional carpenter's tools are still employed today, such as axes, adzes, planes, particularly for use in those ceremonial stages of the building process which celebrate the selection of the site, the raising of the first column, the erection of the ridge pole and the completion of the building.

Below: Four kinds of building joint evolved by Japanese carpenters. These craftsmen kept their methods secret. 1 Gooseneck mortice and tenon joint. 2 Oblique scarf joint. 3 Inserted tenon joint. 4 Mitre joint.

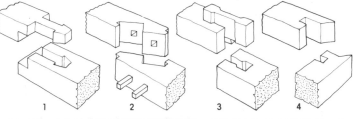

1 2 3 4

Right: Bridge and garden of the Daigoji Temple in Kyoto. To the Japanese, the garden had a 'contrived spontaneity' akin to the 'awakening' of Zen Buddhism.

Humble Origins
Plain Structures-Common Materials

Architectural Importance:
Medieval domestic architecture is essentially the symbolic expression of simple needs and aspirations. It is 'folk art'; popular culture with particular regional or even national variations in design, materials and dimensions. The vast majority of the house types were built by and for agricultural workers and farmers. Later, these houses, sometimes greatly enlarged and elaborated, were taken over by artisans and became entirely residential. Few examples of the earliest types have survived until recent times.

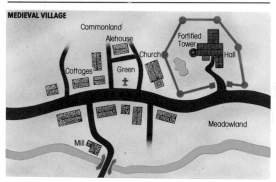

MEDIEVAL VILLAGE

The thatched cottage is a favourite subject for wall calenders, a timeless sentimental conception of life that provides reassurance in a modern world torn by ideological confusion, doubt and technological crises. The Medieval town houses of Germany and the low countries, the log houses of Scandinavia and the old hill towns of France exert a powerful romantic influence on the modern city-dweller.

For both the tourist and the native Englishman, the picturesque villages of south eastern England provide the most evocative symbol of the English way of life—half-timbered thatched cottages nestling around a village green, leaded windows, cosy gardens, a church spire rising in the background, and the gentle thud of the cricket bat on a warm Sunday afternoon.

These simple buildings were constructed to accommodate simple needs: shelter for the

Spans kept short by arranging rooms in a row, except in north Germany, where large spans achieved with enormous members.

Stylistic Essentials: Timber-framed structures (normally exposed) panels filled in with wattle and daub, plaster or brick. Thatched roof, either reed or straw. Generally, small windows; and the earliest versions made use of an open pit for the fire with no chimney for the escaping smoke. Three types became standardized: the Saxon House (Germany) and the Hall and Long House (Britain and France).

Primary Building: Materials: Oak frame, exceptionally hard and weather-resistant; either box, cruck or aisled structure. Joints made by carved interlock, by tenon or dowell joints.

Spread of Influence: The timber-framed, thatched or tiled cottage or farmhouse survived in a variety of forms throughout the Middle Ages and on through to the late 19th century.

family and its animals, storage for their produce. Although not 'great architecture' on the scale of the pyramids, the Pantheon, Santa Sophia or Versailles, the inherent charm of these vernacular buildings gives equal pleasure to the tourist, and their history is as rich as any grandiose monument of regal or religious patronage.

Throughout Europe until the 16th century, there was an abundant supply of wood, the easiest and cheapest material to use for building the structural frames of simple shelters. Even the crudest huts of Neolithic times used timber supports, filled in by mud, branches, bark or whatever came nearest to hand. Remains of log huts have been found in Poland dating from 700 BC, and the abundance of straight pine in Scandinavia introduced widespread log building long before AD 1000.

Timber frame house construction was evolved in Roman times, and may go back even further, to the Bronze Age. The timber frame minimized the need for large members, providing a rigid skeleton that could be filled in with cheap, locally available, materials, such as 'wattle and daub', or more permanent and decorative fillings, such as brick. Where money and skilled craftsmen were available, highly ornamental wood carving, moulded stucco or even plaster were often applied.

The most durable timber was oak, a species in good supply until the demands of warship building in the 16th and 17th centuries seriously depleted the great deciduous forests of Northern Europe. Skillful jointing with dowels or mortices combined with the iron-like hardness and strength of the oak beams created structures that have lasted well through the ages. Their survival is obviously related to their ultra-successful avoidance of fire, and to changing needs that have demanded sometimes radical alterations and additions, if not outright demolition.

The surviving timber framed houses of the 14th to 17th centuries tell only part of the story of vernacular architecture. Besides the farmhouses, manorhouses, churches and cathedrals, there were the other essential buildings of pre-industrial existence: the windmill or watermill, the storage barns, the smithy's forge, the wheelwrights' shop, the bakehouse, most of which have disappeared—superceded by demands of mass production and centralized distribution.

Naturally, there is a vast range of local, regional and national variations in these vernacular architectures, conditioned by the degree of prosperity and stability, by local materials and traditions by social behaviour and by the levels of skill and technology available. Described here are three of the major house types of Northern Europe that illustrate the main principles of Medieval domestic planning and construction: the 'hall house' of South Eastern England, the 'long-house' of Northern France, Northern England and Scotland, and the 'lower-Saxon' house of Germany and the low countries.

From Hovel to Long-House

The Medieval cottages and farmhouses still existing are in general examples of housing used by farmers, husbandmen or artisans. Peasants and farmworkers lived in rude dwellings erected to keep out the weather. Most were single-roomed shelters, often lacking either windows or chimneys; smoke from the fire in the centre of the room was dispersed through cracks in the walls or vents in the ridge. More often than not the smoke simply hung in a thick cloud about the room. The beaten-earth floor was strewn with rushes or lime-ash. These crude structures were scattered around villages all over Europe and, even as late as the mid-19th century, were still the primary form of shelter for the peasantry of Ireland.

Perhaps the earliest, true, timber-frame buildings were built by the Scandinavians; these were developed from stave structures. The structural advantages of the timber truss were first exploited to the full by the Romans, who used them to span great spaces, without requiring intermediate support, in the early basilicas of the Empire. Many Roman agricultural buildings in Northern Europe bore a crude resemblance to the

Below: Bayleaf farmhouse at Singleton in England. This 15th century house has been carefully restored to illustrate the original construction methods.

basilica, with two rows of columns supporting a 'hipped' roof and 'lean to' extensions on all four sides. Pictures of these constructions can be found on a group of carvings on Trajan's column in Rome.

The spans achieved in Medieval times were more modest than those achieved by the Romans, though the larger halls of important houses were covered without intermediate supporting columns. This was made possible by the invention of the 'king post' roof in the 11th century, and the 'queen post' and 'hammer beam' roofs in the 14th, the most famous examples of this being Westminster Hall (1395).

The difficulties of covering wide spans, using timber beams, placed limitations on the dimensions of ordinary houses. The 'long-house' was one common solution, where several rooms are linked in a row so that the building, though possibly extremely long is of modest width. The aisles of the 'basilican' type provided intermediate support for the roof, and the 'cruck frame' imitated a simple tent structure with two inclined vertical members that join at the ridge of the roof, braced with a horizontal tie beam, like the letter 'A'. The 'box frame' system was another common variant; here the house was divided into bays, each framed like an open box with vertical and horizontal timbers. The roof formed a triangular truss that was intended to sit on top of the box.

Right: An English cruck-frame house. The 'crucks' are the curved timbers that lean together. It was one of the earliest Medieval structural systems.

THE AGE OF CONSTRUCTION

Anglo-Saxon Cottage

English Cruck Frame

Spread of Medieval domestic architecture observed in Scotland,

Farm House

Low Countries, Germany and Scandinavia.

Market Hall

| 800 | 900 | 1000 | 1100 | 1200 | 1300 | 1400 | 1500 | 1600 | 1700 |

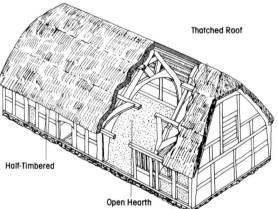

Thatched Roof

Half-Timbered

Open Hearth

Left: Illustration of a typical 'hall house', showing the timber skeletal frame. The rooms are arranged in a row in order to lessen the spans which the roof members had to bridge.

Right: Close-up of the first floor beams of Bayleaf Farm. 'Jettying' may have originated from the need to increase floor areas in buildings located in crowded towns and cities.

All these systems developed during the early Medieval period, with increasing skills in carpentry contributing to the strength and endurance of the structure.

Simple Hall House

In England, a very large number of houses have survived that date from the late 14th to the early 16th centuries. In some parishes, where virtually every pre-modern house dates from this period, it has been calculated that a very high proportion of houses dating from the 15th century have managed to survive.

The ordinary manor houses and larger farmhouses of this period were mostly divided into three parts, known as service, hall and solar, arranged in a line. The service end was usually divided into two equal rooms, the buttery and pantry. Both the solar and service ends very often had upper floors, giving two upper rooms, the solar chamber and the service chamber, but the hall in the middle of the house had no upper floor and was open to the rafters of the roof. In or near the middle of the hall burned a log fire on an open hearth, the smoke finding its way through a vent or louvre in the roof, or simply by percolating through the spaces between the tiles or thatch.

The service end of the house was known as the 'lower' end and the solar end as the 'upper' end, reflecting their positions in the social hierarchy of the plan. At the lower end of the hall was the main entrance, often a pair of doors opposite one another linked by a 'cross passage'. The passage was not divided from the hall but 'spares' screens helped to define the passage and prevent draughts. At the upper end of the hall was the 'high table' at which sat the owner and his family.

The use of the hall itself is fairly well known from contemporary accounts. It was the main living room of the household, certainly, where they ate and where some of the servants might also sleep. Some cooking was done on the open fire but many houses had kitchens in small separate buildings at the service end of the house, presumably to lessen the risk of fire. The hall was also a semi-public space, where visitors were formally received, disputes were settled and, in manor houses courts were held.

The use of the rooms in the service end—the buttery and pantry—is also easy to deduce. It was essentially the preparation and storage of cold food and drink: the word buttery means drink-store and pantry means bread-store, but both would have been used also for other provisions.

The uses of the three rooms at the solar end of the house are less certain. The solar itself was probably a private bed-sitting room for the owner and his wife—it would have contained a bed, chest, coffer and hangings, with chairs and stools and was often the best constructed and decorated room of the house. Paradoxically, the service chamber can be somewhat larger in size: possibly it was the domain of privileged servants or the family's sons, but this is pure conjecture. Similarly, there is little direct evidence for the use of the ground floor room at the solar end: sometimes it may have been used for sleeping, or as a workroom for weaving or spinning, or for storage of goods.

Most rural houses of this kind would have been the centre of a farming operation and therefore associated with farm buildings: certainly a barn, possibly also a granary, cow-house, yard, and stables. It is surprising, therefore, that the houses themselves show little or no sign of farm use and that identical houses were sometimes built in the towns and in the countryside. Compared with other peasant houses in Northern Europe, they are residences rather than farmhouses.

Medieval Noah's Ark

'Long-houses' are found in a recognizably similar form in Cumbria, in parts of Scotland, Ireland and Wales, in south-west England, and in Brittany, but there is good evidence from archaeological excavations and from documents that in the 13th and 14th centuries they were much more widespread.

The explanation for the pattern of survival must lie in particular combinations of conditions. To some extent the upland conditions and wet climate tie the areas together, and an absence of domination by large-scale farmers allowed the smaller and relatively independent husbandman to survive. Taken together these factors partly explain the necessity for secure housing for a few cattle attached to every house. Possibly also there is a tendency in more isolated and hardy communities for the longer survival of folk customs and beliefs, such as the simple but vital ones that cows produce more milk when they are warm, and thrive within sight of a fire. The size of surviving examples varies considerably, from the substantial houses of south-western England, with several living rooms and a byre for several cattle, to the smallest examples in Brittany, with just one living room and space for only two or three beasts.

Long-houses were unmistakeably farmhouses, although few have survived to the present day

with animals still housed under the same roof in the traditional way. In essence, the plans of long-houses are very similar to those of the hall-houses: they consist of three parts, arranged in sequence from 'lower' to 'upper', the entrance passages being at the lower end of the hall. The difference lies in the use of the lower end of the building as a byre for cattle rather than as service rooms. The room at the upper end of the house—the 'inner' room—was sometimes divided into two smaller rooms, possibly as parlour and buttery, making up for the lack of service rooms at the lower end.

Some long-houses still survive which had an open fire in the hall but true Medieval examples are few in comparison with the hall-houses of south-east England. In some remote areas the use of open fires persisted within living memory, for instance in a few Hebridean 'Blackhouses,' but in most examples a masonry fire-place and chimney have been inserted. The usual position for this is at the lower end of the hall, backing onto the cross-passage.

Although the existence of a cross-passage giving internal access between house and byre is a distinguishing feature of the long-house, there was often a separate entrance into the byre for the cattle. The cattle might then stand facing the cross-passage and could feed from hay bags hung in it. Alternatively, the cattle could stand in two rows facing the outer walls, a central drain carrying away

Below: Crofter's cottage on the Isle of Skye, Scotland modelled on the long-house.

Right: 14th century English long-house. The chimney was added possibly 100 years later.

manure through the gable end wall. Because of the problem of manure, long-houses were almost invariably sited across the contours of a slope, the ground falling towards the byre at the lower end, so that inside the house the hall floor level was higher than the byre and the inner room was much higher than the hall.

The Saxon Heritage

In a sense the Lower-Saxon house is also a long-house: men and animals live under the same roof. The prototype undivided house-and-byre plans first appear in excavations of Bronze Age sites on the German North Sea coast:

Below: The earliest Saxon and Medieval cottages were usually one or two-storey dwellings, but later versions were taller.

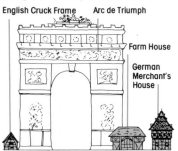

English Cruck Frame · Arc de Triumph

Farm House

German Merchant's House

the two ends of the buildings are distinguished by the presence, respectively, of an open hearth and a drain, and are separated by a walkway between two doors opposite one another in the middle of the long walls. This pattern is essentially the same as the long-house, but by the 12th and 13th centuries the Saxon houses seem to have been differentiated by the incorporation of storage space for corn and hay in their roofs, above the cow-stalls, as a direct result of the increased yields and harvests being achieved at that time. After the deep economic recession of the 14th and 15th centuries, the peasants of North Germany built up their arable husbandry again and the 16th century saw the blossoming of the Lower-Saxon house into a range of related types which remained fundamentally unchanged to the modern period.

The 'Lower-Saxon house' was a considerably larger and more complex development of the principle of men and beasts living under one roof. The type developed in the 16th century as the prosperity of peasants in North Germany revived with the increasing demand for food. Larger fields and improved techniques increased

the size of the harvests and North Germany became an important grain-producing area. The buildings became larger and the roof space was used for the storage of hay fodder and of sheafs of corn. Although great labour was involved in lifting the whole of the harvested crop into the roof space, a resulting benefit was the drying and preservative effect of heat and smoke from the open fire. The cross-passage was forgotten in favour of a highly decorated main entrance in the gable end of the house, through which carts brought the harvest. There was therefore no division between the hearth, which was usually built against the end wall of the 'flett' or living area, and the crop stored in the roof above the 'diele' or threshing floor, so the smoke from the fire could circulate freely. Because of this functional connection between the smoke from the open fire and the crop stored in the roof, the use of an open fire in the living area persisted well into the 19th century.

Beyond the hearth area were the private rooms, with similar functions to the solar or inner rooms in English houses but equipped with a stove so that the family did not rely entirely on

Early Tent-like Frame **Simple Cruck**

Advanced Cruck **Post and Truss Frame**

Above: The evolution of the Medieval timber roof. The tent-like system of converging poles was adapted into the 'cruck' frame, using split timbers. Tie beams helped to stiffen the structure.

the open fire for warmth. To either side of the hearth area the aisles of the building were opened up to form the 'lucht' or dwelling niche, lit by tall windows, and in the wall behind the hearth were sometimes cupboard beds for the family. Cattle and horses were stalled in the aisles facing into the threshing floor from which they were foddered.

Framework of Wood

Timber dominates the construction of each of the three house-types discussed. Most long-houses now have walls of stone but many were originally built of timber. Both the English hall-house and the Lower-Saxon house were timber-built in the great majority

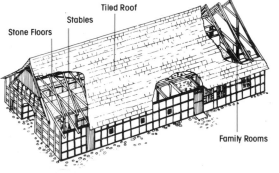

Right: Illustration of a typical Saxon house, showing clearly how accommodation for both man and beast was provided under the one roof.

Below: Late Medieval timber-framed houses in the museum of vernacular architecture in Westphalia. The spaces between the frames were often highly decorated.

Tiled Roof
Stables
Stone Floors
Family Rooms

of examples. In fact, archaeologists have shown that virtually all peasant houses were built of timber until the 13th and 14th centuries, even in areas where building stone was easily available. Relatively little timber framing survives from the 14th century but what does exist is highly developed, suggesting a long history of steady improvement of craft techniques.

The houses described illustrate the three basic forms of timber construction: post and truss (or 'box-frame') in the English hall-house, crucks in the long-house, and aisled construction in the Lower-Saxon house. Aisled construction was used in south-east England for houses in the 14th century, but thereafter only in barns. Crucks, on the other hand, seem to have been used for both houses and barns from the 13th century for at least 500 years, gradually descending the social scale, but still being used for cottages in poor areas in the 18th century. The geographical distribution of crucks in England is interesting and has been closely studied. Of more than 2,000 cruck buildings known to exist, not a single one occurs in the eastern and south-eastern lowland counties. The reasons for this

Below: The Almonry, Evesham, England, a fine example of a picturesque timber frame building; only recently has there been a revival of popular interest in this type of domestic building.

distribution are not known, but the same boundary is known to exist also in other aspects of social and cultural life. Crucks are also found in small numbers in Germany and France.

The aisled timber construction of the Lower-Saxon house was very highly developed and extremely impressive. Very wide spans were achieved for both the nave and the aisles, necessitating extremely heavy beams to support the weight of the stored crop. Roofs came to be constructed on the so called 'bound' system, with each pair of rafters connected with its own tie-beam, a method which was completely unknown in England.

Originally, the timbers used for joists in flooring were most usually laid flat. Although this meant they were structurally weaker than when laid edge on, it was possible using them this way to cover a much greater floor area. Beams which covered the corners were laid diagonally and the floor joists thus projected to create a cantilevered effect, with the upper storey walls supported on top of them. As a result, the first floor overhung the ground floor, thereby generating more internal space at the upper level.

In spite of the large numbers of cruck buildings in some areas, by far the majority of English timber buildings from the 15th century onwards were constructed on the post and truss principle: main posts at bay intervals supported tie-beams which, in turn, supported roof trusses. This system was also extremely common in other areas of Europe and North America, the main differences being in the details of the type of roof truss and in the joint between the tie-beams and the walls.

Bastion of Authority
Focus of Feudal Power

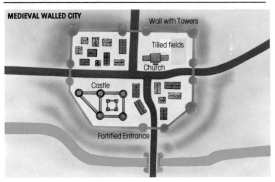

MEDIEVAL FORTIFICATIONS
- Harlech
- Caerphilly
- Tower of London
- Dover Castle
- Coucy
- Louvre
- Vincennes
- Chateau Chinon
- Drachenfals
- Chateau Gaillard
- Carcasonne

Architectural Importance:
The many thousands of castles built in Europe during the Middle Ages absorbed a major part of building expenditure, labour and material resources. Masonry skills developed in the course of building cathedrals were applied with equal enthusiasm to the construction of defensive fortifications. Castles later had a degree of influence on the design of large country houses. It was the arrival of powerful and increasingly accurate cannon that led to the eventual disappearance of the Medieval castle.

MEDIEVAL WALLED CITY
- Wall with Towers
- Tilled fields
- Church
- Castle
- Fortified Entrance

While the outstanding artistic achievement of the Middle Ages is undoubtedly the cathedral, its very magnificence has tended to obscure what is, to many, an equally incredible achievement of the period: the castle. In terms of the labour employed, the construction of tens of thousands of castles throughout Europe between the ninth and 16th centuries represents a feat of organization no less stupendous than that involved in the building of the pyramids.

The concept of the castle originated thousands of years ago, when Neolithic tribes sought the means to defend their territory, families and herds from attack. In time, the hilltop redoubt became the standard type of defensive bastion for iron-age communities around the world.

As societies grew in complexity, so their means of defense became more sophisticated. The hilltop stronghold underwent a variety of

Stylistic Essentials:
Four main categories:
'Motte-and-bailey'
Square or round keep
Concentric
Quadrilateral
With growing inter-
action between East
and West and
improving communi-

cations between
countries within
Europe, a tremen-
dous diversity of
construction styles
evolved. This was
partly also the result
of the military preoc-
cupations of
regional rulers.

**Primary Building
Materials:**
Stone almost every-
where was the
preferred material.
Brick was used
(sometimes with
stone banding)
where good stone
was scarce (eg

Holland and
Germany). Stability
and strength derived
from the massive
solidity of con-
struction, though
later castles often
substituted buttres-
ses and vaulting for
thickness of walls
(buttressing and
vaulting did, how-
ever, increase rigidity
and aid resistance
to mining).

modifications and refinements
until it became a formidable
citadel of military power.
Stockades became fortresses;
mud-brick walls gave way to
timber walls, which in turn were
replaced by thick masonry battlements. Moats were dug and filled
with water to deter soldiers from
climbing the ramparts; forests
were cleared to provide a full
field of uninterrupted fire. Defensive positions were transformed from vulnerable redoubts
into impregnable fortifications:
the castle had arrived.

By the end of the Middle Ages,
castles blossomed over the face
of Europe. Some 40,000 were
built altogether, of which more
than 10,000 were situated in
Germany alone.

The castle offered a number of
advantages, both in a defensive
and offensive sense. Their physical presence alone had a powerful
subjugating effect on a conquered
people; they acted as foci for the
control and administration of
captured territory, guarding
routes and collecting tolls, pro-

viding shelter for armies and
bureaucracies, and a safe refuge,
sometimes even a permanent
dwelling, for the military commander while he was resident
in the vicinity.

As focal points of the feudal
system, castles had a major role
to play in the generation of
economic wealth, the enforce-
ment of political stability and
the creation of resources for
external military activities. Thus,
despite their enormous cost in
labour and materials, castles
more than justified their existence,
and the prestige and security they
conferred upon their owners was
comparable in value to that of
today's investments in satellites
and ballistic missiles.

The evolution of European
fortifications was affected by the
nature of the weapons used
against them. In essence, this
meant the nature of the gun that
was trained upon besieged strongholds. Indeed, before 1480, the
thickness, solidity and height of
the battlements were sufficient
barriers to an attempted seige,

but the invention of gunpowder
and the appearance of powerful
and increasingly accurate cannon
rapidly altered the situation.

The Motte-and-Bailey

As the European Dark Age came
to an end, a new type of warfare
became fashionable in the fields
of France. While mobile armour,
in the form of well-armed cavalry,
was used to crush an enemy
attack, feudal castles were designed to maintain static control
over a conquered race. This is
more or less what happened in
Britain when William the Conqueror invaded the southern coast
of England. Having defeated King
Harold's infantry with his cavalry, William's army then overran
the country, and his followers
erected hundreds of castles across
the land to subjugate the people.

The first Norman castles
consisted of a simple motte-and-
bailey. The motte was a mound,
surrounded by a ditch, moat or
strong wooden stockade. The
bailey was a forecourt, sometimes
protected by a second moat. With
time and money to spare, the
wooden palisades surrounding
the motte were exchanged for
stone walls. The motte and keep,
resistant now to almost any kind
of customary attack, became an
impregnable inner stronghold, a
refuge for its lord useful also as a
treasury and perhaps even a
prison to hold captives.

For hundreds of years the

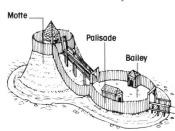

Above: A motte-and-
bailey, the first
type of castle
favoured by the
Norman engineers.

Below: Krak Des
Chevaliers. A
concentrically-
designed castle of
stupendous size.

massive keeps of the early
Medieval castles have remained
almost intact—they are among
the triumphs of Norman architecture. From a military point of
view, the square, stone keep had
a number of definite advantages
over the motte-and-bailey, quite
apart from its ability to resist
fire. To begin with, it could be
built a great deal higher and
defended by a far smaller garrison. In effect, it was more
efficient. Maintenance was reduced, since unlike wood, stone
does not rot nor need to be
replaced. And it was more resistant to the elements. But it also
had its disadvantages. One was
the fact that 'blind spots' existed
at the corners of the square-
shaped castles. The other was the
vulnerability of square-corner
towers to undermining or boring.
These problems were to be overcome by the introduction of
polygonal and round towers in
the following centuries.

Crusader Castles

The main stimulus for the
development of the science of
fortifications came from the
Crusades, a series of Holy wars
proclaimed by Pope Urban II in
his famous speech of 1095. As in
the Norman Conquests of England and Italy, castles became
prime instruments for the imposi-
tion of feudal hierarchy on the
Holy Land, though the most
significant castle building in the
Holy Land was undertaken later
and was an extension of architectural ideas developed in France.

In the initial offensives the
crusaders achieved striking success, mainly because of their
superiority in open battle, where
their armoured cavalry van-
quished the lightly-mounted Saracens. But they soon had to
improve their skill, as they discovered during the siege of
Jerusalem in 1098, where their
craft was tested to the full. The
walls were finally scaled with the
aid of two wooden towers, and

the victorious crusaders celebrated Mass in the Church of the Holy Sepulchre, while the streets flowed with the blood of slaughtered Jews and Moslems.

The commonly held view that all important innovations in Medieval military architecture came from Moslem or Byzantine examples has been challenged in this century (by T.E. Lawrence among others). The extreme shortages of manpower in the Holy Land necessitated the rapid evolution of castle design to counteract the skilled siege-craft of their opponents. Small garrisons, holding out in heavily constructed castles, making maximum use of impregnable natural sites, became the only effective way of maintaining control in the besieged principalities. The castle was much more than a refuge: it was an administrative centre for collecting revenues from the local population and a base from which to mount attacks in a land of incessant warfare.

THE AGE OF CONSTRUCTION

Fortified Byzantine City	Crusader Castle	French Castle	English Castle

| 300 | 500 | 700 | 900 | 1100 | 1300 | 1500 |

Below: The evolution of the castle wall and tower. The square towers of the Normans were vulnerable both to mining and to battering. They also had blind spots. The round tower was more stable, it was stronger and contained no blind spots. The star tower arrived with the cannon, though by now the value of the castle as a means of static defense had consequently deteriorated.

Square Tower   Round Tower   Star Tower

Many of the design improvements may have originated from experiments in Europe. The more important developments came from the need to inflict more damage on the attackers than was possible with the Norman keep or motte-and-bailey. These innovations included the use of numerous loop holes to exploit the more powerful longbows and crossbows; the increased emphasis on perimeter defence with massive, thick polygonal towers, capable of resisting mining and battering rams; impressive gate houses with sophisticated changes of axis to confuse attackers and render them more vulnerable,

and much improved storage and accommodation facilities to resist a long siege.

Krak Des Chevaliers is one of the greatest castles ever built. Most of it was constructed by the fighting monks of the Order of Hospitallers. It is a powerful example of the principle of concentric fortification, where the inner defence ring is high enough above the outer walls to provide simultaneous covering fire. The site forms a steep-sided citadel, accessible from only one side. From its first occupation in 1109, it survived numerous sieges and two earthquakes until finally taken from the last remaining Hospitallers by Sultan Barbars in 1271. At its peak, it had a garrison of over 2,000 troops and was deliberately designed to withstand a long siege. Thus it contained deep stone vaults to hold grain, and a windmill to facilitate grinding and milling.

The main entrance to the outer wall of the Krak was placed so that the enemy had to file along a narrow path, two-thirds of the length of one side, while under constant fire from the walls above. Having penetrated the outer gate, the route to the inner ward was along a narrow vaulted passageway barred by four successive gates and guarded by machicolations (battlements) above. The entrance to the inner ward was barred by a heavy door and portcullis, defended by a guardroom to the rear of the attackers, with further machicolations above.

Left: The White Tower at the Tower of London, the most famous of Norman stone keeps.

Below: The main entrance to the Krak Des Chevaliers, a warren of hidden defensive positions.

In the upper ward there was a banqueting hall, vaulted with three bays and a portico along one side. The chapel was a solid, severe Romanesque structure, vaulted in three bays with transverse ribs and a semi-circular apse. It had to be re-built after an earthquake in 1170.

The Grand Master of the Hospitallers occupied the range of buildings on the south side of the inner ward, which was an independent unit forming the donjon, or last line of defence. Dominating the whole fortress, its halls were richly decorated with rib-vaulting and delicate mouldings. Water storage was of crucial importance; the Krak was equipped with a deep well, nine large, rain-water tanks and an open reservoir located between the inner and outer curtains on the south side.

When the Krak was besieged by the Barbars in 1271, the sultan managed to break through the outer ward only after a month of intensive mining. But the 'battered' plinth of the inner walls (a massive, steeply inward-sloping stone platform) withstood all attempts at undermining, and the sultan only won by trickery. A forged letter, supposedly from a friend of the Grand Master, said that Tripoli had fallen and that further resistance was useless. The exhausted garrison was deceived, and surrendered.

Making Castles Siege-proof

The great fighting kings and princes of the Middle Ages studied military engineering with all the enthusiasm that they showed for hunting, a pastime

they followed with an obsessive passion. They poured over Roman military manuals, and avidly exchanged, borrowed or imported new military concepts. The improvements in masonry technique pioneered in church-building were soon applied to castles: in particular, the use of ribbed vaulting for roofing halls on lower storeys. There was a gradual transition from square towers and keeps to polygonal ones, which allowed improved flanking fire. Drawbridges, portcullises and other mechanical devices became rather fashionable fixtures.

Henry II of England was a prolific castle builder. Constantly on the move, he spent a major part of his income on repairing, improving and building his fortresses, which formed an essential part of his administrative system. His finest achievement was probably Dover castle, a fortified link between the two parts of the Angerin Empire. It was the earliest example of concentric fortifications in England, with inner and outer 'curtain' walls, and rectangular projecting towers.

Construction began in 1179. The keep was a massive square tower with walls over five metres (17 feet) thick. At the base the walls slope outwards, forming a talus or pyramidical podium, used to bounce stones dropped from the top of the keep onto the attackers; it proved highly effective in resisting several important sieges of the early Middle Ages.

Richard Coeur de Lion was a masterful commander and an acknowledged expert in the science of fortification. He took with him to the Holy Land a portable wooden castle which he used to protect himself from attack during the long journey. Chateau-Gaillard, his greatest castle, is reputed to have been constructed under his personal supervision. It was built on the top of a cliff-like spur, with the main keep at the far end of the spur, so that to take it involved overcoming a whole series of intervening defences—several ditches, an outer and inner bailey and then the 'chemise', a series of stout, round towers so close together that only one metre (three feet) of walling connected them. Only one part of the chemise was hidden from the defenders' view and it was here that Philip Augustus' sappers were able to safely pick away at the stones.

Philip Augustus was himself a prolific castle-builder; his famous constructions include the Louvre in Paris. His particular design innovation was the 'quadrilateral' plan, in which defence is concentrated in a carefully designed massive, rectangular outer wall. There was always a temptation in the elaborate designs of castles like Gaillard for the garrison to retire behind the next line of defence if hard pressed on the outer walls. The quadrilateral

plan relied on the brute mass of its outer masonry, together with carefully incorporated narrow slits, towers and hoarding (wooden machicolations) to inflict the maximum possible damage on the attackers.

The years that followed the era of Philip Augustus were the golden age of French castle-building; famous fortifications include the walls of Carcasonne, the keep of Coucy and the 13th century work on Chateau Chinon. The double 'curtain' wall, as at the Krak des Chevaliers, was used to great effect for the town of Carcasonne, possibly the finest remaining example of a city defended by concentric rings of fortifications. It had been a fortified citadel since Roman times, and was further reinforced by, among others, the Visigoths. During the second half of the 13th century, extensive renovations were undertaken by Louis VIII to render it the most formidable fortified town in western Europe. Every device and subtlety of contemporary military architecture was employed. The walls one can see today largely result from a 19th century restoration, though they convey most effectively the original multi-towered majesty and gaunt beauty of St. Louis' masterpiece.

The winding road that forms the approach is well defended by the walls that tower above it and even the two main gates were built like independent castles themselves. Between the two layers of walls the 'lists' or terrace could be brought under constant fire from the inner walls, and was blocked at several points to prevent it from being overrun entirely, should attackers breach the outer

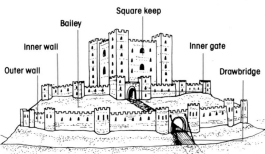

Above: Wooden machicolation used at Carcasonne. Projectiles would be hurled down to deter mineworkings.

Left: Reconstruction of a typical Medieval castle, showing the square keep with its concentric circles of inner and outer walls.

[Diagram labels: Square keep, Bailey, Inner wall, Outer wall, Inner gate, Drawbridge]

wall. 'Dead ground' was avoided by frequent projecting towers and machicolations. If the enemy did penetrate the inner ring, each of the 25 towers would have to be taken individually, an awesome task considering the vast numbers of casualties likely to have been incurred even before reaching the inner wall.

The cylindrical keep at Coucy was one of the most remarkable examples of military architecture of the Middle Ages. It was 55 metres (180 feet) high, with a diameter of 31 metres (102 feet). Though under constant siege from French troops, Richelieu's engineers failed to blow it up. It was finally destroyed by the Germans during the First World War. Its great strength was due

to the heavy internal buttressing, rigidly linking the stone arched vaulting of the three stories inside.

The vaults of Coucy were lit from above by circular openings or eyes in the middle, and the entrance was well protected by moat and drawbridge. A wooden hoarding supported on stone corbels around the top provided arrow slits and machicolations to provide pin-point fire down on to the attackers. The great height of the castle was achieved by leaving holes in the masonry at intervals, into which projecting beams were insected to form a spiral ramp to cart up materials.

Coucy, in common with the Wakefield Tower of the Tower of London, and other towers of this period showed the influence

of Gothic structural principles derived from church building. The thick walls of Romanesque construction were considerably strengthened during this period, with the internal area more effectively utilized by the use of internal buttressing and cross-arching. Thus the walls are tiered rigidly together, and more resistant to mining, since the breaching of a niche between buttresses did not in any significant manner reduce the fighting strength of the structure as a whole.

Mighty Bastions of War

Henry III of England inherited his family's passion for castle-building, though his predilection was for comfort and luxury rather than for strictly military functionalism. The records of the king's works abound with instructions for costly internal decoration, glazed windows and wall paintings. With the help of his son, Edward I, he made the tower of London one of the most luxurious and powerful fortresses in Europe.

Edward I was a military man who had gained considerable combat experience from the

Crusades and the defeat of Simon de Montfort. In the process of conquering the Welsh, he built some of the most formidable castles in the British Isles, including Caerphilly, Caernarvon, Flint, Conway and Harlech Castles.

Edward's extensive experience of sieges abroad led him to favour the principles of aggressive defence, through the concentration of fortifications on massive double perimeter walls, usually rectangular with strong circular towers at each corner. He replaced the keep with a powerful gatehouse, and increased the mobility of troops within the inner bailey to maximize the control and fighting strength of the small garrison available. Another inherent defect of earlier castle planning was also rectified. It was always the case that in the last resort the attacking forces could simply starve the garrison out. If more than one exit was provided, the defenders had a better chance of escape. In many sieges, the personnel were more important than the castle itself—if they got away, there was always the chance of regrouping with reinforcements to counter-attack and drive away the besiegers. Thus many castles of this period were built with several secret entrances, as well as the main one with its massive drawbridge.

Caernarvon castle is one of the most beautiful of all Medieval forts, and with its stark elegant towers and fortifications, still almost intact, is among the best surviving examples of Medieval military architecture. The walls were so massively built that its single line of defence was virtually immune from mining. The towers at Caernarvon are polygonal, with harsh, sharp angles between faces that would have presented a terrifying ordeal to a besieging army. It was named the Eagle Tower because Edward adorned the battlements with stone eagles, symbolic of Roman imperialism.

Other military subtleties at Caernarvon include the arrow

Above: Caernavon Castle, built by Edward I to subjugate Wales. It has a single, virtually unminable ring of defense.

Right: Schloss Neuschwanstein, an example of that curious obsession the Germans have for the mountain stronghold.

'loops' that were designed to allow archers to fire in several different directions; the blocking of the walkway along the top of the walls by towers, so that an enemy could gain access to only one part of the walls at a time; and the arrangement of firing positions so that there could be as many as three tiers of archers simultaneously showering attackers with arrows.

Military science became more specialized, with separate branches of artillery, civil engineering and architecture. Castles that doubled as living accommodations grew steadily more comfortable. Appearance was more carefully considered. Bare stone walls were now covered with rich hangings, giltwork and paintings. Roofs were built higher and were more steeply pitched: both for aesthetic and for military reasons (deflection of missiles). Stone machicolation provided a convenient vehicle for external decoration. and was spread more widely so as to cover the entire ground-level perimeter, thus preventing an attacker from approaching too closely without the risk of being crushed by projectiles being dropped from above.

Natural Impregnability

With the election of Fredrick I (known as Barbarossa) the feuding between Germanic princes was controlled, though not entirely eliminated. The power base of individual German rulers usually depended on the size and wealth of their personal land holdings, and Barbarossa consolidated his by building a stupendous 350 castles and palaces in southern Germany and Switzerland. Administration and supervision of his properties were left in the hands of 'ministriales', many of

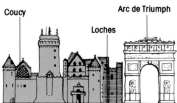

Above: A scale comparison. Heaviness of construction and ability to withstand mining was just as important to the Medieval castle-builders as height.

whom became powerful barons in their own right. German fortresses of the 12th and 13th centuries—including the famous Rhine castles—were characterized by their superior luxury and comfort, compared to French and English equivalents. They tended to rely more on natural defence in impregnable sites than on sophisticated military science.

Decline of the Castle

The Medieval castle enabled a small garrison to withstand a large invading force. But with the development of gun-powder and the onslaught of mining techniques and powder-operated cannon, the invulnerability of the castle collapsed.

Nevertheless, castles still had a vital part to play, and many more were built, for defence and for conquest, for national and for private warfare, as a strategic military network, or as fortified dwellings for the king's landowners. But the context was very different in the 14th century, than in earlier centuries. Now economic decay, famine and the Black Death, and the revolutionary changes occurring in the strategy of warfare altered the emphasis in the role played by castles.

Monarchs now relied more heavily on the skillful use of professional soldiers to fight their wars. At the battle of Crecy, for example, there were as many as 18,000 troops engaged on both sides, a far cry indeed from the 1,000 or so knights assembled for the feudal disputes of previous centuries. In this situation, the castle could provide only the most limited relief against a siege by such large, well-organized armies. They traded their wooden hoardings for sturdy and fire-resistant stone machicolations, and introduced gangways and platforms to speed the movement of groups of defenders to particular danger spots.

Solemn Homage to God
Piety Enshrined in Stone

Romanesque Europe
- Durham
- BRITAIN
- GERMANY
- Caen
- St Etienne
- Worms
- FRANCE
- Pisa
- ITALY
- Palermo
- SICILY

Architectural Importance:
Precursor of the Gothic style. Evolution of stone vaulting, and of 'rib' method of construction. Visual and conceptual unity of design – plan structure, decoration, and the major and minor spaces. Romanesque movement spread from Cluny in France to the rest of Europe, though wide regional variations in style developed, especially in Italy. Romanesque was expressive of a general outpouring of art, following the dark, sterile age which immediately preceded the Medieval period.

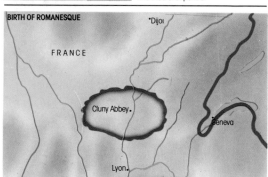

BIRTH OF ROMANESQUE
- Dijon
- FRANCE
- Cluny Abbey
- Geneva
- Lyon

At the beginning of the Middle Ages strange and miraculous powers were attributed to the holy relics of Christendom: the sacred remains of saints, apostles and martyrs—or any humble objects that may have absorbed their spiritual powers—were believed capable of protecting a person from countless diseases, sicknesses or other misfortunes. The tomb of St. James, son of Zebedee (at Santiago de Compastela, in northern Spain), was the final objective of the most famous pilgrim route in Europe. Throngs of the pious risked inclement weather, tortuous roads, robbery, and even murder to lay their sorrows and sins, their gold and their gratitude at the feet of the apostle. Celebrated pilgrim centres like Santiago used the wealth thus accumulated to build huge cathedrals to accommodate the faithful. Here, during Masses and solemn procession, the light of flaming torches and the sound of the monks' chants reverberated

Below: The Church of
St. Etienne, in France;
founded in 1066 by
William the Con-
queror, it is one of
the finest of Norman
churches and a monu-
ment to the power

and wealth of the
Norman dukes. The
east end (shown
here) was rebuilt in
1166. There are nine
towers, emphasizing
the building's
strong vertical axis.

Stylistic Essentials: Heavy masonry construction, sparse ornament, plain walls, with linear decoration directly derived from the line of the structure. Semicircular arches, thick 'moulded' piers.

Multiple towers and subsidiary chapels added to the basic, early Christian basilica. Tall nave, often divided into bays with central piers supporting cross-ribs for the vault: minimal centring needed.

Primary Building Materials: Stone is the major material, with regional variations according to local resources. Brick sometimes used where good stone is scarce—such as the Netherlands

and North Germany Structure assembled from small stones individually-carved to fit. Caen stone was particularly famous for its fine-grained, smooth surface. Marble was only available locally in Provence and Italy.

solemnly from stone to stone.

The stout, muscular masonry of Romanesque architecture evolved from the need to provide larger and more magnificent churches to match the new confidence and maturity of a faith that was the sole unifying force on a divided continent. Apart from a brief period under Charlemagne, Europe, from the fall of the Roman Empire until the Norman conquests, had become a collection of warring principalities, harassed from all sides by barbarians and Moslems. Art and architecture, science, medicine, indeed, knowledge in general, stagnated.

Out of this chaos emerged the great monastic movements that rekindled the arts and sciences, brought a semblance of common purpose to rival rulers and established the Latin Church as the dominant cultural force. Once the 1,000th anniversary of Christ's birth had passed without apocalypse, total destruction or a second coming, the world could, in the words of a contemporary chronicle: 'shake itself, and casting off her old age, clothe herself with a mantle of white churches'.

The strength and purity of Romanesque architecture was largely ignored in the centuries that followed, most historians usually dismissing it as a crude prelude to the glories of Gothic. Although the story of the complex origins of Gothic ribbed vaulting, pointed arches and vertical stone tracery is controversial, Romanesque churches have a solemn grandeur of their own that is nowadays much admired. The plain, massive forms and powerful geometry of their spaces are just as alluring to modern eyes less easily seduced by elaborate ornament.

Coined in the 19th century, the term Romanesque is itself confusing—the architecture of Ancient Rome is only one of many influences, others including Byzantine, Viking, Celtic, Moorish, and Armenian. It is usually applied to

a style of architecture that appeared in western Europe during the 11th century and lasted until the rise of Gothic in the 13th. Within that style there is a wide variety of regional and national differences. Indeed at first sight, it is difficult to find much in common between the Leaning Tower of Pisa and Durham Cathedral. Yet there are several valid connections, and the 11th and 12th centuries have proven fruitful ground for scholars searching for explanations, patterns, theories, and historical controversy—the more so because many of the vital clues are missing.

In that age of unceasing experiment, churches were extended, rebuilt and sometimes drastically altered. Fire, wars, earthquake, and faulty construction took their toll as well, and succeeding generations of improvements have ensured that few Romanesque churches have survived in their original form.

Amongst the regional peculiarities and stylistic variations, it is possible to pinpoint certain key features that distinguish the Romanesque idiom. The Romanesque church reached upwards with a high nave and towers, in contrast to the early Christian basilica, with its long, low emphasis. The simple rectangular space of the basilica became more complex and subtly articulated, by division into compartmentalized bays and by the addition of transepts and subsidiary chapels. Ornament and decoration were directly derived from the strong lines of the structure, rather than applied as a veneer in the Roman manner. The weighty elegance of the masonry itself became a primary form of Medieval architectural expression.

The severe, solemn rhythm of line and space of Durham cathedral, or the stout walls and noble scale of St. Etienne in Normandy, define and exemplify the bold, simple conception of

Above: Interior of St Etienne. Each bay is articulated with a tall shaft that continues the line of the vaulting down to the floor. Two bays make up a square in plan, shown in alternating patterns on the piers.

the Romanesque style—solid stone assembled with a deep sense of religious piety.

The Struggle for Mastery

Charlemagne was crowned Holy Roman Emperor on Christmas day, AD 800. For 14 years he actively promoted Christianity, encouraged the formation of monasteries and gathered artists and craftsmen around him to restore some of the past glories of Roman civilization in Europe. When he died his 'empire' disintegrated into several factions torn by regional disputes and vulnerable to attack from Scandinavians (Normans) in the North, Hungarians in the East, and Saracens

from the South. For a 100 years or more, life in Europe descended to an anarchic level.

In AD 911, Charles III made a treaty with the Scandinavians, bringing a peace of sorts to northern France. The Emperor, Otto I, took some time to deal with the Magyar horsemen of Hungary, but finally defeated them in AD 955. In the south the Saracen pirates had been menacing Europe for centuries from their foothold in Spain. The Mediterranean islands, southern Italy (including Rome itself) and Provence were attacked and taken. Only in AD 972 did William, Count of Provence, stem the flow and begin to force the Saracens back to southern Spain.

Below: West front of Notre Dame La Grande, in Poitiers – a fine example of a French Romanesque sculptured façade. The nave is roofed with a simple barrel vault, punctuated by transverse ribs.

THE AGE OF CONSTRUCTION

Worms

Abbaye-aux-Hommes (St Etienne)

Cluny 111

Durham

Pisa & Leaning Tower

German Romanesque | French Romanesque | English Romanesque | French Late Romanesque | Italian Romanesque

950 | 1000 | 1050 | 1100 | 1150 | 1200

Out of this confusion, several new nations struggled to emerge: France, Germany and Spain; the Scandinavian kingdoms were already established, and by the end of the 11th century, William the Norman had unified England. The Holy Roman Empire became no more than a nominal entity.

The one consistent force that survived the political instability and chaos of the Dark Ages, and kept the spirit of civilization alive, was Christianity. Monks and clergy were the guardians of education, science and the arts. Bishops had considerable political power and even led troops into battle. In the 11th century, the monastic orders (which had started with a few eccentric ascetic hermits in the deserts of Egypt in the first years after the crucifixion) rose to become Europe's most powerful patrons of art and architecture. It was the monks who promoted new methods of agriculture, designed and built the great churches, and dominated science, medicine, education and scholarship.

Religious zeal reached new heights by the 12th century — particularly in France, where a continuous stream of pilgrims risked the dangerous roads linking the great shrines and sanctuaries that housed important holy relics. Pilgrim offerings swelled the coffers of the shrines, financing yet grander constructions. The provision of fire-proof spaces to contain the throngs of the faithful with their burning torches was one of the necessities that gave birth to the Romanesque style of architecture.

Cluny—A New Concept

Cluny was the name of a small Roman villa, about 96 km (60 miles) north of Lyon, the favourite hunting lodge of William, Duke of Aquitaine. When he died, he gave it to the Abbot Berno, to establish a monastery. What the monks inherited was a small complex of buildings around a courtyard, including a chapel. The monastery that was founded here in AD 915 grew to become the most important in Europe, and it had considerable influence in the promotion of the Romanesque style.

Abbot Hugh, the third head of Cluny, was one of the most prolific builders of all time. He ruled for 60 years, visited all the major monuments of western Europe, and personally approved the plans of more than 1,000 buildings. His predecessor, Odilo, had built the second abbey church at Cluny, which inspired the

Above: Durham cathedral, one of the finest of all Romanesque churches in Europe. The siting of the cathedral is equally spectacular: it is perched on the top of an escarpment overlooking the valley of the River Wear.

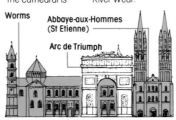

Above: Worms and St Etienne, two fine examples of Romanesque cathedrals drawn to scale alongside the Arc de Triumph.

design of several other churches throughout Europe, and Abbot Hugh replaced this with 'Cluny III,' the spiritual centre of an order that by then had spread as far as Italy, northern Spain, the Alps and England.

A unique feature of Cluny II was the extension of the aisles beyond the transept to form two small chapels on either side of the main apse and its altar. Two additional chapels were created in the east wall of the transept. Extra chapels were needed because of the increasing number of saints requiring worship, and the growing number of priests celebrating individual Mass every day.

At the famous church of St. Martin, in Tours (one of the great pilgrimage churches) the same problem had been solved by adding small semi-circular chapels, radiating from the apse at the east end. A similar solution was used at St. Philibert at Tournus. These innovations are significant because the subsidiary spaces are integrated and unified with the major space, instead of just being

tacked on as an afterthought. The brute simplicity of the basilican rectangle, crossed with a transept, is beginning to be softened by the addition of a series of subsidiary spaces that are united with the whole in a clear, logical manner.

Abbot Hugh took this development a stage further with Cluny III built between 1084 and 1121. It had the longest nave in Europe,

and its soaring space provided perfect acoustics for the famous Clunaic chants. The vault of the nave and aisles was slightly pointed in order to reduce the thrust. This was the first pointed vault in Europe, and provides a distinctive clue to the beginnings of Gothic. Sadly, the church was demolished in 1810.

The limestone of Caen, in Normandy, is one of the finest building materials in Europe. Skilled sailors, the Normans distributed Caen stone throughout northern France, and even as far as England. Once converted to Christianity, the Normans became devout church builders, and through their maritime trading were able to witness the evolution of various architectural movements in Europe. One result was that Norman contacts with the monasteries of southern France extended the influence of Cluny to Normandy, and several of the first Norman churches were modelled on Cluny II. Bernay Abbey was one of the first, a larger and grander version of Cluny II with richer decoration and possibly, a higher standard of masonry.

The great abbey church of Notre Dame at Jumieges was finished in 1066, but had to await consecration for two years while Duke William was away in England. This church established the Norman style: stout ashlar stone walling, strong, simple detailing, and square bays with alternating columns. It had a wooden roof and with the tall proportions of its walls, allowed for high, large windows. The only problem unresolved was the design of the vault. This was to be dealt with by the next generation.

The grandest church of Romanesque Normandy, however, is the Abbaye-aux-Hommes, or St Etienne, started by William in 1068. Originally designed to have a wooden roof over the nave, it was provided with a stone vault sometime after 1100. The vault system used was 'sexpartite', meaning that the square bay was divided into six sections with a transverse arch supporting the crown of the diagonal. This innovation was a key component in the evolution of Gothic (taken one step further by the pioneering rib vaults of Durham). The other great innovation of these Norman churches was the clear articulation of each bay by means of tall, slender shafts that run from floor to ceiling. This vertical emphasis marks the transition between basilican church and Gothic cathedral: the former — horizontal,

Norman Impact on Italy

The Normans moved into Sicily in 1061, and wrested control from the Saracens in 1091. The island had been colonized by the Greeks, the Carthaginians, the Romans, the Byzantine Empire and then, from 827, by the Moslem Saracens. Each culture contributed something to the exotic architecture of this charming island. When the Normans arrived, Moslems, orthodox and Latin Christians, and some Jews, were all living on top of each other. As elsewhere, the Normans absorbed and made use of what they found: the sophisticated comforts and luxury of Moslem palaces, the skills of the Saracen stone-masons, and the mosaics of the Byzantines.

In 1063 the foundations were laid for the cathedral of Pisa. The nave is a double aisled basilica, intersected by two smaller basilicas to form a transept with a dome above the crossing. The exterior is sheathed with brilliant white marble, decorated with superimposed arcades and pilasters. The proportions and massing of spaces reveal a tremendous elegance and simplicity, although structurally the building is straightforward. The delicate white tracery of the external ornament became a well-known Pisan trademark.

The famous Leaning Tower or campinale, was started in 1174. 13 storeys and 54 metres (179 feet) high, it now leans about 3 metres (13 feet) out of true, due to insufficient foundations and differential settling. Once crooked, the load from the top slightly bent the shaft, so that it is now also slightly curved. The problem of preventing further movement has amused and fascinated civil engineers ever since. Stylistically, this wonderful group of buildings is something of an oddity—perhaps rather more oriental in style than Romanesque.

Towers, Turrets and Galleries

The most typical German Romanesque churches are the cathedrals of Worms, Speyer and Mainz but of greater historical importance is St. Michael's at Hildesheim, started in 1001. It was more or less contemporary with that other key monument in the evolution of Romanesque, the second abbey church at Cluny. Instead of elaborating the simple basilica by adding subsidiary chapels—as at Cluny—St. Michael's has two transepts, two apses and two chancels arranged in an almost perfectly symmetrical plan. The nave, situated between the transepts at either end, was divided into three square bays

---

contained, leading the eye ever forward to the altar; the latter—vertical, uplifting, leading the eye to the heavens.

Ruthless Simplicity

Norman rule, like its architecture, was ruthlessly logical. Wherever they conquered (northern France, Southern Italy, Iceland, England), the Normans absorbed local practises and combined them with features of their own.

Church building, given impetus by the foundation of several great Benedictine abbeys, was one of the prime instruments of 'Normanization'. Between 1066 and the year he died (1087), William supervised the building or rebuilding of Canterbury, Lincoln, Old Sarum, Rochester, Winchester and Worcester cathedrals, and the foundation of abbeys at St. Albans, Bury St. Edmunds and Battle. But the most significant Norman cathedral was Durham, where the innovations of Jumieges and St. Etienne in northern France were taken to their logical conclusion. Started in 1093, Durham is located in one of the most beautiful settings in England, and is one of the finest examples of Romanesque architecture to be found anywhere.

The plan of Durham, which follows the Cluny II model, took about 35 years to execute and was based from the start on a vault design. It is this vaulting that has attracted the most historical interest, being the subject of fierce nationalistic clashes between French and English historians as to the exact date of construction. It is the first church to have ribbed vaulting throughout and thus was a key event in the evolution of Gothic architecture.

The plan is made up of a series of bays—eight in the nave, a square bay at the centre of the crossing, and four bays to the east. A slightly pointed arch spans across alternate bays, and the line of its rib is carried down to the floor with a multiple shaft or pier. Two pairs of diagonal ribs are thrown across from the six pillars of each double bay and the seven compartments thus created are filled in with lighter material. Thus, the long-held ambition of church builders to vault tall, wide naves was realized at last. The result was a church with beautiful acoustics and with generous, high-level 'clerestory' windows in the walls. Furthermore, the ribs allowed for a significant reduction of the complicated temporary wood support

Above: The massive masonry of Durham cathedral, begun in 1093 and vaulted some 40 years later.

Below: System of Romanesque bays of the nave: square plan with pier supporting cross-ribs.

or 'shuttering' required for construction. Lastly, and perhaps most important to the cathedral's designers, the visual logic and unity of each bay is completed by the linear movement of abstract pattern and spatial geometry which leads the eye smoothly up to the meeting point of the arches, high above the centre of each bay. The nave becomes a rhythmic procession of spatial compartments.

All these architectural objectives reach their fulfillment in the Gothic style, and yet Durham is entirely Romanesque. Although the decoration is linear and abstract, it always follows the

with two intermediate secondary columns either side. Thus, in contrast to the simple basilica , where a uniform series of columns marched relentlessly towards the altar, the rhythm here is interrupted by a more subtle procession of square, inter-connecting spaces. The bishop who built St. Michael's was said to be 'experienced in painting, excellent in science and the art of bronze-founding and in architectural work': splendid references.

The cathedrals of Speyer, Mainz and Worms have been considerably altered over the centuries. Restoration work on Speyer has better preserved its original stark grandeur. It is assembled almost entirely from square, or nearly square, compartments. Construction is heavy and solid, with walls 6 metres (20 feet) thick at the west end. The total length, east-west, approximates that of Chartres cathedral. Comparison

of the stout, confident masonry of Speyer with the lofty delicacy of Chartres well illustrates the different themes of Gothic and Romanesque.

Worms cathedral similarly is based on a square-bay design and, like Speyer, the crossing of the nave and the chancel is marked with an octagonal tower. Another octagon rises from the west end, flanked with round, slender towers either side, and two additional towers at the east end. A northern Italian influence is also evident in the open arcading and shallow relief plasters encircling the tower — a connection, if somewhat remote, with the Cathedral and Leaning Tower of Pisa.

The Story of Ribbed Vaulting

The fire risk of timber roofing was a major stimulus in the development of masonry vaulting. If a pilgrim's flaming torch or

zealot's candle should catch a roof timber alight, a vast investment in labour and materials could be burnt to ashes overnight. Another advantage of masonry vaults was their superior acoustics. But most of all, there must have been a strong desire to construct a roof that embodied the same symbolic permanence of the massive stone walls, and a structural system that was visually consistent and homogeneous.

Medieval masonry techniques were developed from the need to construct buildings with stones small enough to be carried by pack horse (the only effective means of transport apart from water). Although, if possible, local materials were used, some projects imported stone from considerable distances: the famous Caen limestone of Northern France was taken across the Channel to be used for Canterbury Cathedral and the Tower of London. In the majority of cases though, the materials available locally had a major influence on the development of regional styles and variations — the Caen stone of Normandy leading to the fine-grained, crisply cut ashlar construction of the Normans; the light volcanic rock in the district of Auvergn allowing a variety of colours and decorative treatments; the clays of the Netherlands and Northern Germany, producing bricks that were combined with bands of stone. Marble was locally available only in Provence and Italy.

One of the major problems with heavy masonry vault and arch construction was the need for temporary support during erection. The great Roman thermal and Byzantine vaults needed elaborate and costly 'centring' —

Left: Church of the Apostles, in Cologne, begun in 1035. The east end shown here has 3 semi-circular apses, clustered around a low octagonal tower. The nave has an extremely compact plan.

Above: Cathedral and Leaning Tower of Pisa: Oriental influence added to Romanesque.

Below: Stages in the development of the stone vault, from the Roman vault to the Gothic arch.

Roman Waggon Vault

Waggon Vault with Intersecting Vault

Romanesque Intersecting Vault

Gothic Vault over oblong Compartment

an accurate, temporary wooden framework the same shape as the underside of the vault to hold the concrete or stonework in position while the mortar set.

During construction, the inside of the Pantheon would have been covered by a dense forest of timber scaffolding. The solution was to construct an arch in a series of concentric ribs, each wider than the one below it, thereby making it possible to use the first (thinnest) rib as centring for the wider ribs above it. Thus only the first rib needed a framework of wooden supports, which could be light and easy to construct. This technique led to the evolution of 'moulded' arches and, by a process of extending the ribs downwards, to moulded or 'compound' piers as well. If the central moulding of the pier was taken up to the arch that spanned across the nave, a bay was generated, thus subdividing the nave into compartments.

The development of ribbed vaulting allowed the same advantages of minimal centring, as the ribs could first be constructed on a light timber framework, and the areas in between filled in afterwards. The system was developed to perfection by the architects of the Gothic style.

A New Age Dawns
Threshold to Heaven

Architectural Importance:
Revolutionary style of construction which followed (though in some parts of Europe was contemporary with) the Romanesque. Delicate balance of forces, with the thrusts directed throughout a rigid structural lattice. Gothic enjoyed universal popularity almost from the moment when the Choir of St Denis was completed, and its adoption throughout Europe was extremely rapid. Much later, Gothic enjoyed a peculiar sort of revival when it was 'rediscovered' during the 19th century.

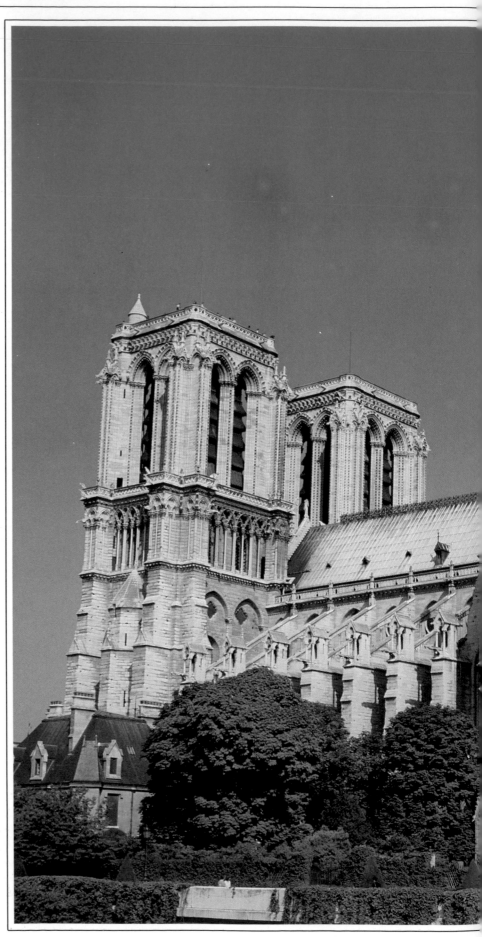

In 1144, Abbot Suger, the most influential churchman in France, consecrated the new Choir of the St. Denis Abbey which is near Paris. It was a revolutionary building; the anonymous master mason who designed it invented the Gothic style. By the 12th century the Catholic Church had become the dominant political and cultural power in Europe, and the Gothic style spread throughout the continent with astonishing rapidity.

Gothic architecture has certain easily identifiable, characteristic features: the pointed arch, the ribbed vault and the flying buttress, each of which had been used before in Romanesque churches of the 10th and 11th centuries. What made the Choir of St. Denis so different from any previous church was the deliberate combination of pointed arch, ribbed vaulting and stained glass used to create a taut and delicate stone cage that glowed with 'heavenly' light, an entirely new aesthetic,

Stylistic Essentials: Pointed arch, flying buttress and ribbed vault, deliberately used together to create a new type of building. Gothic architects planned their buildings to accommodate soaring spires, open walls, and interior spaces filled with light. It is perhaps in this feature that Gothic is differentiated so profoundly from the Romanesque style of which it was the direct offspring.

Primary Building Methods: Fine-grained limestone; its homogeneous texture and high tensile strength made it possible to accurately fit members to mouldings. Gothic style is closely associated with the use of stained glass, employed with grandiose effect in the rose windows of Gothic cathedrals and no less dramatically in the arcades of side windows of the larger Gothic churches.

quite unlike the thick, heavy masonry and gloomy grandeur of Romanesque buildings.

There were significant practical advantages to the Gothic system: the pointed arch enabled architects to vault over almost any ground plan, however complicated and elaborate. Flying buttresses made it feasible to build higher and to open up the solid walls, thereby creating spaces for large windows. Indeed, there was no longer any need for solid walls at all, since now a light framework of stone could be substituted.

Yet these technical advantages were solely a means to an end—it was the spiritual symbolism of the Gothic style that was the driving force behind the universal adoption of the style. To the ordinary worshipper in Medieval France, the Gothic cathedral was a threshold to heaven, an awesome and fearful sanctuary whose beauty was an expression of divine truth. The cathedral was the

Above: The famous rose window of Rheims cathedral. The 13th century west façade comprises a series of magnificently carved stone portals.

House of God—not merely a hallowed place where heads were covered and words whispered, but a representation of supernatural reality created to satisfy an urgent need for architecture that reflected a deep religious experience.

Medieval architects were fascinated with geometry and the theory of proportion. St. Augustus had used musical analogies to suggest that mathematics and perfect proportion could provide a link between the spiritual and temporal worlds: the octave, like the golden section, representing divine harmony, the heavenly beauty of eternal truth. The symbolism of light was all-important too—luminosity was associated with revelation; it was considered the source and essence of all inner truth and beauty.

Deeply influenced by such ideas, Abbot Suger prepared the plans for the first Gothic building, the Choir of the Abbey Church of St. Denis. His ambition was to create a sanctuary that would match the legendary Church of Santa Sophia in Constantinople, or the Temple of Solomon in Jerusalem. He firmly believed that his design for the new church was inspired by celestial vision.

Politically, Suger was the most powerful clergyman in France and within 100 years, Gothic had reached its glorious perfection in the elegant unity of design at Chartres, the delicate stone tracery of Rheims and the magnificent carved portals of Amiens. England, Germany, Italy, and Spain soon absorbed the style to create their own unique interpretations.

Gothic architecture was carved architecture. Every stone was cut to fit its particular position: the linear mouldings and ribs were united with the structure, they reduced its weight and expressed its lines of force. The distinction between structure, function and ornament was eliminated, and each part was integrated within the whole. It was a miracle of conception of proportion and of technical achievement.

The French Connection

At the beginning of the Gothic era, the area under its influence was no larger than the Ile-de-France (i.e. Paris and its environs), for long the royal domain of the kings of France. Within 100 years, a large part of Europe had come under Gothic control, and its sway had even reached the lands of the Middle East. Until the end of the 14th century, an astoundingly unified 'International Gothic' style prevailed.

The Gothic era began with architecture and for about a century—in the age of the great cathedrals—architecture stood at the helm of the Gothic movement. The origins of Gothic architecture can be very precisely pinpointed. It appeared in 1137 in the reconstruction of the Abbey Church at St. Denis, a short distance from Paris.

The man responsible for the rebuilding of the Abbey Church, and hence directly for the origins of Gothis architecture, was Abbot Suger, chief advisor to King Louis VI. Suger was instrumental in establishing a powerful Christian monarchy in France, preserving a delicate balance between Church and state. He helped to ensure French support for the popes in their struggles with Emperor Henry V, and put the Church firmly on the side of the monarchy in its long-running battle with the recalcitrant nobility. On his election as Abbot of St. Denis, Suger worked to further the prestige of the already distinguished monastery.

St. Denis was the patron saint of France, and French kings were buried in the Abbey Church. It was a 'royal' abbey, exempt from feudal and ecclesiastical obligations and subject only to the control of the king. Suger used his political influence to gain even more privileges for the monastery and sought to make it a centre of pilgrimage rivalling that of the Shrine of St. James at Santiago in Northern Spain. When Louis died in 1137, Suger retired from politics and devoted his time to rebuilding his church.

In 1124, Louis had granted his abbey the right to hold the yearly 'lendit', a religious festival centred round the relics of St. Denis, that attracted large crowds of pilgrims and with them a huge fair. The revenue from this fair was considerable, providing many of the funds required for building. The growing number of pilgrims gave Suger the justification for modifying the old Romanesque church, which he considered to be inadequate, and from 1124 onwards, money was set aside for this purpose. He repaired the nave in 1130, and began work on a new west facade in 1137. The choir was started in 1140.

When Abbot Suger began construction, he had neither craftsmen nor materials, and it took time to assemble a team and to find a good quarry for building stone. Perhaps this lack of local experience and tradition helped to forge the concept of such a revolutionary building, for Suger indeed wanted something more than the stoic grandeur of Romanesque.

By the time he had started work on the choir he must have found a master mason of consummate skill. It is a synthesis of Suger's vision and the mason's virtuosity: all the elements used had been tried before—the pointed arch at Durham and the third abbey church of Cluny; the ribbed vault at the abbeys of Caen, and Durham again. But Suger's vision of reaching God and divine truth through a dramatic construction of light and space created something entirely different using the same components.

The plan of the choir consists of a double 'ambulatory' with seven radiating chapels. The ambulatory is like two concentric, semi-circular routes, with the chapels as shallow niches forming a wavy wall round the edge. Each radiating bay is roofed by a ribbed vault with pointed arches. It is, in effect, one space articulated

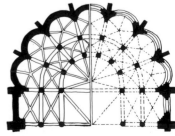

Above: Plan of the New Choir of the Abbey Church of St Denis. The use of the arch enabled the mason to vault over the awkward spaces.

Notre Dame   Laon   Amiens   Wells   Milan

France   France   France   England   Italy

| 1100 | 1200 | 1300 | 1400 | 1500 |

by the five-ribbed vaults. Suger himself described it thus: 'The whole sanctuary is pervaded by a wonderful and continuous light entering through the most sacred windows'.

The result was a new, geometric order; the unity of approach achieved in the Abbey Church of St. Denis is as stunning as it is novel. Although the basic scheme is Romanesque in its elements, the final effect is pure Gothic. The distinguishing features are the incredible lightness and gracefulness of the edifice—it appears almost weightless in comparison with the heavy solidity of its Romanesque forebears. The Abbey Church is abundantly filled with light, the result of the drastically enlarged windows which seem to make the walls themselves translucent. Within, the double ambulatory is experienced as a continuous space, whose shape is delineated by a delicate framework of columns, vaulted ribs and slender arches. The heavy buttresses that contain the outward pressure of the vaults can only be seen from the outside, thus emphasizing the incredible airiness of the interior.

In describing the details of the Abbey Church at St. Denis, one has described the essential features of Gothic architecture, of which St. Denis was the prototype. How dramatic the effect of St. Denis was on those who gazed upon her, we shall never know, but what can be said with confidence is that within a few years of her completion, plans were being prepared for a whole succession of churches to be built across France. Gothic had come of age.

On June 10th, 1194, a huge fire destroyed the town of Chartres, the bishop's palace and the cathedral. Only the west facade survived. Chartres was an important pilgrim centre: in AD 876, Charles the Bold had presented to the cathedral the tunic allegedly worn by the Virgin Mary during the birth of Christ. Its destruction was thought to be an act of God, for the whole life of the city revolved around the relic and its patron saint, Denis, not the least because of the income generated by the pilgrims.

In fact, the relic itself survived the conflagration, and this 'miracle' was taken to signify the patron's desire that a wonderful new cathedral should be erected: a sanctuary worthy of her special residence. The cathedral took 27 years of non-stop construction to finish. There is no record of the name of the master mason, and some authorities claim that towards the end of the project he was succeeded by another. The design shows considerable sophistication in its geometry—the system of proportions is based on the pentagon and the formula called the golden section.

One of the principle innovations at Chartres was the use of simple, diagonal, ribbed vaults, stretched across a bay that is roughly half a square, single—west of the crossing, and double—to the east. The apse has five semicircular chapels. Another innovation concerns the piers: they alternate between a cylindrical and octagonal core, each with four slender shafts. The shaft on the nave side rises right up to where the vault begins. The alternating cores give a subtle indication of the square formed by two of the bays, only slightly interrupting the rhythm of piers marching towards the altar. At the great cathedrals of Laon and Notre Dame, Paris, the piers are circular, and the moulded shafts start from the top. At Noyen, moulded piers alternate with rounded ones.

The effect at Chartres is more unified; nothing intervenes between floor and vault, and the unbroken lines ascend to an immense height. The arches of the aisles also soar, as do the clerestory windows. All this adds

Left: The west façade of Laon Cathedral, a superb composition in the early French Gothic style. On the towers are carvings of oxen which hauled the stone blocks.

Below: Chartres Cathedral, renowned not least for its stained glass windows.

Above: An interior elevation of the nave. The vault is over 36m (120 ft) high.

to the effect of verticality. This three-tier elevation with its uniform moulded piers and diagonal rib vaulting represents the 'high' Gothic style, perfected in the cathedrals of Amiens, Rhiems and Beauvais. They are more daring and architecturally thrilling than Chartres, yet Chartres has a unity of conception and dignified repose that, combined with its well-preserved stained-glass and sculpture, makes it the supreme synthesis of Gothic art.

Separate Development

The first Gothic church in England was Canterbury Cathedral, built by William of Sens in 1174. William had been involved in the building of Sens Cathedral in France, started about 30 years earlier, and some similarities in design can be seen. Gervais, the cathedral's chronicler, tells how four years after work began, William severely hurt himself when he fell from high scaffolding in 1178, and was forced to return to France an invalid. An English architect was immediately appointed to succeed him.

Although the style of construction is clearly French, the compartmentalization of the different spaces is essentially English in character. Another interesting feature is the use of marble for the shafts and 'string courses' (horizontal bands of masonry mouldings). This idea was later taken up by other churches and became a characteristic feature of early English Gothic.

Following the consecration of Canterbury, the cathedrals of Wells and Lincoln were constructed. The vaults of Lincoln are roughly contemporary with those at Amiens. Unlike the English bays, those in French cathedrals are narrow and tall. At Amiens the vaults are a natural, logical extension of the bays; those at Lincoln are a profusion of radiating ribs like the veins of a leaf — only barely connected to the piers supporting them from below.

There are several other differences between French and English cathedrals. While French cathedrals were located in the centre of the town, English cathedrals were generally linked to monasteries in open surroundings, forming the focus of a complex of buildings or 'close' with cloisters and chapter house.

The model English cathedral is Salisbury, built during the span of a single generation and hardly altered since, except for the addition of the spire in the 1450s. From the outside, the impression of height is created by a series of stone structures, some apparently separate, others connected, that culminate in the spire. The interior, with its long, low nave and multiple linear mouldings, is very English. Dark, purbeck marble is used for the decorative shafting, and there is little evidence of sculpture. Again, in comparison to the French cathedrals, the

emphasis in English cathedrals is on the horizontal, rather than on the vertical, that characterizes French Gothic.

In the 14th century, the profusion of linear moulding and the stone tracery of windows produced the English 'decorated' style, foreshadowed by the vaults of Lincoln and Exeter, and the windows of Carlisle. Carved ornament is applied not as a decorative surface, but in a profusion of ribs and stone tracery, always subordinate to and integrated with the structural skeleton. This was the golden age of English Gothic, exemplified by the wonderful and daring octagon of Ely, the extravagantly decorated tower of Canterbury, and later, the stupendous fan vaulting of the cloisters at Gloucester, King's College Chapel at Cambridge, and Henry VII's chapel at Westminster Abbey.

Spreading Throughout Europe

By the middle of the 14th century, French Gothic had become decadent; interior decoration was applied with little regard to the structural frame. The French themselves called this period 'flamboyant'. In its structure, the flamboyant period shows no significant developments of its own: rather, it is distinguished from its high Gothic precursors by the luxuriance of the ornamentation. The network of decoration is so dense and fanciful that it completely obscures the structural skeleton beneath.

The Gothic style arrived late in Germany, and the earliest examples of German cathedrals are stylistically derived from the French. Cologne Cathedral, begun in 1248, with its tall choir and narrow bays, is strikingly similar

Right: Salisbury Cathedral. With its long, narrow nave and two transepts, it represents the classic English Gothic Cathedral. It has the tallest spire in England.

to the cathedral of Beauvais. The extraordinary thing about Cologne is that it took nearly 700 years to complete.

Most German Gothic churches of the 14th century acquired the characteristically 'hallenkirchen' or Hall Church appearance, which became the standard throughout the country. The distinctive feature of the Hall Church is the fact that the roof above the aisles is as high as that above the nave, thus creating a space of great fluidity and expansiveness. There is no impression of pressure, no sensation of order or command

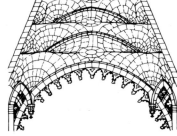

Above and Below: The magnificent pendent or fan vault of the Henry VII chapel, Westminster Abbey, built as a mausoleum for the king. The vault is a miracle of intricate stone tracery, that actually seems to be suspended in thin air.

to proceed in any particular direction. Instead, there is an impression of continuous movement, given impetus by the unbroken lines of pillars.

The Gothic style of Italian architecture is unlike that of the rest of Europe. Indeed, it hardly deserves the label Gothic at all. Yet the structures produced during the 13th century in Italy are as beautiful and impressive as any in France or England which fall in the category of Gothic.

The Italian Gothic was the creation, not of cathedral builders, but of the Cistercian monks, who looked to the great abbeys of France for their inspiration. Noted for their austerity and lack of surface ornamentation, Italin Gothic churches reveal a high degree of harmonious planning; their fine proportions have a Romanesque feel about them, yet they are nevertheless unmistakably Gothic.

The Italians preferred to build with brick, sheathed or banded with marble, and with large plain surfaces covered by elaborate paintings. Gothic pointed arch vaulting was used, but the spaces are wide, open and unencumbered.

Milan Cathedral was built between 1386 and 1485, and is the second largest Medieval cathedral in the world (the largest is in Seville). It is said that over 50 architects were employed, some of them from northern Europe. The exterior is a mass of shining white marble with lacy, intricate pinnacles, flying buttresses and ornamental sculptures. The interior is dark and mysterious with tall, massive moulded piers

Above: Milan Cathedral, the stunning result of the combined efforts of some 50 architects: it took several centuries to achieve its final completion.

and a lofty vault 45 metres (148 feet) high. Florence Cathedral began as a Gothic church, but Giotto and Brunelleschi added a campinalle (bell tower) and dome that are essentially Renaissance in style. The enormous nave, nearly 82 metres (270 feet) long, is divided into four bays.

Delicate Balance

The fine-grained limestones of the Ile de France provided Gothic architects with the perfect material with which to build their cathedrals. It's homogeneous texture and high tensile strength made it possible to accurately fit members and mouldings with, consequently, a considerable reduction in the thickness and therefore the weight of the vaulting.

Gothic architecture relies on a delicate balance of forces, with thrusts carefully directed throughout a rigid structural lattice. To .use an analogy from nature, Romanesque structure is like the heavy shell of a turtle compared to the skeleton of vertebrates imitated by Gothic. The wall becomes a void between buttresses, to be filled by stained glass, framed by delicate stone tracery. The outward thrust of the vault is absorbed by the flying buttress and passed down to the ground outside the building. The

Right: The 3-tiered flying buttresses of Chartres Cathedral, the flying buttresses transfer the thrust of the vaulting to solid buttresses that take it down to the ground.

great 19th-century historian Violet le Duc, proposed the theory that Gothic architecture evolved from structural invention, but nowadays the religious and philosophical symbolism of the pointed arch and stained glass illumination is considered to have been more likely responsible for its birth. During the world wars several ribbed vaults were damaged. In several instances, even though the ribbing failed, the vault was left intact. This has led to the conclusion that the rib had less structural value than was previously thought.

Below: The spires of the great cathedrals have dominated the towns and cities of Europe since the inception of the Gothic style during the early 12th century.

Notre Dame Cathedral

Laon Cathedral

Salisbury Cathedral

Arc de Triumph

Brotherhood of Islam
New Focus in the East

.Medina

SAUDI ARABIA

Red Sea

.Jidda
•Mecca

Architectural Importance:
The origins of Islamic architecture can be traced to two main sources: Mesopotamia and Graeco-Roman/Byzantine. The Islamic religion provided a unifying source of inspiration for art and architecture across a wide range of diverse cultures. The mosque was a major outlet for Islamic artistic design and craftsmanship. Islamic architecture makes much use of symbolic geometry, using pure forms such as the circle and the square. Major sources of decorative design are foliage and writings from the Koran.

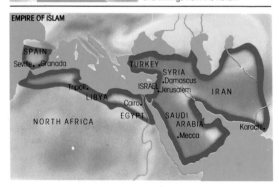

EMPIRE OF ISLAM

SPAIN
Seville. .Granada
Tripoli.
LIBYA
NORTH AFRICA
TURKEY
SYRIA
.Damascus
ISRAEL.Jerusalem
Cairo.
EGYPT
SAUDI ARABIA
.Mecca
IRAN
Karachi.

The growth of Islam after its foundation by the prophet Muhammad in AD 632 was so amazingly rapid that less than a century later the Moslem world stretched from the Atlantic coast of Spain right across to India. As did Christianity in Europe, the Islamic religion provided a unifying source of inspiration for art and architecture throughout this vast and disparate empire with its ever-changing political climate and tremendously diversified cultural complexion.

The most striking feature of Islamic architecture is its sensuous use of texture and colour, coupled with a rigorous logic in the application of abstract pattern and symbolic geometry. The brilliant colour of tilework, the rich texture and patterns of stucco or brick seduce the eye and the emotions, yet at the same time the harmony of proportion, purity of form and powerful symbolism of symmetry have a stimulating effect on the intellect.

Primary Building Materials:
Stonework techniques derived from Roman and Byzantine methods, while brick and tilework had their origins, for the Arabs, in Mesopotamia and the Sassanian dynasty. Plaster made from gypsum, often built up in layers carved and highly polished to give it a marble-like finish. Wood was scarce and highly valued for carving and ornamentation.

Stylistic Essentials:
Plans of most mosques based on a rectangular courtyard, with a prayer hall on the side facing Mecca. Layouts strongly symmetrical, forms repetitive and geometrical. Roofs make much use of the dome. Arches often pointed or horseshoe-shaped. Surfaces richly decorated with glazed tiles, carved stucco, patterned brickwork or alternated bands of coloured stonework. Decoration is perhaps the key element in Islamic architecture. It is used to bring alive flat building surfaces, and often to disguise undesirable structural lines. Representation of human forms forbidden.

Among the bewildering variety of regional and historical styles throughout the Islamic world certain common characteristics emerge. The two major building types are the mosque and the palace. The courtyard is a key feature of both: in the mosque it functions as an assembly area, with a pool for ablution and purification; in the palace it generates a miniature paradise, enclosed and private with sumptuous gardens and gushing fountains. Religious buildings have survived rather better than secular ones, largely because piety has ensured their preservation.

Mosques were laid out with the main covered space or prayer hall on the side of the courtyard that faces Mecca. This direction is marked by the 'mihrab', a niche in the wall towards which the faithful pray. Next to the mihrab stands a high pulpit, approached by a flight of steps, which are often elaborately carved. The prayer hall is usually wider than it is deep, so that a great number of worshippers can be close to the wall containing the mihrab. Outside the mosque are the minarets—tall needle-like structures from which the muezzin calls the faithful to prayer.

The architectural design of the prayer hall took three main forms: the first was the hypostyle hall where the roof was supported by parallel rows of uniform columns, spaced closely together. This was common throughout Islam for the first 500 years and maintained its pre-eminence in the Arab-speaking world. In Iran there developed the iwan, a high vaulted hall open on one side, situated in the middle of the courtyard wall. The four-iwan mosque had an iwan on each side, with the one facing Mecca forming an entrance to a dome-covered prayer hall. In the 15th century, the Ottoman Turks evolved a variety of mosque types where the dominant feature was a large central dome surrounded by smaller domes and semi-domes. The mosque was more than a religious sanctuary—it also functioned as a meeting place, law court and social centre. Some mosques were founded as teaching establishments, with the designation of 'madrassas'.

Palaces were divided into two parts: the public area, an exclusively male preserve where guests were entertained and meetings held, and the private part populated by the women and children. The palaces of Topkapi in Istanbul and the Alhambra in Spain are dazzling evidence of the gracious living and lavish artistic sponsorship of their Islamic rulers. Other secular buildings include fortifications (strongly built and ingeniously defended) bazaars and caravanserais (travelling inns), as well as remarkable engineering constructions such as canals, reservoirs, cisterns and other irrigation systems.

Islamic architecture is highly regarded for the quality of its decoration: the abundance of colour in mosaic, glazed tile and painted stucco, the delicate and intricate carving of plaster and wood, designs for which were derived and abstracted from foliage, calligraphy and abstract pattern. Geometry itself became a major art form, using refinement, repetition and symmetry to create a wide variety of effects. Often it seems as though the structure is sheathed or even disguised by a mantle of ornament, like a rich carpet or textile hanging. Since much of the city and landscape settings are dry and monochromatic, the great Islamic monuments appear as dazzling jewels that flash with colour in an otherwise monotonous environment.

Search for Identity

Islamic chronology starts in the year AD 622, the date of the 'Hegira' or flight of the prophet Muhammad from Mecca to Medina. The prophet was obliged to flee because his revolutionary teachings conflicted with the ruling aristocracy in Mecca. At Medina, Muhammad founded a community with a constitution that broke the stranglehold of tribal customs and leadership. He changed the centre of religious devotion from Jerusalem to Mecca, where the Kaaba (a shrine in the form of a stone cube) had long been an important Arab sanctuary and centre of pilgrimage. In doing so he combined his revolutionary teachings with established Arab traditions and his egalitarian philosophies and strong, simple faith soon won widespread support. He made a triumphant return to Mecca in 630.

Muhammad died in 632 and the community he founded subsequently elected a 'caliph' (meaning a vicar or representative of the prophet). The second caliph, Omar, began the conquests that were to bring large parts of North Africa, the Middle East and Asia within Islamic rule. Damascus was taken in 635, the Byzantine Emperor, Heraclius, was evicted from Jordan, Jerusalem fell in 638. By 641 Egypt was absorbed, as indeed was much of Persia.

Above: The Spiral minaret of the Friday Mosque at Samarra. More than 50 metres (165 feet) high, it was originally connected to the mosque by a long viaduct. In the ninth century, Samarra was chosen as the new capital of the Islamic empire, but only four decades later it was abandoned.

In only 30 years, Islamic conquests stretched from Tripoli to the river Oxus in Kashmir. All that was left of the Asian part of the Byzantine Empire was the Turkish peninsula and the Persian Empire disappeared altogether.

After a period of bitter internal dispute, the leadership of the Islamic world fell to the Umayyad family who founded the first great Islamic dynasty, in 661. The caliph now became an hereditary monarch, and the capital was moved from Medina to Damascus. During this dynasty a degree of unity was forged among the various Arab tribes, and the frontiers were extended to the Indian Ocean in the East and the Atlantic in the West. The adoption of Arabic as the official language signified the establishment of a truly Arab-Islamic culture, and the first signs

THE AGE OF CONSTRUCTION

Great Mosque
of Damascus

Ince Minare
Konya Mosque

Qa it Bay

Suleimaniye Mosque

AD 622 flight of the prophet to Medina

AD 630 Muhammad's triumphant return to Mecca

| 500 | 600 | 700 | 800 | 900 | 1000 | 1100 | 1200 | 1300 | 1400 | 1500 | 1600 | 1700 |

of a uniquely Islamic architecture became evident.

By the middle of the eighth century, the Umayyads lost their grip on the empire, and the Abbasid family, also direct decendants of the prophet, assumed the leadership. The Abbasid dynasty lasted for nearly 500 years and during this time the capital was again transferred eastwards, from Damascus to Baghdad, reflecting perhaps the growing economic and political importance of the eastern sector of the empire.

During the Abbasid dynasty several independent or semi-independent sub-groups of Islamic culture established themselves, each making an important contribution to Islamic art and architecture. These include the Caliphate of Spain, the Tulunid dynasty in Egypt, the Fatimid dynasty in Sicily and Egypt, the Samarid dynasty in what is now Afghanistan, the Seljuks in Iran, the Almorarid dynasties in Spain and North Africa, and the Mamaluks in Syria and Egypt. Many of these were developing contemporaneously with each other.

Baghdad was sacked by the Monguls in 1256. By this time the Islamic world was permanently divided into fully independent nations. Architecturally, the most significant areas were Iran, Spain and India (described in subsequent chapters of the book) and the Ottoman empire, inaugurated with the sacking of Byzantium in 1453.

A Form Emerges

The word mosque means 'place of prostration', though the first mosques were political and social centres, as well as places of worship. Originally, the followers of Muhammad assembled in the courtyard of the prophet's house in Medina. In time, congregational mosques were constructed; simply rectangular compounds, large enough to accommodate the male population. They were often surrounded by a ditch, reed fence or wall. One of the earliest permanent structures was the mosque in the town of Kufa, Iraq, built in 639. The qibla, or side of the compound that faced Mecca, had a simple portico supported by second-hand Roman marble columns and covered by a wooden roof. Like the Greek Agora or Roman Forum, these early mosques functioned as public meeting places, law courts and debating halls.

The new religion initially had no architecture of its own. Indeed, the first mosques were designed by Christian or Coptic architects invited to do the job in the absence of Islamic expertize. With the

building of the Great Mosque at Kufa the pattern was established for the majority of mosques that followed. It had a wall and colonnade on three sides, and a prayer hall five columns' deep on the side facing Mecca.

An exception to this rule was the seventh century Dome of the Rock in Jerusalem, built on the site of the Temple of Solomon. The plan is octagonal with a central dome over the rock where, according to tradition, Abraham sacrificed Isaac, from whom all Arabs believe they are descended.

Below: The Dome of the Rock in Jerusalem, built at the end of the 7th century on the rock that was the supposed site of Abraham's sacrifice of the lamb.

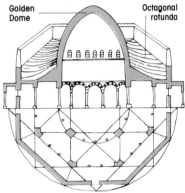

Golden Dome

Octagonal rotunda

Below: The early 8th century Great Mosque at Damascus. The dimensions of the great court were determined by the temple that the Mosque replaced.

Right: The treasury of the mosque at Damascus. The mosaics were executed with Byzantine techniques, using coloured and even gilded glass.

The form of the building and its decoration were directly derived from Byzantine Christian churches in the Middle East.

The most famous of the early Islamic shrines is the Great Mosque at Damascus, built between 706 and 715, and still largely intact. The prayer hall consists of three long naves parallel to the wall facing Mecca, with a dome at the centre. At that time, Damascus was the capital of the Islamic Empire, and the Great Mosque was intended to be a monument to rival the most grandiose Christian basilicas. The interior was covered with a magnificent mosaic extending over half a hectare (an acre) in surface area, though sadly much of it has been destroyed by fire. The techniques were Byzantine, though the imagery contained no animal or human representation, since this was forbidden by the Koran. The Great Mosque at Damascus is one of the finest examples of Umayyad architecture and was the most influential Islamic building of its time.

The Umayyads were responsible for many desert palaces'

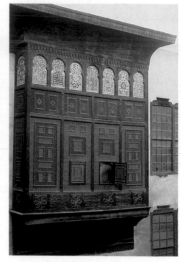

Left and Above: An interior and exterior view of a window in the Sultan Hasan Mosque. Although the screen allows air to pass through freely, it severely restricts the light that filters through the window.

Arc de Triumph   **Selim Mosque at Edirne**

Left: Close-up of a carved lattice window screen. The patterns are derived from the square and circle.   **Above:** A scale comparison of the Selim Mosque at Edirne in Turkey and the Arc de Triumph.

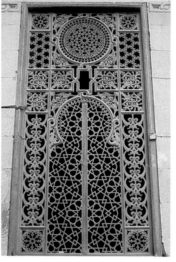

Above: Mihrab of the Sultan Hasan Mosque in Cairo. Here marble and stone are used together to heighten the rich, decorative effect. The mihrab is a niche in the wall facing east, used as a focus for prayer.

(farming centres not unlike Roman country villas) on the borders of the 'fertile lands' of Jordan and Syria, and the Arabian desert. Extensive irrigation works were undertaken to guarantee a water supply for the palace itself and the surrounding fields. The larger palaces were country retreats for the royal family, and were luxuriously appointed in their layout and decoration. One of the best-preserved is at Khirbat al-Mafjar, near Jerico. It was planned around two courtyards, with a mosque, elaborate baths and royal apartments; the finest part was the bath-audience hall, a huge space with a vaulted roof supported by 16 massive piers, and a central dome. It was decorated throughout with richly carved stucco, a technique borrowed from the Sassanids in Persia.

The early buildings of Islam exhibit a logical synthesis of Oriental and Western art: the carved stucco came from Persia, the mosaic from Byzantium and Roman architecture influenced layouts and structural techniques (columns removed from Roman buildings were often incorporated in Islamic mosques and palaces). In the 11th, 12th and 13th centuries these elements were fused into an architecture that was,

despite the many regional variations of style and construction, unmistakably Islamic.

The Elegance of Ibn Tulun

In 868, the Abbasid Caliph at Samarra sent Ahmed Ibn Tulun, the son of a Turkish slave, to Cairo to be the governor of Egypt. Here, Ahmed built a mosque that attracted the admiration of the Islamic world. The Ibn Tulun Mosque built from red fired brick, and faced with carved stucco, is a vast, solemn and grandiose monument. Like the mosque at Samarra in Iraq, there are wide corridors (ziyadas) on three sides of the courtyard. It has pointed brick arches, richly carved ornamental stucco and a spiral minaret.

At Qairouan, in Tunisia, the Great Mosque was extensively remodelled between 836 and 863. It was the key monument of the Aghlabid dynasty, a regime that brought peace and stability to North Africa during the tenth century. Aghlabid architecture is characterized by its purity of form, forceful and simple planning and utilitarian style. The sanctuary of the Great Mosque at Qairouan is a vast hypostyle or columned hall, roofed with a painted wooden ceiling. The Aghlabids were skilled hydraulic engineers, and built many reservoirs to reclaim the once highly-productive desert.

In 969, the Fatimid dynasty

seized control of Egypt and for over two centuries controlled much of North Arica and Syria, taking advantage of the decline of Islamic power in Iraq and the growing commercial importance of the Red Sea and Mediterranean, particularly the trading activities of the emerging maritime Italian states such as Venice. The Fatimids often used stone as a principal building material; the exterior façades of their monuments were richly decorated, usually with shallow, recessed arches that broke up large expanses of walling. They were also fond of monumental arches or portals, to provide dramatic gateways or entrances to their public buildings.

In the 11th century the Fatimids were ousted from Syria by the Seljuk Turks, and threatened in Egypt by the crusaders. The legendary Saladin seized control of Egypt in 1171 and created a powerful empire that threatened the position of the crusaders. This era is called the Ayyubid dynasty, and it was followed in the twelfth century by the Mamaluks. The architecture of these two eras is characterized by the madrassas (theological colleges) and lavish mausoleums erected by the Sultans and Amirs, financed by the prosperity resulting from the Red Sea trade between East and West.

The finest monument of the Mamaluks is the tomb and madrassa of Sultan Hasan in Cairo.

Designed by a Syrian architect, a huge army of craftsmen from Syria and Persia were employed to build this vast complex in only three years (1356-9). There are four colossal arched recesses that surround a central court. The walls are over 27 metres (100 feet) high. The decoration is a supreme example of the integration of decoration with architectural ornamental structure.

Rise of the Ottomans

The Ottoman Empire was founded by the Turkish leader Osman in the beginning of the 14th century. With the capture of Constantinople by Muhammad the conquerer in 1453, it quickly grew to be the dominant empire of the Islamic world, a huge and well organized state that was to last for nearly six centuries. Constantinople, re-named Istanbul, once again became a great city and centre of civilization. With Selim 1's conquest of Syria and Egypt, the Ottoman empire was extended to encompass the holy places of Islam and included most of North Africa and the Middle East.

Ottoman architecture is a synthesis of Byzantine, Armenian and Seljuk (Turkish and Persian) ideas, combined with great originality and inventiveness. The great Byzantine church of Santa Sophia provided a model, where the dome became the dominant feature, combined with Persian minarets

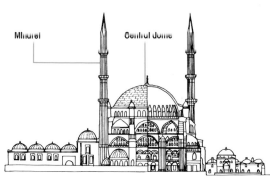

and decorative ornamentation. The Golden Age of Ottoman architecture was the 15th and 16th centuries, a period dominated by the legendary architect, Sinan Agha. One of the great builders of all time, he is credited with the design of over 350 monuments.

The first of his three most famous creations was the Seyzade Mosque in Istanbul, built between 1544 and 1548. Its plan is based on the square with a central dome surrounded by four semi-domes. The central dome rests on four huge arches that span between four columns, and with four small domes filling the space in the corners. The effect is devastatingly simple, a masterful solution to the problem of roofing a large square volume.

Sinan's most celebrated building is possibly the Suleiman Mosque, founded by Suleiman the Magnificent in 1550. The basic form is almost identical to Santa Sophia, built 1,000 years earlier, yet the emphasis is entirely different. With Santa Sophia, the spherical volumes merge into one glorious and mysterious space, but in the Suleiman Mosque, the geometry is clearly revealed and the structure unashamedly expressed. The subsidiary volumes are connected, yet separately defined.

The Great Mosque of Selim II at Edirne was constructed when Sinan was 80 years old, and represents the culmination of a lifetime's experience and experiment. Sinan himself considered it to be his finest work. In this building he finally abandoned the Byzantine prototype. The central dome rests on eight arches that form an octagon. Small semi-domes span the diagonal corners, completing the square. Their interior is sober and elegant, a symmetrical space that radiates from its powerful central octagon. Sinan was much concerned with the symbolism of the circle, square and dome, and the harmony of geometric projection. The Great Mosque at Edirne was the supreme fulfillment of this cult of geometry, and is the most spatially sophisticated of Islamic architecture.

The imperial palaces of the Ottoman Empire were lavish and opulent, filled with pavilions, kiosks, interconnecting courtyards and arcades. The largest and most

famous is the Topkapi palace, Istanbul, started by Muhammad the Conqueror in 1462. The numerous structures are arranged around four great courts. The sultan's apartments are richly decorated with coloured tilework and painted domes.

Skilled Draughtsmen

The more spectacular monuments of Islam, usually based in the major centres of civilization, were designed by skilled professional architects. Some of them travelled great distances to carry out particular commissions. Architects often achieved a high social standing. Most Islamic professions and crafts were passed from father to son, and since the basic form and design of the majority of mosques were constantly repeated and refined, many buildings were probably designed by ordinary craftsmen. Drawing instruments that have been found during excavations show that Islamic architects and engineers were skilled draughtsmen, and well able to conceive their ideas on parchment or paper and accurately communicate them to their craftsmen. Some designs were even tested first with small scale models.

The autocratic Moslem rulers were able to assemble large teams of workmen and quantities of materials in order to build their monuments very quickly, and some famous mosques were built in less than three years, in stark contrast to the much slower constructions of Europe. However, the costs were often enormous and a severe drain on the economy.

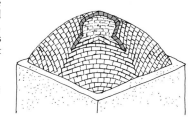

Jewel of the Faith
Isfahan-'Half the World'

SOVIET UNION

Mashad.

•Tehran

•Baghdad

•Isfahan

IRAQ   I R A N

•Shiraz

SAUDI ARABIA

Architectural Importance:
Iranian architectural styles have had an immensely powerful effect on the rest of Islamic architecture. This is particularly true of such important details as the decorative treatment of patterned brickwork, coloured tiles and moulded stucco. Indeed, the blue tiles used in the Friday mosque and other Islamic shrines and palaces have earned the Persians the world's admiration for the brilliance of their ceramics. Other important aspects of Iranian building concepts are the 'stalactite vaults'.

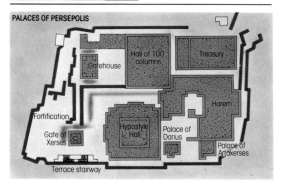

PALACES OF PERSEPOLIS

Gatehouse · Hall of 100 columns · Treasury · Harem · Fortification · Gate of Xerxes · Hypostyle Hall · Palace of Darius · Palace of Artaxerxes · Terrace stairway

For almost 1,000 years, the city of Isfahan has presented a welcome sight to the weary merchant or pilgrim wending his way over the vast semi-desert tracts that separate this city from others in Persia. Isfahan lies on a huge plateau and only at the end of the journey is the traveller confronted with a view of the shimmering blue domes and spikey minarets of the city's mosques.

Isfahan owes its magical beauty to the inspiration and dynamic vision of one man, Shah Abbas the Great, who assumed the title of king of kings in 1587. Until then, this southern Persian township was little more than that — a drab and unappealing community beside such other centres of Islamic culture as Mashad, Tabriz and Baghdad. Abbas transformed it into a beautiful and powerful capital, and made it almost overnight the envy of the Islamic world.

The focal point of the city is the Maiden,

Below: View of the Maiden, the enormous square conceived by Shah Abbas as the focus of a unique urban development project. It is fully enclosed by a screen of double-tiered archways. In the foreground is the Royal Mosque, on the right the Ali Qapu Palace, and opposite, the Shaikh Lutfullah Mosque.

75

Stylistic Essentials:
Wide use of mud or fired brick domes. Richly decorated surfaces, patterned brickwork, brightly-coloured tiles, moulded stucco, the four-Iwan mosque is the typical Iranian layout.

Primary Building Materials:
Since good stone was hard to obtain, most buildings were made of burnt brick. Domes often constructed layer by layer without shuttering. Invention of tri-lobed squinch

led to the 'stalactite vault', a characteristic Islamic feature. Dome of the small sanctuary of the Friday mosque in Isfahan represents one of the world's most dramatic examples of sculptured brick design.

Spread of Influence:
While the form of the classical Persian mosque was still being developed, the minaret was evolving into the star form that had such a marked influence later on the Indian sub-continent.

an enormous square. This was Abbas's greatest achievement. Twice the size of Red Square in Moscow, and seven times the area of the Piazza di San Marco in Venice, the Maiden is enclosed by a continuous line of two-storey arcades, richly decorated with the blue tiles that have made Persian ceramics renowned throughout the world.

At one end of the Maiden is the bazaar, at the other the Royal Mosque, dominated by a vast blue dome. Everywhere the eye is feasted with the richly-textured patterning of ceramic designs of floral or abstract patterns embellished in intricate calligraphy of scripts taken from the Koran, the Holy Book of Islam.

Isfahan is unique among Iranian cities in having managed to preserve so many of its wonderful monuments. Partly this is because it does not lie on the earthquake fault line that has caused the destruction of so many other Persian cities over the centuries. Indeed, Isfahan seems to have

been miraculously saved from all manner of natural and man-made acts of destruction.

The architecture of Iran has been a crucial source of inspiration to the architecture of Islam. Gradually, the skillful integration of brick vaults and domes and the engineering brilliance with which Persia's stupendous mosques were constructed influenced the development of building styles throughout the Middle East and North Africa. It culminated in such masterpieces as the famous 'stalactite vaults'—the clustering of hundreds of miniature vaults about a central pillar like the stalactites found hanging in limestone caverns.

Yet again, the classic problem of fitting a dome over a square chamber was solved with elegant simplicity in Persia: witness the burnt-brick dome of the Friday Mosque. It was a solution obtained without the benefit of calculus, or concealed chains or buttresses.

Isfahan is the jewel of Iran, 'half the world' in the words of an Iranian poet. It was a city built in the image of one man, Shah Abbas.

Powerful Contrasts

In climate and terrain, Iran can be compared to Spain. Both countries have a wide, flat central table land, dry in summer and bitterly cold in winter. Both have wild, rugged, mountainous areas, and both countries have absorbed the effects of the Islamic faith. In

Iran, though, the contrasts are stronger—the summers are hotter, the winters colder, and the colours of the landscape more vivid. Cyrus the Great said that at one end of his kingdom people could be dying of cold, while at the other they could be simultaneously parched with heat.

Iran lies on the main route between the Far East and Europe. Before Vasco de Gama opened up the Cape seaway in 1497 (and the Suez Canal shortened the sea route still further 400 years later), the great caravans between Cathay and the West filed across the northern territories of Iran. They brought with them the wealth of the Orient: precious stones, silks, spices and rhubarb, to be exchanged for velvets, glassware, iron and gold thread.

The first Persian dynasty was founded by Cyrus the Great in 550 BC. His successors, Darius and Xerxes built the extraordinary palace at Persepolis, near Shiraz. This era was brought to a close when the country was invaded by Alexander the Great in 335 BC. One hundred years later, the Parthians (nomads from the north east) established a royal house that lasted for 500 years. Then followed the Sassanian dynasty (a time of great experiment with vaults and domes) that survived

Below: The ceremonial stairway that leads to the palace of Persepolis in southern Iran. This enormous imperial residential complex, was built by King Darius I about 2,500 years ago.

Great Mosque at Samarra — Iraq

Gunbad-i-Qabus — Iran

Mausoleum of Oljeitu — Soviet Union

Royal Mosque of Isfahan — Iran

| '600 | '800 | '1000 | '1200 | '1400 | '1600 | 1800 |

until the conquest of the Caliph Omar, who brought Islam to Iran in 642. Iran was ruled by Seljuk Turks from 1037 until 1187, when the Monguls invaded from the east.

It was under the Safarids (1499-1736) that Isfahan was transformed from a small market town into one of the finest capitals in the world. A tolerant and humane ruler, Shah Abbas established a court that attracted merchants and ambassadors from all over the world. The Safarids were eventually overthrown by Afghans in 1722, and the capital transferred to Mashad.

City of Kings

King Darius I began the construction of his magnificent palace in 518 BC. A short distance south of his capital, Pasargadae, it presents a most dramatic setting. Travelling across vast areas of arid plain, north-west of Shiraz, the ruin suddenly appears in the distance. It is raised on a tremendous stone platform, with a great cliff-like spur of rock behind. The platform is 457 by 274 metres (1,500 × 900 feet), standing something like 14 metres (50 feet) above the plain.

Persepolis was conceived by Darius, but completed by his

Below: Royal Mosque of Isfahan This view is of the north Iwan or portal, as seen from the inner courtyard of

the mosque, which is set at an angle to the main square so that the prayerhall faces towards Mecca.

successors, Xerxes and Artaxerxes. The palace is particularly renowned for the impressive low relief carvings on the stairways, the finely wrought window openings and the stately entranceways—a dignified procession of repetitive figures, nobles, courtiers and tribute bearers. Originally, the carving was painted in brilliant colours. Although impressive, the ruins are too sparse to give a true impression of the grandeur of the palace: most of the walls of polychrome mud-brick have gone, as have the painted stucco-covered timber columns that supported the roofs of the lesser apartments.

Unlike the earlier, widely-spaced and landscaped Persian palaces, Persepolis was dense and compact. It had two main audience halls, including the legendary 'Hall of 100 Columns'—a throne room with stone columns and a cedar roof, supported by teak beams imported from India. The columns were finely fluted with capitals derived from Greek and Egyptian models. Each of the three emperors built a palace, and there was a separate hareem and treasury.

In general, most of the important

buildings in Iran that have survived have been religious. Islamic sacred buildings were usually more soundly constructed than palaces, which tended to be regularly altered and re-built by successive rulers. Also, the Iranian palace was a collection of pavilions in a landscaped park or garden, rather than a single unit, for the Islamic way of life has favoured adaptability of internal spaces, with little distinction between eating, sleeping and living areas.

The oldest mosque in Iran is the eighth century Tarik Khana at Damghan: a square courtyard with a single, tunnel-vaulted arcade round the side. The side which faces Mecca has a deeper arcade, thus forming a sanctuary. The plan is Arab-Islamic, although the massive piers and pointed

Right: A comparison of the heights of various Persian buildings with the Arc de Triumph.

Below: The sanctuary minaret of the Royal Mosque, with its elaborate floral and Koranic motifs.

arches seem to be pre-Islamic, possibly Sassasian in style and construction.

The Great Mosque at Samarra was started in 847, and is the largest Islamic shrine ever conceived. Its courtyard is a gargantuan rectangle, 238 by 156 metres (784 × 512 feet) surrounded with a high 'bastioned' wall made of burnt brick (the bastions are solid, semi-circular buttresses that project at regular intervals). At the sanctuary-end there were nine rows of brick piers, supporting a flat roof with teak beams. The vast brick minaret, some 49 metres (163 feet) high, still dominates the site. A ramp spirals up the side.

The city of Samarra was the capital of Iran for only 50 years; little more than an elephantine

Oljeitu — Gunbad-i-qabus — Arc de Triumph — Entrance portal of Royal Mosque

building project on a virgin site, abandoned before it was finished.

At this time the essential characteristics of Islamic surface decoration emerged—principally the use of painted and moulded stucco, glazed tiles and (particularly in Iran) decorative brickwork. Two further features that evolved in the ninth and tenth centuries were to influence eastern Islamic architecture: the mausoleum and the Iwan. The Iwan was originally a shallow niche used for prayer, and the earliest example to be found is in the Friday mosque at Shiraz. It developed from a far grander opening made in a vaulted hall, with one side always facing the courtyard.

Mausolea were not initially permitted in Moslem architecture, it being considered that no one tomb should be more magnificent than another. In the tenth century, however, the Iranian pre-Islamic tradition of building lavish tombs asserted itself, and the mausoleum became a legitimate form of tomb. The Gunbad-i-Qabas (1006), built in north eastern Iran by a prince named Qabas, is one of the most incredible tombs in the world. Over 55 metres (182 feet) high,

legend has it that the prince's body was suspended from the roof in a glass coffin.

The other innovation of architectural significance in the 11th century was the so-called 'tri-lobed squinch'. The difficulty of fitting a circular dome over a square chamber is a recurring problem in Western and Eastern architecture. The Byzantine pendentive, which evolved a few centuries earlier, was one solution. The tri-lobed squinch achieved the transition from square to circle with three hollowed niches spanning the corners. It formed the source of the extraordinary muquarnas or 'stalactite' mouldings of later Islamic architecture. The earliest-known example is the mausoleum of Arab Ata, just over the Iranian border, in what is now the USSR.

A Masterpiece of Masonry

The first mosque to adopt the 'Four Iwan Plan' (later to become the standard layout of the classic Iranian mosque) was the Masjia-i-Juma, or Friday mosque in Isfahan. It has a long history of alterations and additions, but

before its final conversion, it possessed two remarkable domed chambers located at either end of the complex. The first was constructed by Nizam al Mulk, a powerful visier of the Seljuk monarch, Malik Shah. It was built of brick and its dome rests on 12 pillars.

Soon afterwards, between 1088-9, a rival of Nizam called Taj-ul Mulk built the 'Brown Dome' at the northern end of the mosque. Smaller than Nizam's sanctuary, it is a miracle of brickwork, and one of the masterpieces of Iranian architecture. Here the classic problem of the transition from square chamber to circular dome is solved in possibly the most elegant of ways. At the base there is a broad arch in the middle of each wall, with two narrow arches at each corner. In the storey above, larger arches span across the corners linking up with four arches in the sides to form an octagon of eight arches. Above this again, there are 16 smaller arches, rounding off the corners of the octagon to join effortlessly with the circular drum of the dome.

The effect is austere yet magical. The pattern of small, brown-

grey bricks forms the main surface decoration, with some delicate calligraphy traced around the drum of the dome and above the lower arches. Structurally, the system of squinches is simple and effective, avoiding the concealed chains, hidden buttresses or cones that were necessary at St. Peters, Rome or St. Pauls Cathedral in London.

Tyrant with a Tender Touch

The brutal conqueror Tamerlane captured Isfahan in 1386, massacring its inhabitants and piling their skulls in a bloody heap. His capital was Samarquand (in Russia Turkistan) but his descendants transferred the centre of his empire to Mashad. The finest buildings of this period are in northern and western Iran, including Tamerlane's tomb (th Gur-i-Mir), the blue mosque in Tabriz and the Ganhar Shad mosque at Mashad. It was the Timurids who developed the tri-lobed squinch into the pendentive, thereby creating the elaborate 'stalactite' mouldings so characteristic of later Islamic architecture. They also evolved the technique of 'faience' tiling, a

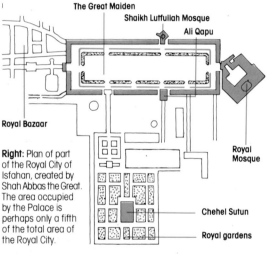

The Great Maiden
Shaikh Lutfullah Mosque
Ali Qapu
Royal Bazaar
Royal Mosque
Chehel Sutun
Royal gardens

Right: Plan of part of the Royal City of Isfahan, created by Shah Abbas the Great. The area occupied by the Palace is perhaps only a fifth of the total area of the Royal City.

Right: Part of the tile mosaic of the Royal Mosque. The patterns are derived from simple, geometric forms which are based, in turn, on the square and the circle, and then overlaid with floral motifs.

Below: The dome of the prayerhall of the Shaikh Lutfullah Mosque, so-named after the father of its creator, Shah Abbas. The rich decoration of the dome creates an illusion of appearing to be floating above the courtyard.

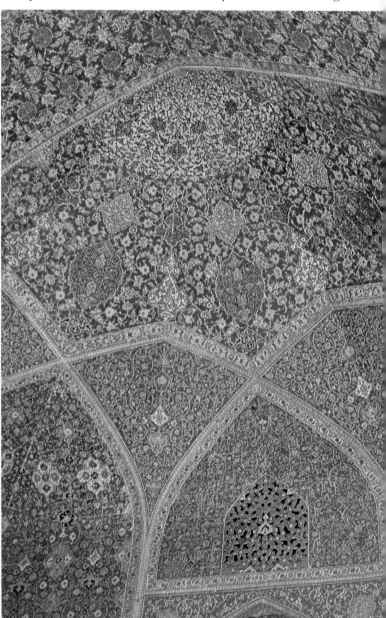

jigsaw of monochrome tiles for covering large, flat areas. The first colour used was turquoise, though other colours were added gradually to the range, including black, white, lapis lazuli, yellow and finally green.

Shah Abbas the Great made Isfahan his capital in 1598. His court has been described with picturesque detail by the many ambassadors, merchants, scholars and dilettantes from Europe who periodically visited Isfahan. Abbas was just as curious about Western culture, and treated his visitors with great respect. To his own subjects he was a cruel and ruthless ruler, as frightening as Ivan the Terrible of Russia who reigned at about the same time. Extremely energetic, he despised laziness in others. He loved to hunt (often cooking the game he had caught himself) and was skilled at various kinds of craftwork.

Abbas's building programme is divided into two periods, separated by wars with the Turks between 1606 and 1612. The Great Maiden, his principal creation, occupies over 8 hectares (20 acres). It contains four principal buildings — the Royal Mosque, the Shaikh

Above: The entrance pavilion to the Ali Qapu Palace, which originally served as a summer 'throne room' and viewing platform during festivals for the emperor.

Below: The madrassah of the Shah Mosque. This was a teaching annex in this case dedicated to the Shah's mother. It was built in the 1700s.

Lutfullah Mosque, the Ali Qapu Palace and the enormous portal of the Royal Bazaar.

The shah's first project was to refurbish the palace now known as Ali Qapu. The gateway faces into the main square, with a high gallery or balcony above supported on slender wooden columns. The interiors were richly decorated with landscapes, hunting scenes and erotic figures, though successive restoration and repainting have obscured much of the original work.

Abbas began the Royal Mosque in 1612, the largest individual project of his reign. The entrance portal was completed first — it is nearly 27 metres (90 feet) high, and sheathed in richly coloured exotic tilework. The 'stalactite' pendentives hover above the intricately tiled vault and the arch is framed with a triple ceramic 'rope' ornament. Two lofty minarets either side guard the entrance. The mosque itself is twisted off the main axis in the square, so that the main sanctuary faces Mecca. The effect is surprisingly ingenious. In the inner court are the four Iwans, the largest of which forms the entry

Below: Close-up of a stalactite vault formation in the Sotoun Palace in Isfahan. This example is decorated with pieces of mirror.

Above: The brown dome of the Friday Mosque, where the transition from square floor plan to round dome is achieved simply.

to the sanctuary, which is crowned by a huge turquoise dome that dominates the whole city. Every visible surface is covered with brilliant blue tile work.

Decoration against Structure

The use of burned brick for constructing vaults and domes goes back to the Babylonian period, and partly, the lack of good building stone may have encouraged the use of brick. Decorative brickwork first appears in the extraordinary tomb of the Samarids at Bukharel. There is an intriguing duality of attraction between the structural and decorative functions of bricks used this way, since neither is entirely subordinated to the other. In fact, different parts of a building could be marked off by using various patterns of brick laying. A common form for domes was a zig-zag pattern. Stucco had been used to cover rubble or mudbrick walls in pre-Islamic times, carved or moulded with patterns or figures, an easy and cheap way of giving an impression of magnificence. Islamic architects made wide use of the technique, in some cases moulding the plaster when wet, in others carving it when set.

Glazed tiles provided a more lasting and permanent surface decoration, with the advantage of having brighter colours. Colour indeed had been used in early Iranian architecture to pick out and stress particular lines or parts of the structure. When brightly coloured tiles were widely used, the surface decoration tended to dominate the three-dimensional shape it covered. In the best examples, though, there is a harmonious balance between architectural mass, decorative design and colour. At worst, it was a useful way of disguising shoddily built and ill-designed buildings.

Stronghold in the West
Spain-Land of Magic

FRANCE

CHRISTIAN SPAIN

.Salamanca

.Toledo

MOORISH SPAIN-AD 910

.Cordoba

Seville .Granada

.Almeria

Mediterranean

Architectural Importance:
Moorish architecture in Spain and Morocco was somewhat insulated from the major aesthetic developments occuring in the rest of the Islamic world. Early buildings were influenced by Mesopotamian brick and stucco techniques, and the basic layout of mosques followed traditional forms, but an independent spirit prevailed in the use of decorative carving, pattern and colour, which shows in a striking way the powerful influence of Roman and European ideas of design on a basic Islamic model.

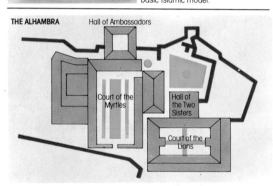

THE ALHAMBRA — Hall of Ambassadors

Court of the Myrtles

Hall of the Two Sisters

Court of the Lions

The Palace of the Alhambra in Granada is, without exception, the most famous example of Western Islamic architecture. It is a miracle of intricate filigree, rich colours and tranquil courtyards. The physical counterpart of the magical Tales of the Arabian Nights, the Alhambra powerfully evokes the poetic decadence of its pleasure-loving Moorish inhabitants. While wandering through the gardens and courtyards of this gigantic palace, with its peaceful patios and mysterious grottoes, one seems to hear the echoes of long-forgotten love affairs, and of the assassinations, feuds and intrigues that surrounded the dazzling court of the Nazarid dynasty.

At the summit of its power, the empire of Islam controlled almost as much territory as the Roman Empire 1,000 years earlier. From Spain in the west to Samarkand in the north and Africa in the south, the empire that gave

Stylistic Essentials: Frequent use made of horseshoe arch and the multifoiled arch, both of which less common in Egypt and Asia. Minarets are large square towers, rather than thin, polygonal spires.

Many Moorish buildings made use of Roman columns and capitals. Vaults and arches developed into highly complex and ornate forms, culminating in the spectacular vaults of the Alhambra Palace.

Primary Building Materials: Brick is the major building material, used both decoratively and structurally (in combination with marble) and stone was used for decorative effect

by contrasting it with brick, as in the Great Mosque at Cordoba. The antique columns used in many Moorish constructions were also of limestone or marble. The Alhambra makes extensive use of stucco or plaster to build up richly modelled surfaces, painted with bright colours and sometimes even gilded.

allegiance to the memory of Muhammad controlled the destinies of tens of kings, hundreds of principalities and millions of people.

An empire founded upon the fanaticism and militancy of the Moslem religion, it arose in the deserts of Arabia and spread rapidly throughout the Middle East. The Arabs were skillful, often brutal fighters; eventually their conquests brought them to the very shores of Europe, a continent seething with internecine wars and fratricidal conflicts.

The Arabs invaded Spain from North Africa in the eighth century and, within a decade, were threatening France. But this was as far as they reached. Stopped at the Loire, the Arab soldiers retreated to their strongholds in Spain and turned their Iberian conquests into the core of a Western Islamic Empire.

In time, the Moorish civilization of Spain achieved a remarkable level of cultivated existence, yet it never completely outgrew its brutal origins. The Arab nobles who spent so much of their time reading, writing poetry and patronizing the arts, science and medicine, were also capable of the most bizarre acts of cruelty. Just as they were generally tolerant of the Christian and Jewish minorities in their midsts, so they could be spitefully bigotted towards those who challenged the accepted precepts of the Moslem faith.

Like Byzantium, Moorish Spain acted as a bridge between the cultures of Islam and Christianity and, during the 800 years of Arab occupation, the arts, in general, and architecture, in particular, were strongly influenced by the intermingling of these two cultures.

In Cordoba is observed the first flowering of the Moorish culture, and its architecture exhibits the conquering spirit of the Caliphate. Here stands the Great Mosque, where the faithful in their hundreds could dwell among a forest of columns in contemplation or prayer. The city of Cordoba, with its quiet, whitewashed courtyards and small, secluded squares, still retains the flavour of the Moorish presence.

Seville, the second great city of the Moors, has changed radically since its Arab conquerors finally relinquished control to the invading Christian armies. Yet Granada, the fabled setting of the 1001 Nights, is a city so characteristic in its Arabic influence, that it might have been transplanted from the Middle East.

By their naturalistic gardens and rock pools, their patios and grottoes, and their courtyards and squares, the Moorish architects have earned the world's admiration. The faithful Moslem is a fatalist; his concern is with the present, not the future. The buildings of Moorish Spain, as well as others of the Islamic Empire, were assembled from delicate materials, such as plaster, wood and light (sometimes mud) bricks, and were consequently extremely fragile. The wonder is that so much of Islamic architecture has survived.

Moorish buildings are conceived on an informal arrangement, based on a plan of numerous, intimate courtyards, rather than one grand square. Ornamental emphasis is exclusively internal, based on the refinement of natural designs or elaborate stylizations of writings from the Koran (Holy Book), since representations of the human form were proscribed.

The Court of Lions in the Alhambra Palace is the supreme example of the architecture of Moorish Spain—an intimate space, formal yet relaxed, reflecting the Moslem concept of paradise as described in the Koran.

Arab Threat to Europe

In AD 710, the Arab leader Tarif, searching for plunder beyond the shores of his African possessions, launched a series of successful raiding parties to Spain. The first Arab incursion into the Iberian peninsula, it met with hardly any resistance, due to the relative weakness of the Spanish and Visigoth kings who were in control of the country.

One year later, Tarif's successor, Tarik, embarked on a much larger expedition, this time involving an army of 20,000 men. He made rapid progress and was soon in possession of the entire peninsula.

Mercifully for everyone concerned, resistance to the Arab invasion was shortlived. In many cases, to avoid losing their lives and estates, the Spanish nobles acknowledged Islamic supremacy while the common people seized the chance to escape from the certainty of serfdom by embracing the new religion. With such support, the Moors crossed the

Above: The Court of the Lions, the most notable of all the various courtyards of the Alhambra Palace. This luxurious residence of the Caliphate was conceived as a series of individual cells.

Pyrenees with the intention of marching to Paris. Their progress was checked at Poitiers in AD 723.

The Islamic army in Spain, for all its bravery and fighting skill, was still rather small, and its continued domination of the country depended more on peaceful negotiation than on the use of arms. Cities, towns and individual estates, rather than risk a massacre of their inhabitants, agreed to unconditional surrender. In return, the Arabs consented to leave them in peace (except for financial exactions and the appointment of an Arab official to take charge). In time, this process worked

THE AGE OF CONSTRUCTION

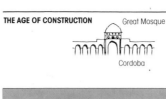
Great Mosque
Cordoba

Giralda Tower
Seville

Alcazar
Seville

Alhambra
Granada

700	800	900	1000	1100	1200	1300

Above: The famous gardens of the Alhambra. The design endeavours to give physical reality to the elusive Islamic conception of paradise: water courses, lush greenery, scented plants, cool breezes.

Below: An example of the spectacular 'stalactite' vaults of the Alhambra Palace. The myriad, miniature, decorated vaults tend to enhance the feeling of space, a feature common to Islamic shrines.

inhabitants were of Spanish origin, though many different races and religions co-existed to create the richest culture in Spain until the 17th century. By the first half of the 10th century, the population had reached nearly half a million.

The most famous construction of this period is the Great Mosque. There had been a church on the site long before AD 785, when Abd al-Rahman purchased the land. Several features of the Christian basilica were retained, perhaps because of the urgency with which the first part was built. There were four main building periods, each extending the area covered.

Many of the 1,200 pillars made of jasper or marble, were taken from Roman and Visigoth monuments. In its final form there are 19 parallel naves, running north-south. The arches are horseshoe-shaped, made from alternating bands of red brick and white stone. Extra height was gained by the use of double arches to support the complex vaults above, an effect that was probably copied from Roman aqueducts.

The initial sections of the Mosque were rather austere, but later additions brought richly decorated mosaic and intricate stone lattice carving, using stylized floral motifs. Ornament and structure are interlaced to create an hypnotic effect, while the repetition of the red and white arches acts as a unifying force on the spatial conception.

Moorish Stronghold

The distinctive Moorish style of architecture reached its ultimate expression in the patios and gardens, and above all in the Alhambra Palace, of Granada, the final stronghold of the Western Islamic Empire on the Iberian peninsula.

It has been suggested by travellers and historians that Granada could well have been the paradise on earth described in the innumerable mythologies of past cultures. It is hard to refute this conceit, for certainly Granada is a beautiful city, and one perfectly situated. It is surrounded by the peaks of the Sierra Nevada, and is watered by the River Guadalquivar and its tributaries. To the west lies the Vega, a vast fertile plain that provides the city with a bountiful harvest of fruit and vegetables.

The conquering Moslem warriors from Africa must have found the lush green garden of Granada a startling contrast to the arid deserts of their homeland. Historians suggest that this coastal Eden gradually tempered the war-

so well that the Arabs created 'vassal' states in northern Spain: autonomous regions which acknowledged the sovereignty of the Caliphate.

Several towns, such as Barcelona, Gerona and Pamplona, on payment of tribute, were granted semi-independence. The payment of taxes was compulsory for every non-Moslem, so it was financially expedient not to press conversion of Christians with too much vigour.

Over a period of decades, the south of Spain became a settled Arabic community, with Cordoba at its centre, and loosely subject to central control from Damascus, the capital of the Islamic world. In AD 755, the Emir Abd al-Rahman, the last ruler of the imperial Umayyad dynasty that was overthrown by the Abbasids,

fled to Spain and established an independent Islamic state. It was Abd al-Rahman, a particularly ruthless tyrant, who authorized the construction of the Great Mosque at Cordoba.

The treasures of Moorish Spain—the architecture, the writings and the illuminated texts of the Koran—are the result of a unique fusion of Eastern Islamic, Christian and African cultures that survived both the Catholic conquest of Spain by Queen Isabella and King Ferdinand in 1492 and the unremitting march of modern technology.

Bridge Between East and West

Emir Abd al-Rahman's most grandiose building project was a fortified palace outside Cordoba,

called the Medina Azzahra. Recent excavations have confirmed the enormous scale of the complex described in contemporary Arab chronicles: 10,000 men, 5,000 camels and 15,000 mules were employed in continuous construction, absorbing one third of the Caliph's annual income. Materials were imported from Europe, Asia and Africa, and the site covered 115 hectares (280 acres). Among the marvels of Medina Azzahra was a room with a pool full of mercury. When agitated, the pool produced dazzling reflections which danced round the walls and ceiling of carved marble, with gold and silver ornament.

The city of Cordoba itself flourished under the Caliphs. It stood at the crossroads of East and West. The majority of the like spirit of the North African Arabs, and encouraged in them a more poetic, sensual and contemplative attitude towards life.

Granada had formerly been an important Roman town, and the Roman network of roads, bridges and irrigation channels form the basis of much of the layout of the Moorish city.

In the 11th century the Berber rulers began to enlarge the city. On the site of an old Roman fort called the Alcazaba, they built a palace, and improved the fortification of the hill on which it sits. Further building was undertaken by the Almohads, but the grandest period of Granada's history was inaugurated by the first of the Nazarid dynasty, Mohammed Banu 'L-Ahmar.

For 200 years, Granada was an enclave of rich Islamic culture, fostered by the 20 Nazarid monarchs who enlarged and nurtured the halls, gardens and fountains of the magnificent palace of the Alhambra, started by Banu 'L-Ahmar.

The founder of the Nazarid dynasty was obsessed with water, perhaps a throwback to the desert origins of his ancestors. He built a water course over 1.6 kilometres (1 mile) long to supply the palace; it is essential to realize that the fountains, pools and channels form an integral part of the architecture of the Alhambra. Furthermore, he took great pains to provide an efficient water supply for the city itself and the surrounding fields, and built public fountains and baths. Banu 'L-Ahmar was an efficient ruler and the economy of the province, consequently, flourished.

Citadel on a Hill

Ferdinand III, with the powerful Christian army of Castille, was the major threat to this prosperity and stability. Banu 'L-Ahmar brought peace with Christians in exchange for annual tributes and military service. He started work on the Alhambra soon after the capture of Seville.

The Alhambra is an ancient fortress or castellated palace, though the palace itself occupies only a small portion of the citadel, the walls of which, punctuated with towers, follow an irregular line around the crest of a tall hill that overlooks the city of Granada.

During the Moorish occupation, the fortress was reputed to be able to contain an army of 40,000 soldiers within its walls, and served on several occasions as a stronghold against the sovereign's rebellious subjects.

The plan of the Alhambra is arranged in three sections—the Alcazaba (the military citadel), the Royal Palace and a now ruined village containing what were once the dwellings of the courtiers and royal servants.

The palace consists of two units, each surrounding a rectangular courtyard. Unlike with western European palaces, there seems to have been no overall plan or conception, parts being added if convenient at the time. The first courtyard is called the Alberca, or the 'court of the Myrtles', containing a large pool that almost fills the space—a delightful blend of water, vegetation and architecture. At the north end is the Tower of Comares (the highest building of the complex) above the Hall of the Ambassadors. Once used as a throne room, it is 11 metres (37 feet) wide and 17 metres (59 feet) high, with a ceiling made of richly carved aromatic cedar wood panels, and the walls covered with tiles and intricate stucco decoration, intertwining floral motifs with Kufic inscriptions. In its original state, the stucco was brilliantly coloured and gilded, and the windows were filled with stained glass.

The other main courtyard is called the Court of Lions, the only part of the complex to have survived almost intact. In the centre is the famous fountain—a delicate arrangement of alabaster basins supported by 12 lions. The court itself is laid out in flowerbeds and surrounded by arcades

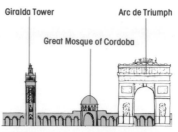

Giralda Tower   Arc de Triumph

Great Mosque of Cordoba

Below: A detail of the Great Mosque of Cordoba. It was converted into a church in 1238.

Above: A scale comparison of the Giralda Tower and Great Mosque with the Arc de Triumph.

Below: The Giralda Tower, originally the minaret of a 12th century mosque in Seville. It was built / of brick and modelled on the towers attached to churches in Syria. The belfry was added later.

of filigree-work, supported on slender pillars of gleaming marble.

The style of the Court of Lions is characterized by grace and elegance rather than grandeur, suggesting a disposition towards indolent enjoyment. It is difficult not to express amazement at how miraculously the fragile fretwork of the walls had not long ago been destroyed by earthquakes, the quiet removal of pieces by souvenir-hunters or even by the violence of war.

Three very fine halls lead from the Court of Lions. One, with a lofty ceiling, and paved in white marble, is called the Hall of the Two Sisters. Here the walls are encrusted with the renowned Moorish tiles, many of which are emblazoned with the coats-of-arms of Arab monarchs. About the courtyard are various recesses for couches and ottomans, and above one alcove is a balcony leading to the women's apartments. In the centre of the Hall of the Two Sisters is a small fountain.

The Hall of Justice is another spectacular room. From the ceiling are suspended three square lanterns enclosed in an elaborate web of plaster 'stalactite' vaulting—the space is a forest of smooth, vertical columns that support an airy cloud of richly-decorated stucco ornament.

The magical quality of the Alhambra rests on the subtle interplay of light and shade, alternating between bright sunlit patios, cooled by flowing water and lush vegetation, and dark halls richly decorated with intricate plaster work. As one sees it now, the spaces are more interconnected than they would have been in Moorish times, because many of the finely carved doors have been removed. The delight of the palace, and of Granada as a whole, is in the small intimate patio, neatly landscaped with water and flowers—a place for quiet contemplation and reflection.

The Koran describes paradise as a heavenly garden, shaded by leafy palms and pomegranate trees, cooled by running water. The Sultan's summer palace, the Generalife, has the intimate quality of such a paradise, enclosed and private, away from prying eyes. The Generalife is more garden than architecture, for water and foliage dominate its small pavilions and patios. The Moorish garden is a complete contrast to the formal, open landscaping of the Western European tradition; space is enclosed, and the aim is seclusion rather than public grandeur.

Decline and Revival

By the 11th century, the Caliphate had crumbled into anarchy, and the consequent power vacuum was filled by a motley band of adventurers and nobles who set up their own petty kingdoms; a pattern that corresponded with that of the rest of contemporary Europe. In the chaos that followed, Cordoba lost its position as the principal city of the Western Islamic Empire. Its place was taken by Seville and Granada.

Little remains of the tremendous Arabic artistic culture that once dominated this southern Spanish city, except for the stunning Giralda Tower and the Alcazar Palace. Built as a minaret of the Great Mosque of Seville commemorating the victory of the Almohad dynasty, the Tower was converted into a Christian edifice when the Mosque was consecrated as a cathedral. it is 13 metres (44 feet) square and nearly 70 metres (230 feet) high. In 1568, it was capped with a Renaissance belfry.

The walls of the Giralda Tower are a massive two metres (eight feet) thick, and there is a ramp—which reputedly carried King Ferdinand and his horse—leading from a platform to the top, via 32 separate landings.

Below: One of the doorways of the Alcazar, the palace in Seville built by Pedro the Cruel (a Christian) with hired labour. The palace is renowned for its carved ornament.

The Alcazar Palace was built by Moslem craftsmen on the orders of the Christian ruler, Pedro the Cruel, between 1350 and 1369. Though greatly altered, it is possible to observe the 'Mudejar' style of its architecture, in which Arabic designs and decorative materials (brick, carved wood and plaster) were applied to Romanesque or Gothic structures. Some beautiful intricately moulded stucco-work remains from the oldest parts of the building, but a combination of fire, earthquakes and drastic alterations by generations of Christian monarchs have all but obliterated the original conception of the palace.

Obsession with Detail

The materials used to build the Alhambra were both inexpensive and insubstantial and the architects who built the halls and laid out the patios and gardens were able to extract the maximum decorative potential out of these resources. The 'stalactite' vault, with its myriad of richly decorated surfaces, originated in Persia. It was derived from the decorative brickwork of the Sassanians. Glazed tiles were used on internal floors and on the lower parts of the walls.

The Moors were renowned for their luxurious baths, which were equipped with elaborate plumbing using lead and copper pipes for the distribution of hot and cold water, supplied in the case of the Alhambra by a huge copper boiler. The baths had both religious significance and sensual qualities, with brightly coloured tile work and ornate statues of animals that spouted water into the pools. The buildings were kept scrupulously clean by being constantly swept with quicklime and sawdust, and were illuminated by wax candles.

Moorish craftsmen were renowned for their woodcarving, leatherwork and ornate weaponry. The finest products of Granada exhibit an extraordinary preoccupation with meticulous detail using extremely fine filigree, repousse and engraving. Moorish fabrics and carpets as well as silk embroidery and lacework were in great demand throughout Medieval Europe.

Right: Cut-away section showing the construction of a stalactite vault. The primary structure is composed of rubble and mortar. A secondary timber frame supports the plaster ceiling with hangers.

Below: A courtyard in the Alcazar, revealing something of the palace's original grandeur.

March of the Moguls
Islamic Dynasty in India

Architectural Importance:
Indian Hindu and Buddhist architecture has had a strong influence on religious architecture throughout the Far East. Hindu temples are found in Kampuchea, Sri Lanka, Burma and Thailand. Buddhism spread to China, where the Chinese pagoda is seen as a development of the Indian Buddhist stupa. Mogul Indian architecture is a unique branch of the architecture of Islam and has its own ethnic characteristics. Hindu masons and craftsmen were often employed on the construction of Islamic buildings.

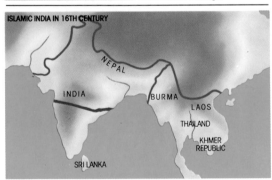

It would be hard to find two buildings as radically different as the Taj Mahal and the Hindu temple of Brahmeswara at Orissa. These two architectural masterpieces reflect the extreme polarity between Hinduism and Islam—two religions that are opposite in every manifestation of belief, practice and ritual. Yet these great buildings are unmistakably Indian, and belong to a culture that has succeeded in absorbing a myriad foreign styles and making them her own.

The highest goal of the devout Hindu is the realization of self—the ultimate state of Nirvana is a strictly private and personal achievement won through contemplation and meditation. Communal worship is practised only on certain specified occasions.

Islam is strictly monotheistic, a religion that makes (in theory) all equal before God, whatever their birthright; a religion that places strong emphasis on communal prayer,

Below: The Great Stupa at Sanchi in central India. A Buddhist shrine, it was built in the 1st century BC and is one of the oldest surviving monuments in the country. The giant brick dome is surrounded by a carved stone processional walkway, with four gateways facing the four compass points.

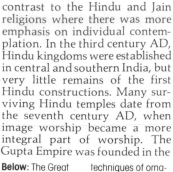

Primary Building Materials:
Few Hindu or Buddhist temples used mortar in construction. Stone was rough-cut to size and assembled using gravity to hold it together, and the fine detailed carving done in situ. The abundance of high quality wood in early times had a strong influence on architecture, as wood carving techniques were directly transferred from wood to stone.

Stylistic Essentials:
Buddhist stupa: hemispherical mound or shrine with a processional path round the perimeter, and elaborately carved gateways The chaityas: assembly halls cut from rock, ornately carved within and without. Hindu temples: elaborately carved stone shrines with the exterior considered more important than the interior. The entire building a focus of worship. Hindu temples more sculpture than architecture proper. Mogul plan of mosques similar to Persian. Islamic religious forms, though often decorated with motifs largely influenced by or absorbed from Hindu art.

architectural forms. The finest examples of Mogul art, such as the Taj Mahal, combine Moslem purity of shape and formal planning with unmistakably Hindu-inspired surface decoration.

The magical quality of the Indian landscape and its rich cultural heritage has continued to inspire architects: the city of Chandigarth is a new city designed and planned by the architect Le Corbusier, who has interpreted ancient Indian forms of construction in a modern idiom.

Cities of the Indus

The very earliest civilizations in India were concentrated around the valley of the River Indus, in cities laid out with neat gridplans of houses built of baked brick. Archaeological excavation has shown that domestic arrangements were quite sophisticated, as exemplified in their use of drains and even garbage disposal chutes. Later many large cities were also built in the valley of the River Ganges, throughout the first milenium BC.

A Buddhist empire was founded in the third century BC from parts of India conquered by Alexander the Great. Known as the Mauryan Empire, its architecture was strongly influenced by Western building traditions, making use of Greek-style capitals and temple sculpture. The oldest surviving monuments in India are the 'stupas' (Buddhist monumental shrines in the form of hemispherical mounds) which date from the second and third centuries BC. Buddhist shrines were designed to accommodate large groups of worshippers—in

contrast to the Hindu and Jain religions where there was more emphasis on individual contemplation. In the third century AD, Hindu kingdoms were established in central and southern India, but very little remains of the first Hindu constructions. Many surviving Hindu temples date from the seventh century AD, when image worship became a more integral part of worship. The Gupta Empire was founded in the

Below: The Great Stupa at Sanchi; the carving exhibits techniques of ornamentation derived initially from wood.

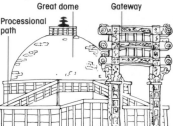

led by laymen. Above all, Islam provides a universal political law, a brotherhood of co-believers, quite unlike the self-orientation of Hinduism or Buddhism.

The Hindu temple at its simplest is a village shrine, a sacred object that may be anything from a knarled tree stump to a water well. Prestige may be gained by the addition of a simple shelter, a statue or image of a deity. The more elaborate temples are still little more than a shrine—the temple itself is a focus for worship, or pilgrimage, not a meeting place or congregation hall like the Islamic mosque. Hindu and Buddhist Indian architecture is carved architecture—the interior is subordinated to the exterior which is ornately patterned and often covered from top to bottom with delicately sculpted figures depicting various scenes from Hindu mythology.

Islam made its main impact in India from the 13th century onwards, when much of northern and central India was conquered by Moslems who came from central Asia, Persia and Afghanistan. Although architectural styles were imported from the Middle East, the work itself was often executed by Hindu craftsmen. Only the ruling elite actually practised Islam. The vast majority of the population remained Hindu.

Although Hindu temples were systematically destroyed by Moslem rulers throughout the five centuries of Mogul occupation, much Hindu art was saved from ruin and was gradually assimilated into Islamic traditions. In the case of the greatest Islamic ruler Akbar, artistic collaboration was positively encouraged. Indian carving—foliage, abstract pattern, even human figures in rare cases—was applied to Islamic

Below: The Hindu temple of Brahmeswara in Orissa. To the right is the Jagomohan or assembly hall and behind is the sanctuary. Both are elaborately carved inside and out.

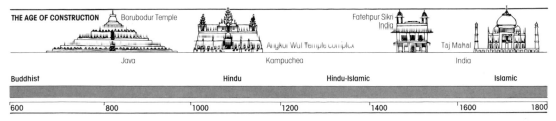

| THE AGE OF CONSTRUCTION | Borubodur Temple | | Fatehpur Sikri India | | Taj Mahal |
| Buddhist | Java | Hindu | Angkor Wat Temple complex Kampuchea | Hindu-Islamic | India Islamic |

600 800 1000 1200 1400 1600 1800

fourth century, and for the next 200 years expanded outside the Indian subcontinent into the Far East, bringing with it artistic influences that later produced the extraordinary Hindu and Buddhist monuments found in Kampuchea, Java, Burma and even Thailand.

Islam first penetrated northern India in AD 712, but initially made little headway. The real impact of Moslem influence on Indian architecture came with the establishment of Delhi as capital of an Islamic Empire in 1195, and the first mosques were built by Hindu craftsmen using components from Hindu and Jain temples destroyed by the conquerors. Moslem architects from Persia introduced more orthodox Islamic architecture which was blended with local styles in the 13th century. The greatest period of Indo-Islamic architecture was inaugurated by the Mogul empire,

which lasted from about 1550 till the British arrived in 1858. The most famous building in India, the Taj Mahal, belongs to this era.

Carved Mountain

Siddhartha, or Gautama Buddha, was born about 563 BC in Northern India. His teachings claimed that salvation (Nirvana) was available to everyone, regardless of caste. Buddhists built monastries for contemplation and shrines where the relics of those who had actually achieved Nirvana were deposited. The stupas are the

earliest monuments of Buddhist India: the largest is the Great Stupa of Sanchi, a huge mound of solid brickwork with a tiny shrine perched on top and a processional path around the perimeter. There are four gateways, at the four cardinal points—similar to the Chinese 'pai lons' or Japanese 'torii'. The elaborate carving shows craft techniques transferred directly from wood to stone with intricate detail and finely sculpted figures. The 'chaityas' or assembly halls that survive have all been cut from rock—long halls with closely spaced columns down each side and a small stupa at the far end forming a shrine. A fine example is the chaitya at Karli (78 BC), 38 metres (126 feet) long and 13 metres (45 feet) high and lined with octagonal columns supporting capitals carved in the form of elephants.

The quest for gold that led to Indian expansion into the Far East was accompanied by Buddhist missionary activity. This led to the construction of the Borubodur temple in Java at around 800 AD, and constitutes the ultimate development of the stupa: a whole mountain carved into an enormous ornate temple representing the universe. The temple is constructed as a series of concentric terraces, each richly decorated by miniature stupas and friezes. At the summit the central and largest stupa is surrounded by 72 smaller stupas in three concentric rings, each one containing a stone statue of the

Buddha enclosed by a bell-shaped open lattice carved in stone.

Riot of Ornament

A typical Hindu temple has a small shrine, above which is a tall, spire-like construction. Around the shrine there may be one or more halls, or 'mandapas', for religious dancing and music. The earliest Hindu shrines were probably carved in wood: when stone became the primary building material, wood carving techniques were simply applied to stone, creating linear decoration which is thrown into sharp relief by the strong sunlight.

There were once over 5,000 temples around the sacred artificial lake at Orissa in north western India. Only 500 remain today, of which the best known is the Temple of Brahmeswara, erected towards the end of the ninth century AD. The sikhara is a tall, curving tower with vertical fluting broken by horizontal bands of carving. In front of it is the assembly hall, a lower building roofed with strong horizontal lines formed by terraced layers of carved stonework. The bold geometry of the basic forms provides a dramatic counterpoint to the richness of the carving.

The Kailasa Temple at Ellora in central India is the largest and most spectacular of the rock cut temples. It has been estimated that over 200,000 tonnes of rock had to be removed in order to carve this monument. It is more a

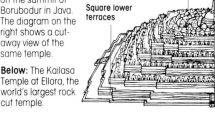
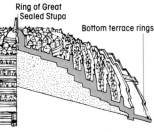

Left: Stone buddhas on the summit of Borubodur in Java. The diagram on the right shows a cut-away view of the same temple.

Ring of 72 stupas / Ring of Great Sealed Stupa / Square lower terraces / Bottom terrace rings

Below: The Kailasa Temple at Ellora, the world's largest rock cut temple.

Left: Angkor Wat, a vast complex of Hindu-Buddhist shrines occupying an enormous area within the Khymer Empire.

Right: Ranakpur Temple, a Jain monument. Jainism was a breakaway sect of Hinduism that preached salvation through ascetism.

gargantuan piece of sculpture than a work of architecture; the small enclosed internal spaces are over-powered by the profusion of highly detailed carving on the façades: dancing human figures, and a grand variety of intricate foliage and animals in a fantastic riot of ornament.

Hindus followed Buddhists into the Far East, spreading the Indian culture abroad, and Kampuchea especially adopted Hindu architectural forms. In the 12th century, Suryararman, king of the Khymer Empire, built a vast temple complex at Angkor Wat. Among the largest religious structures in the world, it was dedicated to Vishnu and was to serve as the king's mortuary shrine. Angkor Wat was erected from blocks of plain stone, and then sculptures were carved on every surface, including the roofs. At the centre, there is an enormous tower, approached by very steep steps. The tower rises from a high terrace with steps on all sides and smaller towers at the corners. Two vast concentric courts surround the terrace. A monumental gateway with three pavilions, approached from a causeway across a huge artificial lake, forms the entrance. The galleried cloisters of Angkor Wat are filled with delicately carved bas-relief illustrating scenes from Hindu mythology. According to Hindu custom, pilgrims who visit every part of the temple have to walk over 20 kilometres (13 miles).

The Hindu temple is the very opposite of the Greek temple: Hindu sculptors made every effort to ensure that each carved element was unique, even if some overall repetition was used to provide a unifying context. There was no attempt to evolve a single, formally perfect type of pillar or column. Much of the carving was designed to be white-plastered or painted with bright colours. Even without applied colour, the Indian Hindu temple, with its wealth of detail and the sensual portrayal of the human form in the figure sculptures that decorate every surface, is a spectacular apparition. The fact that stone was usually assembled rough-cut and carved in its final position further demonstrates the premise, if proof were needed, that the Hindu temple is very much more sculpture than architecture.

Fusion of Ideas

The earliest surviving mosque in India was erected in Delhi to commemorate the decisive military victory of Islamic over Hindu forces in 1193. Tradition has it that the Quwwat al-Islam (meaning 'might of Islam') Mosque was built from materials looted from 27 demolished Hindu temples with all human and animal representation removed. To the south east is a mighty minaret, the Qutb Minar, originally over 72 metres (238 feet) high. It was erected as a tower of victory, and its inscriptions proclaim that it was to spread the shadow of god over the conquered Hindu city. Local Hindu craftsmen were used for the carvings, which combine writings from the Koran with native Indian floral designs. The pointed arches in the mosque were constructed by old Hindu 'corbelling' techniques, evidence of the fact that Hindu masons were employed to use their own skills on imposed foreign forms. The result is a sort of hybrid art, a combination of Moslem planning and Hindu detail.

The first 400 years of the Islamic occupation of India is a complex history of successive dynasties of varying instability and political unity. Architecture during this period alternated between imported orthodox Islamic styles from Afghanistan or Persia and local idiosyncratic interpretations—often incorporating fragments from destroyed Hindu temples. The Friday mosque at Aumadabad is an example of the latter. Built between 1411 and 1424, the construction technique is Hindu, while the forms are Islamic. There are 15 stone domes built by projecting each horizontal course of stone a little farther than the one below it. Much of the decoration and carving are clearly derived from Hindu or Jain temples.

The greatest flowering of Indo-Islamic architecture was heralded by the Mogul invasion of Babur in 1526. Babur was related to the notorious conquerors Timurlane and Chinghis Khan: he was a ruthless soldier who yet tempered his warrior's instincts with a scholarly and aesthetic sensitivity. Barbur and his son, Humayun, were too busy enlarging and defending their territories to leave much of an architectural legacy, but Akbar (Babur's grandson) grew up to be the greatest of all Mogul patrons of Indo-Islamic architecture.

Akbar ruled India for nearly half a century—a golden age that was roughly contemporary with the Elizabethan era in England. Akbar also was a paradoxical and eccentric combination of soldier and artist: he founded a faith based on what he considered to be the best features of several established religions. The success of his empire was much enhanced by his policy of tolerance to non-Moslems, and his desire to assimilate native Indian culture.

The first significant building of Akbar's reign was a tomb he had built for his father, Humayun. Constructed of red sandstone with decorative white marble inlay, it stands within a magnificent, formal water garden. The tomb is a

Right: Scale comparison of Indian buildings with the Arc de Triumph.

Below: The Gol Gumbaz, or round dome at Bijapur. The dome covers the largest domed space in the world.

Gate of Victory Fatehpur-Sikri   Humayun's Tomb   Arc de Triumph   Taj Mahal

large, domed octagon, 38 metres (125 feet) high, surrounded by four square towers. The architect was probably Persian but the monument is the first to show signs of a uniquely Mogul-Indian style, and was to be the prototype for many later buildings including the Taj Mahal.

Akbar founded a royal city at Fatehpur-Sikri near Agra, and held court there for the first half of his reign. Hindu and Islamic elements were deliberately combined in order to express the emperor's desire to integrate his culturally diverse nation. The Friday mosque there has a huge courtyard, surrounded by an arcade decorated atop with little kiosks that have a very Indian flavour. The main gateway is especially magnificent. It is over 39 metres (130 feet) high, and richly decorated with intricate carvings. The emperor's citadel was lavishly appointed with formal courtyards, quiet pools, hareems and audience chambers—decorated throughout with opulent Hindu-inspired carvings of flowers, trailing vines, figured reliefs and murals. Sadly, the city was abandoned soon after it was completed, probably because of an inadequate water supply.

Akbar was followed by his son, Jahangir, who suffered from a variety of weaknesses, including one involving wine laced with opium. During his reign, and that of his son, Shah Jahan, there was an attempt to reassert Moslem orthodoxy in architectural style. This led to a preference for white marble as the main building material with simple 'pavilion' style buildings formally arranged in courtyards or geometrical gardens. The most famous monument of these times is the Taj Mahal, a mausoleum erected by Shah Jahan

to perpetuate the memory of his favourite wife, Mumtaz Mahal.

The Taj Mahal was started in 1632 and finished 16 years later. The mausoleum itself is square in plan with the corners chamfered. It has a central dome 17 metres (58 feet) in diameter and 24 metres (80 feet) high, surmounted in turn by an outer dome that is slightly bulbous and nearly 60 metres (200 feet) high. (This system of using a double dome is Persian in origin). Around the central dome are four, two-storied aisles with a small dome at each corner. An ornately carved marble screen, whose delicate patterns are barely illuminated by the half-light that filters through the pierced marble latticed windows, surround the tombs of the Shah and his queen.

The mausoleum is mounted on a square podium with four 41 metres (137 feet) high minarets, around which is the great outer court containing formal ponds and geometrical gardens filled with the scent of cyprus trees and the soft trickle of water courses. The main building is delicately carved with tracery of abstract patterns and Islamic inscriptions cut into the warm white marble from the quarries of Mukrana. In fact, the marble is only a veneer, though the effect is so magical that it is hard to believe the building is actually made of rubble.

A contemporary Mogul writer called the Taj 'an ocean of descriptions'—and no words or two-dimensional photographs can do justice to a monument that is one of the great works of architecture of all time. It is the extraordinary harmony between building and landscape that gives the tomb its ethereal, mystical quality: the repetitions of reflections, the geometry of the formal gardens and cyprus trees and the luminosity of the marble itself, glowing under the Indian sun.

Shah Jahan left several other fine buildings, including a Friday mosque at Delhi and the 'Pearl Mosque' at Agra. The Delhi mosque is the largest Mogul mosque, its prayer hall dominated by a huge 'iwan' or entrance portal and three bulbous domes of white marble inlaid with black. The Pearl or 'Moti' Mosque at Agra was part of the Imperial Palace. Like the mosque at Delhi, it has a prayer hall with three marble 'onion' domes inlaid in this case with various kinds of red sandstone.

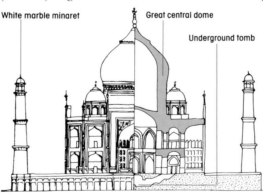

White marble minaret   Great central dome

Underground tomb

Left and Below:
Taj Mahal, India's most renowned monument. It was built in 1648 to house the body of Mumtaz Mahal, Shah Jahan's favourite wife. The tomb is faced with white marble, behind which is rubble.

New World-Ancient Cities
Empires of Blood and Slavery

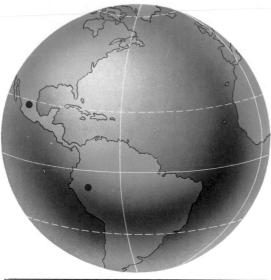

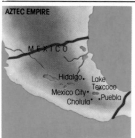

AZTEC EMPIRE

MEXICO

Hidalgo. Lake
Texcoco
Mexico City•
Cholula• •Puebla

Architectural Importance:
Aztec, Mayan and Inca architecture is generally radically different from anything that evolved in the Old World, except in the conceptual basis of the pyramid, which obviously correlated with ancient Egyptian ideas. The predominant volume of building examples which have survived tend to be of a religious nature, ie temples, shrines etc. All three civilizations of the New World conceived of their architecture in monumental terms, even to the extent, in the case of the Aztecs, of building a city on a lake.

MAYAN EMPIRE

Chichen Itza

Yucatan

MEXICO

GUATEMALA

HONDURAS

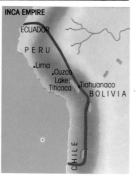

INCA EMPIRE

ECUADOR

PERU

•Lima
.Cuzco
Lake
Titicaca Tiahuanaco
BOLIVIA

CHILE

In November 1519, the Spanish explorer-soldier Hernando Cortes led his invasion force of men into the vast central valley of Mexico and arrived at the city of Tenochtitlan. It was an act that changed the face of America and had a dramatic affect on the affairs and fortunes of Spain, the rest of Western Europe, and the Catholic Church.

Tenochtitlan was the capital of the Aztec Empire. Built on an island at the centre of a vast lake, the city was laid out in an orderly grid of roads and courtyards, sparkling white palaces, temples and houses, all but the religious monuments splashed with the vivid colours of gardens filled with tropical flowers and exotic shrubs. In the centre of this wondrous complex was a vast, open plaza; here stood a group of towering pyramids, all intricately carved and painted in glowing colours. Crowning the pyramids were temples, their interiors black with the smoke of burning

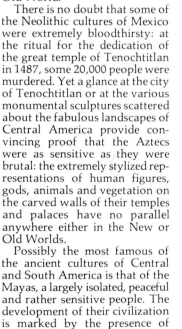

Stylistic Essentials:
Aztec style: strong gridplans, monumental scale, brightly coloured exteriors, often with highly stylized surface carvings of human figures, floral patterns and gods. Mayan styles: Legacy of monumental architecture – pyramids, huge walled enclosures, vast stone cities used only for festivals. The Incas: Though lacking in many vital technological devices and tools, the Incas nevertheless managed to achieve a high level of building skill. Inca architecture impressed through the stark grandeur of its irregular-shaped accurately-cut blocks of stone.

Primary Building Materials:
Stone was the building material favoured by all three New World civilizations. In many cases, design features were simply transferred from earlier, wood structures to hewn stone monuments, ie from domestic to monumental architecture. Use made of moulded stucco, lime-whitened mud, sometimes rubble faced with cut or dressed stone.

incense, and their walls caked with dried blood of human hearts torn from living victims in mass sacrificial rituals to the gods.

This metropolis was built by a civilization that had no wheels, no tools of iron, no beasts of burden, no scales or weights, and that had never apparently discovered the principle of the arch or the dome. Only in astronomy and measurement of time did they approach the contemporary intellectual achievements of the Old World.

There is no doubt that some of the Neolithic cultures of Mexico were extremely bloodthirsty: at the ritual for the dedication of the great temple of Tenochtitlan in 1487, some 20,000 people were murdered. Yet a glance at the city of Tenochtitlan or at the various monumental sculptures scattered about the fabulous landscapes of Central America provide convincing proof that the Aztecs were as sensitive as they were brutal: the extremely stylized representations of human figures, gods, animals and vegetation on the carved walls of their temples and palaces have no parallel anywhere either in the New or Old Worlds.

Possibly the most famous of the ancient cultures of Central and South America is that of the Mayas, a largely isolated, peaceful and rather sensitive people. The development of their civilization is marked by the presence of thousands of strange structures scattered throughout the vast, steamy forests of the Yucatan Peninsula. There are so many, in fact, that only a handful have been fully examined.

In the uplands of the Peruvian Andes are the archaeological remains of the third great empire of the ancient Americas: the Incas. Although they failed to discover the wheel or other vital technological devices or skills, the Incas nevertheless achieved an extraordinary level of civilization. The quality of their masonry, for example, is possibly unequalled anywhere, and such craftsmenship was acquired without the use of iron tools. The Incas founded a strong, centralized empire that stretched down the length of Peru and into parts of present-day Bolivia and Chile. They evolved a highly efficient administration and accounting system, and their artistic achievements are still largely unsurpassed.

Sacred Games

The earliest human remains yet found in Mexico date from about 10-12,000 BC. It is thought that prehistoric man crossed from Siberia to Alaska and spread rapidly throughout the Americas at around this time. Most of these peoples remained nomadic—only in Central America did they settle and develop a primitive agriculture, based primarily on the cultivation of maize.

Recent excavations have established that the earliest major work of architecture was the sacred city of La Venta, built about 3,000 years ago. The scale and conception of this monument implies a civilization already highly organized and structured: blocks of stone weighing as much as 50 tonnes are believed to have been hauled from distant quarries. La Venta contains the first examples of two building types that were to dominate Central American architecture: the pyramid and the ball court (a stadium for playing a religious game using a heavy ball made of latex).

La Venta was built by the Olmecs, the first of eight major civilizations in Central America. Each had its own unique culture, often determined by the wide variety of climate and terrain in Mexico, yet there were many common characteristics, in particular a unity of religious belief which gave rise to similar functional requirements for religious buildings.

The golden age of ancient Mexican architecture spans from 100 to 900 AD, concentrated in two main areas: the Yucatan Peninsula, inhabited by the Mayans, and the civilizations of the central plateau. The latter is sometimes loosely described as Aztec, though in fact, the Aztecs were originally simply one of many small tribal groups occupying the area. Their capital city was Teotihuacan (the present site of Mexico City), and they later conquered most of Mexico.

For a thousand years the Mayans evolved in isolation, and their architectural development continued uninterrupted for several centuries. In particular, they discovered how to roof their monuments with rubble and stone using the corbelled arch (a triangular vault made by projecting each stone a little farther than the one below, like a stack of dominoes, until both sides met at the apex).

In the 10th century one of the groups of the central plateau became dominant: the Toltecs, a militaristic and highly organized dynasty that spread across Mexico and conquered the Mayans. In the 14th century, the Toltecs were replaced by the Aztecs, who were eventually crushed by the Spanish invasion of 1519.

The culture of the Andes in South America that later developed into the powerful Inca Empire started as a number of separate regional civilizations. The earliest monument is the temple complex or ceremonial centre at Chavin, built between 1200 and 400 BC. During the following 800 years the culture developed rapidly with increasing skills in stone masonry and weaving. The highest

Below: A group of pyramids at the Great City of Teotihuacan. The city sprawled over an enormous area, but all that now remains are the pyramids.

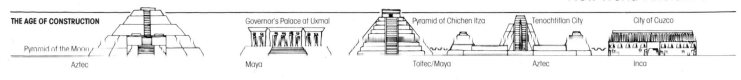

THE AGE OF CONSTRUCTION

Pyramid of the Moon — Aztec

Governor's Palace at Uxmal — Maya

Pyramid of Chichen Itza — Toltec/Maya

Tenochtitlan City — Aztec

City of Cuzco — Inca

500   700   900   1100   1300   1500   1700

development of Peruvian architecture was reached between AD 400 and 1000, when the enormous stone pyramids of Trujillo were built. The Inca Empire grew to prominence in the 11th and 12th centuries, with its capital at the sacred city of Cuzco. The Inca civilization was a highly organized state where each region was commanded by a noble subject to the rigid control of the royal family and the official religion was closely tied to the government. This authoritarian regime began to crumble in the early 15th century, and was finally crushed by the ruthless armies of the Spanish conquest led by Francisco Pizarro in 1532.

'Houses of the Gods'

The first of the great pre-Hispanic cities was Teotihuacan, high up on the central plateau, about 40 kilometres (25 miles) north of Mexico City. Known as 'the place where the gods are born', Teotihuacan served as a model for subsequent Maya and Aztec constructions. There is no record of who built the city which, in the seventh century AD, came to a violent and abrupt end for reasons unknown. This sacred city is now one of the most spectacular archaeological sites in America— several of the monuments have been partially restored so that it is possible to get some idea of the vast scale and conception of the original plan.

The most imposing construction is the Pyramid of the Sun, a five-tiered mound some 667 metres × 685 metres (730 × 750 yards) at the base, rising 60 metres (200 feet) above the plain—a volume of one million cubic metres (35 million cubic feet). Unlike the majority of other Central American pyramids, the Pyramid of the Sun was built at one time. All the pyramids served as dramatic artificial hills to raise temples perched

on top high above the congregation assembled below. Few if any of the original temples survive, but it seems that they were mostly small thatched buildings not unlike contemporary dwelling houses. Like the Greeks, the Aztecs thought of their temples as 'houses of the gods'. The pyramid was a raised stage upon which the religious dramas were enacted. It was probably faced with stone and coated with plaster, and then painted in brilliant colours. The sacred complex of the city was laid out with great precision: there was a central avenue, 'the way of the dead', absolutely straight throughout its length.

Other important buildings include the Pyramid of the Moon and the Temple of Quetzalcoatl, decorated with high-relief sculptures.

Before the destruction of Teotihuacan, several other cities in Central America had risen to prominence, among them Monte Alban, the sacred city of the Zapotecs. The city had a long history, being continuously inhabited from 500 BC to AD 1450. Most of the surviving monuments date from the 8th century, the peak of the development of the Zapotec culture. The site crowns the summit of a small mountain. Today only the limestone facing of the structures is left; the monuments must be imagined in their original sheathing of moulded stucco, brightly painted with dazzling colours. Over 170 Zapotec tombs, cut into the rock, have been discovered at Monte Alban. They have been a rich source of information on the Zapotec life-style, for the bodies were buried with jewellery, metalwork and sacred urns. Some of the walls are covered in polychrome frescoes depicting processions of priests and divinities. The most important structure was the 'south platform', a huge table 140 m (462 feet) square, with two pyramids astride it.

The Aztecs, who succeeded the Zapotecs, Toltecs and Chichimecs,

Above: The Temple of the Warriors at Chichen Itza. The plumed serpents carved on the columns guard the entrance to this Toltec monument.

established their capital in Tenochtitlan, an island on Lake Texcoco, and within 100 years dominated the central plateau. By the time the Spanish arrived in 1520, the Aztecs had control of the whole of Central America. Their architecture was a blend of existing pre-Columbian styles, adapted to suit their own particular needs. A characteristic of almost all Aztec temples was the use of twin sanctuaries.

City of the Lake

The greatest Aztec accomplishment was the sacred complex in the capital city of Tenochtitlan, destroyed by the Spanish and now buried beneath Mexico City. From the first-hand accounts of the Spanish invaders it seems that it was a complex logically planned on a scale that far exceeded any contemporary European city.

The island was connected to the mainland by three great dykes, and the city was divided into regular sections by canals, with the temple complex and royal palace in the centre. According to Spanish description, the palace occupied an area 200 m (660

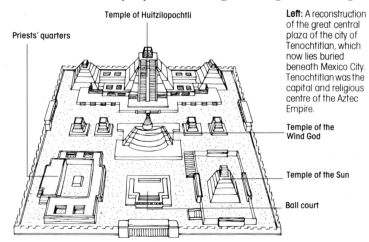

Temple of Huitzilopochtli

Priests' quarters

Temple of the Wind God

Temple of the Sun

Ball court

Left: A reconstruction of the great central plaza of the city of Tenochtitlan, which now lies buried beneath Mexico City. Tenochtitlan was the capital and religious centre of the Aztec Empire.

feet) square and was filled with interior courtyards and patios. The emperor's accommodation was on the first floor, with the administration, judiciary and treasuries below. There were a number of reception halls of enormous dimensions, which were flat-roofed, supported by rows of columns as in a hypostyle hall. Inside the walls were richly decorated with coloured stucco and tapestries, outside, bright white-lime walls contrasted with the lush vegetation of the gardens. The Spaniards arrived when Aztec culture was still making rapid strides, both in art and technology, and the slaughter that followed brought these developments to a sudden and bloody end.

The Mayan civilization was more a loose federation of city-states than a centralized nation. Much of the area was dense humid jungle, sprouting from a thin layer of soil over chalky limestone rock. The limestone was the Mayans' main building resource, providing easily carved stone and a simple plaster and cement made by burning crushed stones. Apart from a recent discovery of oil, there are and were no mineral deposits. Tools had a cutting edge of flint.

The huts built by the present-day inhabitants of the Yucatan are probably no different from the dwelling huts of Mayan times. A rammed earth platform 600 mm (2 feet) high reached by means of a small staircase forms a plinth to preserve the hut from damage in the tropical rains. Plaited branches supported by vertical wooden posts form the walls, while the roof is thatched with palm leaves, and there is only one opening, the door. The walls were covered with mud, sometimes whitened with lime.

As in Ancient Egypt and Greece, the basic form and constructional details of domestic architecture had a strong influence on monumental buildings in stone. The Mayan temple was directly derived from the dwelling hut. Thus the plinth with its steps was expanded to encompass the vast scale of the pyramid, raising the temple high enough to dominate its surroundings. The lack of openings (common in domestic construction in tropical climates in order to keep them cool) is echoed in the stone temples and palaces. The steep-pitched roof is paralleled by the tall triangular 'corbelled' vault that is a unique feature of Mayan architecture.

The earliest surviving Mayan temple to be constructed of permanent materials, was a pyramid at Vaxactun (labelled by archaeologists as the Pyramid E VIII) dating from the second century BC. Quite different from the pure

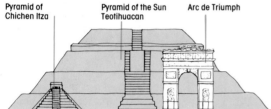

Pyramid of Chichen Itza   Pyramid of the Sun Teotihuacan   Arc de Triumph

Left: The ancient empires of the Americas conceived their architecture in monumental terms.

Below: The massive pyramid that forms the House of the Magician', at Uxmal in Mexico.

geometric forms of pyramids on the central plateau, Pyramid E VIII is a tightly controlled sculpture, where the ascending steps are skillfully interwoven with gigantic carved masks and interconnected horizontal stages.

The city of Tikal was the largest in the Mayan civilization. There were eight huge pyramids, and some 80 lesser public buildings and 'houses' for the nobility and priesthood. Some theories propose that the stone monuments of the great Mayan sacred cities were inhabited only during ceremonial occasions, and that at all other times the population lived in traditional mud and wood dwelling huts outside the city.

At the centre of Tikal is a large

Above: Detail of the astonishing relief carving on the frieze of the 'Nunnery' at Uxmal. Repetitive stylized symbolic motifs form an impressive façade.

open court, at either end of which are two steep pyramids with temples perched on the top. The structures are nearly 47 metres (156 feet) high. The temple has three small chambers within and above the entrance is the 'roof comb', a characteristic feature of Mayan temples thought to originate from decorated wooden boards used to adorn the houses of the nobility. The comb is an elaborately carved stone crest that rises high above the roof, adding to the apparent size and grandeur of the temple. Throughout the city there are various sculptures and intricately carved reliefs, architraves and panels recording the sacred beliefs and philosophies of the priesthood who built it.

The palace of the Governors at Uxmal is widely considered to be the crowning achievement of Central American architecture. The city of Uxmal was built during the 8th-10th centuries. It is situated in a low-lying, dry plain covered with scrub vegetation. The palace is 98 metres (322 feet) long, 11 metres (39 feet) deep and 8 metres (28 feet) high, divided into 20 vaulted chambers, each about the size of a traditional dwelling hut. The most remarkable feature is the great stone frieze, made from over 20,000 blocks of sculpted limestone, covered in repetitive geometrical patterns, some of them stylized representations of the gods.

The Toltec invasions of Mayan territories in the 10th and 12th centuries produced a blend of foreign and native styles, where Mayan decorative treatment was combined with the technical finesse of Toltec stone masonry. Chichen Itza was a Mayan city considerably expanded and rebuilt by the Toltecs. Here the triangular Mayan vault was supported by pillars rather than solid walls, and inter-

nal spaces were opened up to create hypostyle halls.

The most famous construction of Chichen Itza is the Castillo, a symmetrical pyramid and temple with four stairways, built at the end of the 12th century. The richly-carved temple at the top was dedicated to the plumed serpent god, Quetzalcoatl, the serpent motif which is represented throughout the carvings. In the simplicity and symmetry of its plan, the Castillo is remarkably akin to that of the villa Rotundo in Italy, by the architect Palladio.

The Mayan civilization began to falter in the ninth century, prompted by successful revolts by the peasants who were overburdened by the demands of the ruling priesthood. There was a short renaissance in the 10th and 11th centuries when new invaders, the Itzas, revived Toltec and Mayan cultures, but tribal warfare followed and, by the time the Spanish armies arrived in the 16th century, the Mayan civilization had already vanished.

Andean Masterpiece

The most remarkable achievement of the Inca civilization is its stone-

Above: The terraces of Machu Picchu, the Inca city high in the mountains of Peru. The house has been thatched in the style used by the peoples of the Inca Empire.

work. At the Castillo at Chavin de Huantar, a complex that established the principles of construction and layout for highland sites in South America until the Spanish conquest, can be found the earliest evidence of Inca masonry technique. The Castillo comprises a series of galleries and rooms made of rubble, faced with cut stone. There is a decorative cornice, carved with linear patterns that depict simple objects, such as flowers and faces, in a highly stylized manner.

The Pyramid of the Sun at Moche is a massive edifice some 228 metres (750 feet) long by 137 metres (450 feet) wide, reaching a height of 41 metres (135 feet). It would seem that the society that built such structures was obviously highly organized.

The Inca Empire was established by the foundation of Cuzco, its capital city, at the beginning of the 13th century AD. Inca architecture was devoid of the bright colours of Mexican styles; it relied instead upon the stark grandeur of accurately cut stone of irregular

shape, ground to fit perfectly. These fantastic walls form the foundation of modern Cuzco: many of the newer buildings grow out of their amazingly solid and substantial base.

Stone was used by the architects of Central America to emphasize their sense of permanence. The quarrying and carving of stone without the benefit of metal tools was possibly the most incredible technological achievement of the pre-Columbian masons, especially when considered with the fact that they had no wheels or animals to help with transport. Also remarkable was the Mayan invention of concrete, made from burned crushed limestone. The limestone was placed on top of a circular

pile of wood, which was set alight and burned for 24 hours. The resulting lime was made into plaster or mixed with water and rubble, setting to a hard concrete that enabled the construction of the Mayan vault. Although called a corbelled vault, this is not strictly accurate, as the structure depended on the strength of the concrete rather than on the balancing of static forces in the facing stones.

Aztec civil engineering was quite sophisticated, providing their capital city with fresh water through aqueducts of quite considerable length. Both Aztec and Mayan palaces boasted hot steam baths. The ancient Mexican cultures also developed complex calenders, derived from extraordinarily accurate astronomical observations: the 584-day orbiting cycle of the planet Venus was calculated to within a matter of a few hours.

In addition to their skills of stonecraft, the Incas were great road builders. The royal road of the Andes was 5200 km (3250 miles) long, until the 19th century it was actually the longest arterial road ever conceived, planned and constructed.

Below: This drawing of a section of an Inca wall shows the quality of the stonemasonry, where polygonal blocks were painstakingly cut to fit with extremely close tolerances.

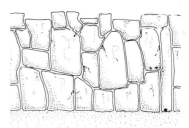

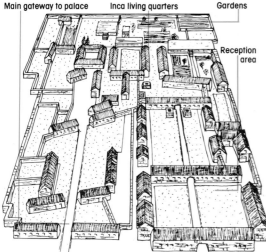

Main gateway to palace — Inca living quarters — Gardens — Reception area

Left: Reconstruction of a typical Inca palace; stone walled buildings with thatch roofs, arranged round open courtyards. Besides the royal quarters, there were food stores, guard houses and even convents.

Right: Temple of the Sun, Machu Picchu, constructed from ultra-hard granite blocks. Machu Picchu is thought to have been a sacred city reserved for the exclusive use of the emperor and his priests.

Old Forms–New Ways
The Italian Renaissance

Architectural Importance:
A return to the models of Graeco-Roman antiquity and the first instance of man's self-conscious searching the past for inspiration. The degree of dependence on classical types waxes and wanes throughout the period. Provoked great changes in both church and secular building and probably had more effect on the physical face of European cities throughout 300 years than any other cultural phenomenon. Established a series of models of proportion and harmony which are now regarded as archetypes.

REPUBLIC OF FLORENCE

ITALY

.Pisa .Florence

.Siena

CITY OF FLORENCE

Medici-Riccardi
Laurentian
library

Rotunda of
Brunelleschi

House of
Michelangelo.

Ponte
Vecchio

Renascentia means, quite simply, rebirth. It was an idea which was self-consciously pursued, as is indicated by the confident proclamation of one early 15th century antiquary: 'I go to awake the dead!' Of course this man and his contemporaries were most selective about which particular dead were to be revived—nothing was more out of date than the Middle Ages (which is, itself, a term coined in the late 15th century). The desire to expunge the recent past and start anew is one which we have witnessed in our own century and one which has been fundamental to certain ages down the years. It need hardly be said that this is a lengthy process and that to state a date for the beginning of what was, in the broadest sense, a new way of thinking would be rash. As early, for instance, as the late 13th century the precursors of Giotto were assiduously rediscovering the classical world in the shape of Graeco-Roman sculpture.

many Roman ruins were plundered for their stone.

Spread of Influence: The great patrons of the early Renaissance were the merchant princes of Florence and they were succeeded by the Papacy in Rome. The Italian architects took the new forms to France at the turn of the 15th and 16th centuries and thereafter it spread throughout Europe.

Stylistic Essentials: The early period in Florence is characterized by massive, rusticated palaces which are sparsely decorated and fortress-like. A more adorned and fantastical architecture is typical of the high Renaissance in Rome and the classical orders were often employed in novel ways.

Primary Building Materials: Despite its obvious debt to the many Roman monuments in Italy Renaissance building methods continued in a direct line from the Mediaeval. Even though there existed such a wealth of fine natural materials

But it was getting on for a century and a half later before what had begun as the preoccupation of a few men of taste would metamorphose into a 'movement' whose influence was to be felt throughout the world.

Though the Italian Renaissance was by no means essentially an exclusively architectural phenomenon, it is not surprising that it should have left us with so varied and marvellous a complement of buildings. The quintessential style of the Middle Ages, the Gothic, achieved in Italy nothing like the magnificence that we can still witness in France, Germany and England; indeed, even the most impressive manifestation of the Gothic there, Milan Cathedral, is not innocent of classical Roman detail. It is almost as if a persistent racial memory of Rome afflicted the men who sought to work within the alien, Gothic tradition; there was, if you like long before the widespread formal exploration of the classical world began, a sort of unconscious will to move in that direction—which is shown in the way that the jagged soaring angularity of high Gothic was always tempered in Italy by the older, native styles. But despite Roman forms never having quite died, it took a catalyst to prompt their wholesale exhumation; and this catalyst was, initially, literary.

The Latin Connection

Dante took Virgil as his model; Livy was a source of inspiration to historians; tragedians looked to Seneca; comic writers to Plautus and Terence. Familiarity with Latin became the *sine qua non* of aspirant writers. Thus the young men who were to become the designers of buildings in Rome, Florence and Venice were exposed to the classical spirit. These men were not architects in the modern sense, nor were they akin to the masons of the Middle Ages. They were painters, metalsmiths, sculptors by training; their appreciation

of Roman buildings was based upon appearance and proportions, upon the notion that such buildings fulfilled an ideal of cultural perfection and rationality, rather than upon any particular admiration for the virtues of Roman engineering (which were considerable) or even utilitarian properties.

The conception of the architect as artist rather than as artisan or craftsman is at least partly due to the sort of patronage the architects

of the early Florentine Renaissance received. The great mercantile dynasties, like the Medicis and the Pitti, fostered an architecture that was worldly, expressive of their wealth and power, inassociable with ecclesiastical norms, and humanistic. To them we owe too the cult of the artist as a man of unusual gifts, someone apart, someone of godlike attributes—such a cult would have been unthinkable during the Middle Ages and the fact of its existence emphasizes the worldliness and anthropocentricity of Renaissance Italy, and may perhaps be regarded as indicative of the abrogation of a striving towards an after-life: better, surely, to create a marble heaven on earth. And the same humanism informs religious buildings of the time—which is not as paradoxical as it might seem when it is recalled that these churches were less shows of piety than monuments to their patrons. To many churchmen of the time the new ecclesiastical architecture appeared irredeemably pagan; but with the exception of infrequent and fanciful flowerings, the Gothic was effectively buried till the early 19th century, when its revival would be promoted on the precise grounds that it was the true Christian style, untainted by pagan associations.

These associations did not, of course, inhibit the Papacy's patronage of the greatest Renaissance

artists. One result of this patronage is that while the early Renaissance is best seen in Florence, Venice and, to a lesser extent, in Milan, the high Renaissance is best represented in Rome, where the most accomplished artists tended to migrate after the turn of the 16th century.

Something Old, Something New

A hundred years earlier, in 1401, the goldsmith, Filippo Brunelleschi, failed to win a competition for the Florence Baptistery doors and set out to study Roman antiquities. This event is frequently seen as marking the beginning in earnest of the architectural Renaissance. When he returned to his native city, he gained, as a result of another competition, the commission to design a dome for Florence Cathedral, work on which began in 1420. However, Brunelleschi did not win this competition because of his knowledge of ancient forms or his keenness to put classical ideas into practice, but because he knew how to make such a dome work. It can hardly be deemed a Renaissance structure, though is none the less remarkable for that—in fact it belongs to no particular tradition and draws on Moorish,

Below: The dome of Florence Cathedral by Brunelleschi. A Renaissance body stretched on Gothic bones, its arresting appearance was a great deal more influential than its engineering.

Byzantine as well as Gothic principles in its construction. Just a year later, though, Brunelleschi's Foundling Hospital in the same city was getting started; it was completed in 1426.

Now while it is quite evident that this building exhibits those characteristics which we have come to recognize as belonging to the early Renaissance, it is equally evident that its debt to any particular building of ancient Rome is at second hand; it does not belong to that strain of revivalism which has rather inelegantly been styled 'archaeological' or copyist. Its elements—pilasters, capitals, Corinthian columns—are certainly drawn from antiquity, but they are disposed in an entirely novel way; and those contemporary spectators of the building who believed that they could see in it various Roman buildings which they knew only as ruins deceived themselves. The Hospital and Brunelleschi's subsequent buildings (many of which were not completed till after his death in 1446) are certainly magnificent, but theirs is hardly a Roman magnificence. They lack pomp, are slender, more 'feminine' (if one may apply such a word to buildings) and even at their sternest—the Palazzo

Below: The court-yard of Brunelleschi's Foundling Hospital shows as much the influence of Tuscan vernacular building as it does of ancient Roman models. It was taken as being 'correct'.

Pitti for instance—display a lightness of touch that successive generations were to lose. This lightness is, no doubt, in part due to Brunelleschi's not having so thoroughly absorbed the lessons of the ancients as his fashionable contemporaries believed he had; he was at least as dependent, though not perhaps deliberately, upon Tuscan Romanesque buildings of the 11th and 12th centuries; i.e., part of the local tradition he had grown up with, and of which the masons he used would, of course, have had copious knowledge. If Brunelleschi was an architect who achieved new ends by mostly traditional means, his younger contemporary, Leon Battista Alberti, was an absolutist and a theorist whose dogma was as influential as his buildings.

The printing press was invented in 1440 and in 1486, 14 years after Alberti's death, his *Ten Books on Architecture* was published. It comprises a series of dissertations which purport to show that perfect design may be determined according to a rational programme. Of course, designs

based upon verbally expressed theory will differ greatly depending upon who executes them; but even allowing for this the actual quantity of building which follows directly from Alberti is not that great. One reason is doubtless that the disciple found himself working in a strictly formulaic way; and even if they had been so minded many of the architects who came after Alberti

Below: The notion that ideals of proportion might be established by reference to human form was characteristic of and fundamental to Renaissance architecture.

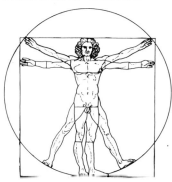

might have had difficulty since they did not share his learning.

Turning Theory into Practice

Unlike most of those whose work is discussed here, Alberti was not originally a craftsman but a scholar of music, the classics and mathematics; he was also a priest. Just as utopian schemes are liable to produce static societies so would Alberti's idealistic precepts, had they been adhered to, have produced a static architecture. Alberti's buildings bear the same relation to Brunelleschi's as do those of say A. W. Pugin to the playfully incorrect Gothic of the Regency and the 1830s—that is to say that they are far more reliant on previous models, even though elements of different sorts of building may be incorporated within one structure.

Alberti's theories were primarily aesthetic, concerned with harmony and proportion rather than with the exigencies of structure; so it is perhaps not surprising that his buildings should sometimes be guilty of that crime against the

narrow spirit of modernism—'facadism'. They are picturesque compositions whose structures are not revealed by their exteriors. His Palazzo Rucellai in Florence, built for one of the great commercial families of that city, is curiously like a stage flat; from a distance it looks as though it is a life-size painted model.

Alberti was not a prolific architect; he did, late in life, design two buildings of considerable importance, both in Mantua, both of them churches, both of them in different ways uninhibited by his own dicta. St. Sebastiano (1460) is built on a central plan, that of a Greek cross—the first instance, probably, of its revival. St. Andrea is an undeniably more impressive church whose portico is closely modelled on a Roman triumphal arch (a device he had employed in his reconstruction of St. Francesco, Rimini). The building did not begin till 1472, in which year the architect died, and there are very likely disparities between conception and execution; but whatever they are, they do not disguise the originality of the means by which the church's effects are realized. The exterior triumphal arch and pilasters are repeated on the interior as the nave walls and aisles are dispensed with; in their stead are chapels which correspond to the recess in the exterior facade.

As is invariably the case when a new style becomes apparent, it attracts imitation of a kind which by the standard of the original is inaccurate and inept but which has an undoubted appeal of its own. The 'artisan mannerism' of the 17th century in England and the 'moderne' of everywhere in the 1930s are characteristic of this trait; so too are the early manifestations of Renaissance modes in northern Europe—these were actually anticipated in Italy at the time when Alberti was working. The mid-15th century portal of the Medieval Castel Nuovo in Naples is a splendid example of the way in which the classical fashion was extravagantly 're-interpreted' without the least concern for ancient precedent.

Past Glories

Variations less wayward than those apparent at Castel Nuovo appeared everywhere. Brunelleschi and Alberti were, if you like, akin to a couple of usherettes whose torches, bright though they were, failed to prevent most of the enthusiasts falling over each others' feet on the way to their seats. Among those who understood as well as appreciated these men's achievements were Antonio Filarete, a contemporary of Alberti who was an enthusiastic

Right: The busy façade of Alberti's Palazzo Rucellai – all pilasters and rustication – gives it a curiously theatrical quality that is mitigated only by the equally curious but undeniably weighty cornice.

proselytizer for the adoption of classical styles, and of a younger generation Luciano Laurana and his pupil Donato Brasmante.

Laurana's best known work is the Ducal Palace at Urbino, but his greatest achievement in the spread of the Renaissance was that he trained Bramante who, after achieving designs such as that of the dome and choir of St. Maria delle Grazie in Milan, began, at the very end of the 15th century, to work in Rome. The eternal city was at that epoch

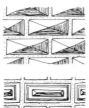

Left: The architects of the Renaissance were constantly inventing new and more elaborate forms of rustication with which the façades of their buildings might be decorated. Rustication is confined almost exclusively to secular building.

suffering what a 20th century sociologist would very likely call an urban stress build-up; i.e. it was a slum and had yet to regain the sort of grandeur with which it had formerly been synonymous. This it did under the patronage of a Papacy which, for the first time since the return from Avignon, was determined to outdo its secular rivals. The popes of the 16th century were a pretty profligate lot and got into terrible debt with their keenness to commemorate themselves in marble

and stone, to raise monuments that would rival those of imperial Rome. Not for nothing does Peter literally mean stone.

Julius II was elected Pope in 1503 and, ignoring the claims of such architects as Giuliano da Sangallo, commissioned Bramante (whose Roman buildings such as St. Maria della Pace and Tempietto he must have known) to draw up the first plans for the rebuilding of St. Peter's. The history of this edifice is a paradigm of the development of the later Renaissance period.

A year before he died, in 1514, Bramante was succeeded as architect of St. Peter's by Giuliano da Sangallo, Raphael and Fra Giocondo. Over the next 30 years a number of architects, including Antonio da Sangallo, each of whom had ideas which differed from those of Bramante, took over supervision of the vast church. Yet its expense was such

that work on it tended to proceed with no great haste. In 1546, Michelangelo took over.

A Master Unsurpassed

Michelangelo was then in his 70s, and had not taken up architecture till well on into middle age. Previously, he had done his best work on his back, but even the ceiling of the Sistine Chapel cannot compare with his architectural achievements which are, unquestionably, the greatest examples of the Renaissance. They are peerlessly dramatic, sculptural, not notably concerned with structural matters and bewilderingly rich in their effects. Although his plans for St. Peter's were altered by his successors it would not be rash to claim that it owes more to him than to any other individual who worked on it; and the great dome, though it was finally completed after his death, is still essentially his work.

The connection between the work of Michelangelo and that of Alberti is tenuous at best. His designs are frequently called perverse and it is difficult to differ from this view — but it is a perversity analogous to that of, say, Shakespeare, who shakes off classical shackles because they inhibit. Such masterpieces as the Lauren-

tian Library and the Medici Mausoleum in Florence and the Porta Pia and the Capitol in Rome abound in tricks and contradictions — again, like Shakespeare's tragedies, they resist summary. Michelangelo's successors were the English Baroque architects of the late 17th and early 18th century — Vanbrugh and Hawksmoor whose style went out of fashion in the 1720s when England became infected with the spirit of Palladianism.

Palladio's architecture is a gazelle beside Michelangelo's elephant; it is light, determinedly graceful and, while its precursors include Alberti's work it is not derivative in any obvious way. Though Palladio never worked on the scale of his great contemporary, his influence was greater, though, because of his book of his own designs which provoked the English fashion for his work, and made Vignola, whose designs included those for the Gesu Church in Rome and Pope Julius III's villa, also very influential abroad.

Because of its coincidence with the spread of printing, the diminution of the hold over men's minds of the Catholic Church, an age of mercantile expansionism and a host of other historical factors, the architecture of Italy during the period from, roughly, 1460 to 1560 became or gave rise to the first international style — something a great many of us have since come to rue.

Left: The grandiose façade of Alberti's S. Andrea in Mantua incorporates a portico which is reminiscent of a Roman triumphal arch. This rather austere exterior masks an interior of great richness and ingenuity. The dome was added by Juvarra.

S. Maria della Pace

Palazzo Pitti

Arc de Triumph

Above: Two typical Italian Renaissance buildings compared in size with the Arc de Triumph.

Below: Palladio's Rotunda at Vicenza was the model for countless villas in Italy and England; though as this photo shows the low dome and tiled roof give it a more rustic air than its progeny.

The Great Migration
Renaissance Spreads to France

.Valladolid
.Salamanca
*Escorial
*Toledo

S P A I N

Seville   Granada

Architectural Importance:
The first collision between the new, classically based Italian styles and stubborn workmen, masters of Gothic crafts. The result is a hybrid architecture whose appeal partly lies in the incongruity of its juxtapositions. Despite one or two buildings which are essentially displaced Italian ones, it was not until the mid-16th century that the French assimilated the lessons from the south. That such assimilation was not total, has much to do with the fact that much of France is climatically unsuited to Italianate buildings.

FRENCH RENAISSANCE

.Paris
Fontainebleau.
Blois. .Chambord
Chenonceaux

Atlantic

F R A N C E

Mediterranean

As a result of its military adventures France's contact with Italy at the end of the 15th century was close and lengthy. It is no doubt a matter of eternal embarrassment to the French that the subject of their greatest pride, their cooking, derives from—indeed, was the invention of—Italians at the court of Francois I. Likewise their Renaissance architecture, while it is quite obviously not in a direct line of descent from the Gothic, is equally not a feat of collective plagiarism from Italian models. It is rather the first important instance—there are many more to come—of the widespread misapplication of character-istically Italian notions about harmony and proportion. Just as the Florentine architect, Brunelleschi was rather promiscuous in his borrowings from the ancients so were French masons (brought up in a Gothic tradition) in their interpretation of designs by their Italian contemporaries. The result of this is that there

Stylistic Essentials:
The Gothic tradition of harsh, spiky carving and finials continued unabated in marked contrast with the cool, restrained language of columns and pilasters. And even

when Gothic devices were abandoned restlessness and variety were not – they were provided by wild roofscapes composed either of spirelets or of sculpturally lumpen mansards.

Primary Building Materials:
France, and especially her northern parts, has an abundance of good building stone which was the natural material for the earliest Renais-

sance chateaux. Adherence to Gothic methods of construction was largely responsible for the character of the architecture.
Spread of Influence:
The important early buildings concentrated in the Loire valley. Patrons were secular and noble. Paris and other cities had to wait till mid 16th century before they began to get a complement of significant buildings.

is no very obvious break between the two styles in France, but a slippery elision, which produced something both original and, for the most part, rather ponderous.

The gap between the earliest examples of Renaissance design in France and contemporary work in Italy is accentuated by the matter of site. Quite simply, the Italians built mostly in towns while French patrons—nearly all of them were secular—demanded chateaux in the countryside, or at least in urban parks. The chateaux of the Loire valley (which are large country houses rather than castles or fortresses) were the first important manifestations of

the Renaissance in France, and they were created for a clientele very different from that which employed such men as Alberti and Bramante in Italy. And when these same nobles built town houses (hotels), they were generally less magnificent than those of their Italian counterparts—power, or, at any rate, architectural display of power was confined to the country. Thus would be born the idea of the picturesque.

Obviously any large, rural building of note forms some sort of picturesque relationship with its environs in a way that one in town might not; it took nearly two centuries before the notion

of recreating a landscape to fit a building became popular. What is important in this regard about the Loire chateaux is that they were perhaps the first major unfortified rural buildings in Europe and were thus the precursors of countless country houses whose designers were constantly to refine the old ideas of building and landscape and, it follows, of man and nature—the latter is first ignored, then tamed, then finally made to ape itself.

Historical Rivalry

The very earliest Renaissance works in France are beyond the scope of this chapter—they are, if you like, displaced Italian buildings and are to be found in Marseilles, La Major Church and the Chapel of St. Lazare. Their architect is not known, but at the epoch of their construction (c 1480), Francesco Laurana was working nearby at Aix-en-Provence where he carved statuary for the Church of St. Didier; they are of little historical importance nor—and it is not at all the same thing—are they of much artistic importance. They do illustrate, though, the fact that styles can survive transition to foreign parts and that style has much more to do with the begetter of an artefact than with exterior conditions. This begs the question: who actually built those Marseilles churches? One is forced to opine that Italian labour must have been introduced, for what gives the buildings of the early French Renaissance their singular flavour is the mix of French workmanship

and Italian ideas; it, of course, has to be observed that the flamboyant, late Gothic which these French workmen in the Loire continued to practice in a covert way never had much of a foothold in southern France—the staggering Cathedral of Albi and the lumpenly restored walled towns of Carcassone and Aigues Mortes belong mainly to the 13th and 14th centuries.

It is arguable that the presence of Italians at the court of Francois I and his predecessors, Charles VIII (1483-98) and Louis XII 1498-1515), is something of a red herring. These artists who formed 'schools', the best known of which is that of Amboise, were mostly of Milanese and Lombardic origin and knew the Florentine styles only at second hand. It is worth noting that these artists were migrating north to France at a time when their Florentine contemporaries, heirs to a greater tradition, were moving south to Rome. Both movements were impelled by the same causes—money and opportunities.

Just how much these Italians were responsible for is moot; it would be rash indeed to ascribe to an Italian the design of any of the three major early Loire chateaux—Blois (begun in 1498), Chenonceaux (1515) or Chambord (1519). The additions to the Medieval chateau at Blois are in a sort of pared down flamboyant style and the Renais-

Below: The bizarre roofscape of Chambord has perhaps never been emulated though it has spawned many copies both in its own age and also during the 19th century.

sance is apparent only in a few decorative motifs that might have been gleaned from a pattern book; the place is more noted for its spiral staircase than for any particular evidence it provides of an appreciation of Italy; subsequently, reliance on the flamboyant style was to wane, but, in one respect, nothing much was to change for almost two centuries. The endemic French preoccupation with roofs and fantastical roofscapes was never very inhibited in its expression by the new fashions. No roof of this period presents a more restless and varied sight than that of Chambord: tourelles, pavilions, lanterns, cones, domes, dormers are recklessly juxtaposed to achieve an effect that is wild and vertiginous, willfully against nature and looking as if it is going to teeter and collapse. In fact, it is all just about symmetrical, but unlikely to be perceived as such unless it is seen along its north/south axis. Chambord had none of the homogeneity of contemporary Italian work, and the myth that Leonardo da Vinci who spent the last three years of his life in that part of France, dying at Amboise in 1519, was responsible for its design is very likely no more than that.

The Italian furniture maker, Domenico da Cortona, is often attributed with the design, the notion being that Francois's masons were unable or, more likely, unwilling to execute something with which they were intuitively unsympathetic and which did not incorporate their own tradition. Like Blois, Chambord had a remarkable staircase, this time a double spiral, for which a design by Leonardo exists—though his lacks the decoration of that at Chambord; but the principle is kindred and shows that he did have some hand in the great palace, a posthumously interpreted hand most likely.

Art of Deception

The matter of ascription is inescapable in any review of the buildings of this first phase of the Renaissance in France. It is, however, more or less agreed that Francois I's mason for the re-

Right: In this scale drawing we begin to see how French Renaissance buildings are gradually adopting the impressive size with which later examples, such as Versailles, are associated.

building of Fontainebleau was Gilles Le Breton and some of his work there, viz the north side of the Cour du Cheval Blanc, is precursive of that which would dominate France throughout the next couple of centuries—it is a simple, two storey range and the pediments of its dormers are segmental and clean, in marked contrast to the busy, overworked creations of Chambord and most of the other Loire chateaux. This splendid overworking was to continue to inform buildings in the grand manner for some time to come. It was in more modest piles that Le Breton's example was followed; they can be seen all over France save in the far south, frequently dignified by the prefix 'chateau' when really they are no such thing—a clear case of lamb being dressed as mutton.

As St. Peter's comprises a well integrated patchwork that is representative of the various stages of the Italian High Renaissance

Chateau de Chambord   Arc de Triumph   Louvre

and early Baroque, so is the Louvre possibly the best exemplar of the French Renaissance which began later and went on longer. Francois I's first architect here was Pierre Lescot who worked, as he had at the Hotel Carnavalet (also a museum now), in conjunction with the sculptor, Jean Goujon. His talent for delicate decoration is what enhances Lescot's otherwise prim and rather academic design for the west side of the square court of the Louvre, a design which is more correctly indebted to contemporary Italian influence than any which had preceded it in France. Francois died in 1547, the year after the Louvre was begun; the products of his patronage, even without those buildings that were lost during and after the Revolution, are impressive and far outstrip those of his kingly rival, Henry VIII of England. The only royal palace of the 16th century that can match Chambord is the Escorial which was built for Phillip II of Spain, started in 1559 and standing to this day as a monument to pious pomp and to the

Below: Le Breton's work at Fontainebleau was a model for French builders for 200 years; by comparison with much contemporary work it is restrained and dignified though hardly exciting.

A Law Unto Itself

The Escorial's exterior austerity and implied asceticism is by any measure notable; by Spanish standards they are quite extraordinary. The palace's architects were Juan Bautista de Toledo and Juan de Herrera, but the source of their inspiration is something of a puzzle. The Escorial is *sui generis*—

it follows nothing and nothing follows it. It may almost be regarded as a magnificent aberration; it recalls a sort of holy barracks which, given the belligerence of Philip II towards the Reformation, is apt. Despite its proximity to Italy and the strength of its trade links with that country during the 16th century, Spain (or the mutually antagonistic and equally haughty regions which composed it) was peculiarly resistant to new and foreign ideas,

Above: The most forbidding building in Christendom? The Escorial is a monastery, a palace and the seat of a holy tyrant. No building is more clearly indicative of its inhabitant's peculiar zeal.

especially to those which involved restraint in pursuit of a culturally and temperamentally ill-suited ideal. Spain excelled, and was to excel again in an architecture whose surface decoration was of paramount importance; at the beginning of the 16th century this confidently flashy style which derived from the later stages of Gothic was known as Plateresque—*plateria* means silverwork.

Quite the most famous surviving example is La Casa de las Conchas at Salamanca, though other buildings in that town, in Seville, Valladolid and Toledo are as characteristic. The Spanish pre-occupation with decoration was such that, the Escorial apart, the country has no major buildings which can be deemed to display the symptoms of a local Renaissance. (There are of course a few essays in Italian imitation, notably Charles V's palace at Granada, which is remarkable solely for the fact that it is situated in Andalucia rather than Tuscany.)

While Spain adamantly resisted Italy, France, during the second half of the 16th century was developing an architecture that at last owed nothing to late Gothic and very little to a misunderstanding of the new dicta. Adjacent to the Louvre there was con-

Left: Casa de las Conchas at Salamanca is one of the great works of the Plateresque style which combines Gothic, Moorish and Renaissance elements to produce a rich style.

structed for Catherine dei Medici the Palais de Tuileries. She was the widow of Henry II who had succeeded Francois, and her architect was her late husband's superintendant of buildings, Philibert de l'Orme (or Delorme). Like Lescot, de l'Orme knew Italy, especially Rome, at first hand, and his work (little of which survives) is that of one who knows the rules and breaks them. His book *L'Architecture* shows his playful variations on the classical orders, and a bay of the Tuileries (which was destroyed in 1871) resurrected on its former site shows that he practised what he preached; its columns are rusticated for the very good reason that the joints in the stone are thus disguised. Of his buildings that are still extant, the Chateau of Anet is the one that demonstrates most clearly that he had arrived at a classicism which relied upon a sophisticated

Above: French divergence from Italian examples and a degree of practical playfulness are manifest in this illustration from de l'Orme's 'L' Architecture' which enjoyed wide popularity.

marshalling of mass rather than the wayward and charming approximations of his predecessors.

Our knowledge of what de l'Orme's work looked like is partly due to the record of them made by another architect, Jacques Androuet du Cerceau the Elder, whose own Chateau at Verneuil sur Oise was destroyed during the Revolution. In his own drawings—and one may assume that it was not his intention to misrepresent the building—it looks quite frightening, like a lunatic asylum designed by its inmates. It was not a building which was influential at the time; one has to wait till the 19th century to find such hard and perverse piles, but its combination of brick and stone did become popular throughout the 17th century. It is to be found, for instance, in the Parisian hotels and squares (like Place des Vosges) of the early 17th century and reaches its zenith with Francois Mansart who lent his name to a roof that he neither invented nor used much, but who achieved some of the most harmonious of all French buildings. It was at the Chateau of Balleroy in Normandy that he combined brick and stone to such marvellous effect. If the roof is misnamed, it is only meet since the use of stone quoins and facings on brick was something that he perfected and which has become part of the European architectural vocabulary of the last 400 years.

The Grand Style

Mansart's Orleans wing at Blois is his most famous work, but it is

Above: The reliance on its gardens of Vaux le Vicomte cannot be too strongly stated. Andre Le Notre designed them and they include statues after Poussin.

Right: Designed for a man who suffered delusions of grandeur Verneuil was a morbid place adorned with gigantic statuary.

both incomplete and tacked on to an already heterogeneous group of structures. That he was not as prolific as his talent merited was at least partly due to his boorishness and rather unorthodox business practices—at Maisons Lafitte he caused the half-built chateau to be demolished because he was not pleased with his design. Mansart was also responsible for one of the comparatively few important French churches of this period, Val de Grace in Paris. It is more obviously Italianate than anything else he did, though this illusion is fostered by the church's dome, which is not his work but that of Jacques Lemercier, one of the Louvre's many designers, who completed the church after Mansart had been sacked. Lemercier is on better form here than at the Louvre where his work is rather nugatory.

We have already compared the Louvre to St. Peter's as a guide to French architecture of the period. This comparison demands qualification; St. Peter's may be, as we have said, a patchwork but it dissimulates the

fact. The Louvre does not; it is piecemeal and looks it. The architect who succeeded Lemercier there was Louis Le Vau, and again he made little attempt to 'fit in'. Le Vau's forte was the grand statement; he can be accused of all sorts of things, but never of reticence. He had some hand in the east façade of the Louvre—which is mostly the work of Perrault—as well as in the square court, but is best remembered for two piles which are among the grandest, if not the most refined, in the world. Vaux le Vicomte was built for the finance minister, Fouquet, who was corrupt and was dismissed from office before he could occupy his opulent palace. Le Vau worked here with the garden designer, Andre Le Notre, and it is the conjunction of formal parterre and house which is so effective; without its surrounds the house would seem curiously urban; witness those drawings of it which omit the gardens. It is a rather lumpen pile, topped by a squat lantern and bulbous roofs. Soon after the completion of Vaux Le Vicomte, Le Vau and Le Notre

Above: By the standards of Rome Mansart's church of Les Invalides is unremarkable but it is notable as one of the few entirely native French Baroque buildings of the first order.

began work on the planning of extension of the royal hunting chateau of Versailles.

This palace for Le Roi Soleil is as arid as it is vast. One reason for this is that the newly created French Academy under the presidency of the painter, Le Brun, was antipathetic towards the Baroque which was then in its ascendancy throughout the rest of Europe and was busily pursuing, rather late in the day, Alberti's ideals. So the garden façade, stripped of the most characteristically French feature—a varied roofline—is an interminable range of institutional pomposity and of no real magnificence. Versailles's interiors are, of course, peerless and so are Le Notre's gardens; architecturally, what is noteworthy is the work of Mansart's great nephew, Jules Hardouin Mansart and of Jacques Ange Gabriel.

Mansart was about as close as France ever came to a first rate Baroque architect and by the standards of neighbouring countries his work is rather mean. St. Louis des Invalides and the Versailles chapel are his best creations, but he worked at a time when French architecture was in decline. With a few exceptions, like Gabriel's Petit Trianon at Versailles and Soufflot's Pantheon, the greatest French works of the 18th century belong unequivocably to the history of interior design and town planning.

Northern Lights
Dutch and English Renaissance

Architectural Importance:
The Gothic went on longer and had more stylistic influence on imported architecture in these countries than it had in France. Both countries achieved a sort of native Palladianism early in the 17th century and the Dutch was initially more influential. Perhaps the greatest single achievement in these countries was the creation of a small-scale, almost homely, domestic classical architecture, an architecture which, in its basest form, is still practised.

It is quite probably misleading even to use the word 'Renaissance' with relation to the sort of architecture which developed in Holland and England after about 1550 and which derives far more than that of contemporary France from a continuation of Late Gothic; indeed the further one gets from Italy the less the debt to the original Renaissance is evident. This is not simply the effect of poor communications and of a world in which people's horizons were far more narrow than are conceivable today; nor is it due to the mistrust of things Italian engendered by the Reformation, Henry VIII's break with Rome and so on. However, it is surely proof that a mode of design is ultimately more powerful than the associations it bears that the Baroque, which came to be identified as *the* style of the Roman Church, its trademark, if you like, should have flourished so thoroughly in Germany, Protestant parts as well. The

development of style in the northern countries is really not akin to that of France where, as we have seen, there was a gradual assimilation followed by the emergence of a peculiarly nationalistic architecture. The extent to which Holland and England resisted the example of France and Italy is at least as important as that to which they embraced it.

A generalization about the spread of the Renaissance might divide the countries of Europe, apart from Italy which is a sort of parent in this case, into three groups: France, as we have seen, stands alone. Germany and Spain and, to some degree, Belgium were only mildly afflicted by the mainstream of the Renaissance and took little notice of Italian models till the establishment of the Baroque (which, in the instances of these countries, follows on

the heels of a similarly highly decorated Gothic). Holland and England, whose ties at the time were close, adapted Italian modes at second hand (via France) and added them to what were essentially Medieval structures before they achieved a small-scale classicism of their own and eventually retreated, like France, into an academic classicism: Palladian rather than Albertian.

Northern Climes, Southern Styles

It is, however, as well to attend first to Belgium which was the financially stronger part of the Netherlands during the 16th century. Belgium and Holland were united till the latter threw off the Spaniards at the end of the century, but even before that division there was a marked disparity between their architectures. This

was, perhaps, to be expected; a natural progression from the Middle Ages when public buildings of great richness and elaboration were constructed in Belgium and were rare further north.

During the third quarter of the century Brussels and Antwerp saw the construction of a number of buildings of undoubtedly southern inspiration; the earliest and most impressive of which is Antwerp Town Hall by Cornelius de Vriendt. It is in a way quite Italianate; the orders are disposed in a way that evidences the architect's close study of Italian models. But atop it all is a pitched roof with tiny dormers and a stepped gable whose classical niches and pediment do not disguise its unmistakably Brabantine Gothic origin. The design is very gay (in the old sense of that abused word) and would eventually be copied, without much regard for fineries, all over the Low Countries and Denmark; or, rather, it would be transmitted there by those who fled Spanish rule by means of a northerly migration. Such a case is the Town Hall of Leiden by de Key, the façade of which is graced by a form of decoration called strapwork (so called because it is alleged to resemble bands of cut leather) which was to gain considerable popularity in the great houses of England.

The Leiden Hall lacks what is perhaps the most obvious and *northern* feature of the Antwerp Hall, namely the large amount of glazing. It goes without saying that the sun, in such climes, is something to be sought rather than shunned as it is further south; and all building in the

Below: Guild houses in the Grand Place, in the old section of Brussels. Built at the very end of the 17th century they still exhibit, in a rather striking manner, a sort of late Gothic exuberance.

North which takes as its model foreign archetypes is bound to attempt to resolve style with climactic exigencies. Rather one might say *should* be bound, because during certain periods all sorts of building that have originated in warm countries have been imported without suitable amendment—the classic case is the white box of the 1930s which became the grey box of the 1940s.

Resisting Foreign Influence

For the most part the Dutch and English resisted the temptation to imitate and refine the Italian style till well on into the 17th century. Belgium remained predominantly Catholic and either, because of this or because of a sort of national predisposition to extravagance in ornamentation, was pervious to the Baroque. Compare the Guild Houses of Antwerp, built at the end of the 16th century with those of Brussels, built at the end of the 17th. The former are almost entirely devoid of any detail that might reasonably be termed Renaissance: they are straight out of a native tradition which goes back through such elaborate creations as the Town Hall of Louvain (mid-15th century) and that of Bruges (mid-14th). And the Brussels houses continue this tradition. The sculptural fantasy may be classical, but it is disposed in a way that is quintessentially Belgian.

This exuberance did spread to Holland but only gradually. It also spread to England by means of pattern books published in Antwerp during the second half of the 16th century and, it is to be presumed, as a result of English eyes cast on that city in the course of trade; Italian and French pattern books were also known in England, and there was even a native one, *The First and Chief Grounds of Architecture* by John Shute, which he wrote on his return from Italy in 1550. But it is only those who are determined to discern the Renaissance (which is dubiously connectable with 'progress') at every turn who can so term the great houses that sprang up all over England during the reign of Elizabeth I.

In such compositions as Longleat, Hardwick Hall and Wollaton (all of them the work of Robert Smithson) and Burghley, which were among the grandest of the period, strapwork and columns do give some hint of foreign knowledge. But what is remarkable about these piles is: a) the sheer amount of glass that is to be found in their façades—hence the rhyme 'Hardwick Hall, more glass than wall' and b) the delicate faerie of their skylines. This latter characteristic may perhaps recall the Loire chateaux of which, no doubt Smithson and his contemporaries were cognisant, but these English houses, even Wollaton, which is a bit pompous, are neither wild nor crazy. The spires and domes of Burghley suggest grace

and dignity and a sense of chivalry beside which Chambord appears neurotic and *busy*. It might be argued that this sort of serenity puts the great Elizabethan houses closer to the Italian than to the French. Of course, the stateliness of the places is comparable but—like the French in this respect only—they are mostly country houses and therefore simply big. All that glass renders their walls frame-like and, anachronistically, gives them the superficial appearance of those modern blocks, which are, not surprisingly, all glazing and plainness.

Their comparative sweetness alongside French chateaux is in some measure due to the way they are sited. Even in contemporary prints showing the houses in parks far more formal than those which surround them nowadays, there is no evidence of that French mania for crushing nature and ensuring that man's hand is

ubiquitously apparent. This talent, peculiarly English and widely imitated, for conceiving of a house as a sculptural object in a landscape should not, perhaps, be discernible at so early an epoch, but so surely do Longleat and Burghley fit into their parks that one may fancifully attribute precognition of 18th century landscaping to their creators.

Medieval Heritage

The first Elizabethan era was not much of a time for church building, but the late 15th and early

16th centuries had been, and it is from the extensively glazed chapels of that period (King's Cambridge, St. George's Windsor, Eton College) that the style of fenestration of Hardwick etc. evolved. Smaller English houses of the time show even less foreign influence and are in a straight line of descent from Medieval manors—they are commonly very plain with triangular gables, mullioned and transomed windows and pitched roof. By the end of the century Dutch gables were getting more frequent, but they have more to do with Dutch native tradition than with assimilated Italian styles.

After Holland gained independence from Spain at the end of the 16th century, the wealth in the Netherlands passed to her, and an architecture began to evolve that had little to do with Belgian

ostentation. The absence of good building-stone in Holland accounts for the character of the cosy neo-Palladianism that became current during the 1630s. Its fairly sparing use of stone dressings is akin to, though less sophisticated than, that employed in France by Mansart at exactly the same time. The Mauritshuis at the Hague is the classic work of this sort, and it was widely copied throughout Holland and became the norm in England after the restoration of the monarchy in 1660. One of its architects was Jacob van Campen and his Town Hall in Amsterdam—now the Royal Palace—is perhaps the grandest Dutch building of

Left: Strapwork, so called because it aped the kind of decoration applied to leather, is characteristic of the low countries.

Below: Built as the Town Hall the Royal Palace in Amsterdam was designed by Jacob van Campen in a modest and chaste classical style which was much copied throughout Holland.

the century. What is remarkable about Dutch classicism is that it consistently maintains a human scale: grand gestures are few and far between and towns like Delft seem like models of themselves. They are very reasonable places, the last thing they are liable to provoke is awe; quite the contrary, they are more likely to foster contempt for a mentality seemingly unable to conceive of anything greater than Man.

England, with its predilection for the small and comfortable, might have suffered a similar legacy had it not been for Inigo Jones' extraordinary act in transplanting an Italian palazzo in London. The Banqueting Hall on Whitehall had an influence out of all proportion with its inventiveness—it is a very good copy of a Palladian building and not much more, but the sheer *strangeness* of it in the early 1620s is what is of moment. Jones was primarily a designer of masques for the court and his architectural output was not great. The Queen's House, Greenwich and the Chapel of St. James' Palace are the only other entire and unaltered works whose attribution to him cannot be questioned. But the point about Jones and his followers, John Webb and Rober Pratt, is that they had partially established a kind of architecture which tempered the Dutch designs that cropped up everywhere just before and after the end of the Commonwealth. For about 80 years till the 1720s when, rather ironically, Jones' master, Palladio, became a posthumous dictator of style, the marriage of Jones' and Dutch architecture produced something very splendid and original. The greatest artists of this period—Wren, Hawksmoor and Vanbrugh devised something that is perhaps beyond this blend, but countless lesser men, many of them unknown to posterity, created a complement of country houses, town houses, halls and public buildings which are, at the very least, of great charm. Speculative builders such as Nicholas Barbon put up terraces in central London to a standard that few of today's architects seem capable of emulating, and architects such as Hugh May and William Talman, whose Uppark in Sussex is a gem of the period, constructed country seats of elegance and simplicity. One of the best early examples of the meeting of Jones' classicism and the Dutch tradition is also in Sussex, called Barnham Court, a house whose author is not known.

Town-Planner to the King

Christopher Wren was 28 when the monarchy was restored in 1660, and a year later he was appointed Assistant to the Surveyor, a strange post perhaps for a mathematician and astronomer. The Great Fire of London could not really have occurred at a more propitious time for him; he had already designed Pembroke

College Chapel, Cambridge and the Sheldonian Theatre at Oxford and had spent some time in Paris where he had met Bernini, Le Vau and their contemporaries and had seen Perrault and Le Vau's east façade of the Louvre being built. It is possible that he had also visited the Netherlands, but maybe not, for a first hand experience was no longer necessary to a comprehension of that country's architecture. Wren was a prodigious designer but little of his work was domestic—the sort

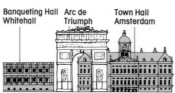

Banqueting Hall Whitehall   Arc de Triumph   Town Hall Amsterdam

of house that is commonly referred to as 'Wren style' is actually the Dutch Palladian box and has little to do with Wren himself.

Nine days after the Fire Wren presented Charles II with his plans for the rebuilding of the City of London and over the next half century saw the place come to resemble the model he had had in his mind. He built 50 odd churches there, St. Paul's, the Monument; up river he was responsible for the Royal Hospital, Chelsea and the garden front of Hampton

Left: Elegant finale. The tail end of the Renaissance in Holland and England is still concerned with fine proportion: less so with the statuesque.

Below: Sir Christopher Wren's Fountain Court at Hampton Court is executed in one of the many styles of which he was an outstanding exponent.

Court; downstream he completed the Greenwich Hospital and designed the Gothic observatory that overlooks it; he also worked extensively at Oxford and Cambridge. Wren's output is in an astonishing variety of styles, but it rarely looks like the work of anyone else even though the sources are often quite patent; he was quite unhindered by rules and thus went in a very different direction to his French contemporaries who were fast retreating into what was to prove a fairly sterile academicism.

Wren worked in conjunction with a number of architects and artists of whom the most notable were the great wood carver, Grinling Gibbons and Nicholas Hawksmoor. Hawksmoor's own work has a massiveness, a heaviness,

that Wren would not have aspired to; his churches in the East End of London are quite the equal of Wren's in the City. The connotation 'Baroque' seems eminently unsuitable for him as it does for John Vanbrugh. Both of them embraced a sort of weighty mannerism whose step-father might be Michelangelo. Hawksmoor's work at its plainnest and more sturdy anticipates the utilitarian industrial architecture of the 19th century. Vanbrugh's, on the other hand, anticipates the hugely self-confident piles of the self-made Victorian industrialists. He was *inter alia*, a playwright and his

Below: The sash window was the dominant method of fenestration in English domestic architecture from the Restoration till about 1840 and is a vital component of Georgian façades.

Below: Vanbrugh's talent for weighty grandiosity is well shown in the remaining parts of Eastbury House. The heavy, pseudo-Medieval arch is turned into a sort of theatrical prop by the tree.

great houses, Blenheim, Castle Howard, Seaton Delaval, and Eastbury are nothing if not theatrical. At Eastbury in Dorset (of which only a wing remains) he put trees on the roof for his ostentatious client, the dubious financier Bubb Doddington. Seaton Delaval stands near the bitter north east coast, outside Newcastle, like a prop from a play too horrible ever to be presented again; it is a sinister spectacle.

Apropos Hawksmoor and Blenheim, it was written that he was 'like a nurse who thinks the child her own.' The extent of his collaboration is moot as is the nature of his influence on Vanbrugh, who was evidently a much less experienced architect. The overall conception is undoubtedly Vanbrugh's — Blenheim is picturesque even though it wears classical clothes. It is perhaps the first great building to be self-consciously made as part of a scene. And even if the generation of Palladians who reacted so strongly against Vanbrugh despised his building, they learned a great deal from his painterly ways.

The great pity about Palladianism as It was practised in England from about 1720 till 1750 was not only that it quashed the magnificent tradition begun by Wren and continued by Vanbrugh but that it was a dead art — excellence was achieved by

Right: St George in the East is among the group of remarkable London churches built by Nicholas Hawksmoor during the 18th century. They are among the most stately ever built.

Above: Seaton Delaval House stands largely neglected on the exposed north east coast of England. It is the most uncompromisingly forbidding of all Vanbrugh's great houses.

adherence to a pattern set a century and a half previously. The splendour of English houses of this period is the product of inspired landscaping and siting rather than of architectural prowess. Prior Park, Stourhead, Stowe, Holkham, Wardour, and many others are instances. There is much to be said for a copybook style when it replaces something

that is worthless, but in the circumstances of the second quarter of the 18th century such a last ditch aesthetic programme was, quite simply, a very bad idea. The tradition of Wren and Vanbrugh continued as — dreadful word — a 'vernacular' form ie, it was adopted by builders up and down the country who in their not always rude manner created 'Georgian', the stolidly elegant and worldly mode of thousands of modest houses of the period constructed almost entirely out of local materials.

Catholicism and Illusion
Italian and Spanish Baroque

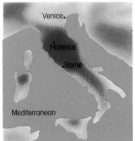

Architectural Importance:
Deliberately wrought in order to impress and overawe. The servant, in this respect, of Catholicism with which it was closely identified, hence the countries in which it is most common. It is the most lavish of all styles, both in its use of materials and in the effects it achieves. Is not at its best in the hands of the second rate – and relies very strongly indeed on individual talent rather than received rules. There are thus considerable variations in the competence of the execution of Baroque buildings.

EUROPE IN THE AGE OF BAROQUE

The Portuguese and Spanish words 'barroco' and 'barrueco', whence Baroque, mean a rough or irregularly shaped pearl. It is apt that this style should bear an ultimately Iberian name for it was in that peninsula and in the South American colonies that it reached its zenith in the early 18th century. As we have already seen, the Baroque grew out of that non-academic, Michelangelesque strain of Renaissance architecture called, for no good reason, Mannerism and was adopted and taken to its *reductio ad absurdum* in the very countries which had resisted the theoretically based design of the high Renaissance—as well as Spain and Portugal, these include Germany and Austria, Belgium and the southern part of Italy and Sicily. In these places the degree of dependence upon classical precept is markedly less than in Rome and the affinity with the Gothic more marked. The work of Vanbrugh, Hawksmoor and their

Below: The great
monastery at Melk
on the Danube was
built during the early
years of the 18th
century to the designs
of Jakob Prandtauer
who took every
advantage of a
magnificent natural
site. It is, by the
standards of German
Baroque building, a
fairly austere creation,
yet it retains a
certain grandeur.

Catholicism and Illusion

Stylistic Essentials: The sine qua non of the Baroque architect was a copious understanding of classical architecture combined with an impatience at its rules, and a desire to see how it might look in a distorting mirror. So pediments are swollen and broken and open; façades undulate; churches seem to abound in tricks which make them appear almost unashamedly theatrical.

Primary Building Materials: The desire to work materials is always evident. There is no great virtue made of materials being themselves. Polished marbles, porphyry, gilt, paint (especially in Germany) were used extravagantly. Artifice is more important than substance.

Spread of Influence: Rome is the Baroque city and it spread thence all over Italy and notably to Naples and Syracuse. It is 'hot-blooded' and was most accepted in southern countries, the same countries in fact which took up art nouveau in the late 19th century.

contemporaries which was discussed earlier has little in common with that which will be reviewed here—it was concerned far more with volume and architectural abstraction than with ornament, although it does share one fundamental quality; it is, if you like, manipulative of its beholder. This is a point we shall return to.

Like Gothic architecture, but unlike that of Alberti and his disciples, Baroque architecture is reliant on its three dimensional existence. Buildings of the High Renaissance work well on paper, those of the Baroque do not. Much Baroque architecture is, to be sure, concerned with the creation of façades and often with the mere addition of façades to existing buildings, but its illusionism goes far beyond that of the Renaissance palazzi which, in spite of their aspirations, look for all the world like backdrops. It reintroduced perspective within the elements of a building and, perhaps most important of all, was never submissive to its material. The idea of 'truth to material' is a dreary Puritan dogma which has had much currency since the late 19th century and has become one of the standard ideés recus of modern architects. It is a dogma significant of a certain pusillanimity of spirit, of a reluctance to overcome 'the natural order', of a dull ascription to inanimate objects human qualities. One of the great glories of the Baroque masters is that they never subscribed to such notions (which are implicit in the Albertian tradition); Bernini sculpting in marble would never have dreamed of treating the block before him as some sort of mute collaborator—so far as he was concerned it was a slave to be wrought till it was flesh or wood or silk. This practice of overcoming material is one reason—others include its self-conscious magnificence and its restlessness—why the style has often been considered 'decadent'. Would that all decay was so

spirited. Would, too, that it was so playful and *engaging*.

Even more than flamboyant (or perpendicular) Gothic, this art of the 17th and 18th centuries was designed to provoke the participation of its spectators; this is not to say that the spectator should experience some sort of extra-aesthetic reaction, but that his reaction to or perception of the work should be gauged just as the maker of a thriller film gauges his audience's terror as he constructs the piece. He creates with an audience in mind and, depending on his prowess, has a more or less sure grasp of how an audience will respond to each ingredient of his story.

The Art of Pleasure

The architecture of the High Renaissance is passive, does not court the involvement of those who gape at it; it is cool, its begetters did not intend to trouble those who used it, even less to trick or cheat them—it was simply enough to please. The work of Bernini, Borromini, Guarini, Juvarra in Italy, of Churriguera and Tomé in Spain, of a host of German and Mexican architects is wilfully aggressive and intended to disconcert. The means used to achieve this goal are many and various and, of course, they changed through the years.

It would be pleasant to pretend that Baroque achieved effects for their own sake, for the pleasure of knowing that they worked, and to some extent this is so—the raison d'etre of a tour de force is to be a tour de force, and to be a monument to its begetter's artifice. The fact of the matter is, rather, that it found patrons in Italy and the Catholic world because its very opulence was an ideal instrument of propaganda for a fairly beleaguered church embarking on the Counter Reformation. This use, any use, does not necessarily alter the way a building is made, but it probably amends our vision of it. Take the façade of the mid-18th century Cathedral at Murcia in southern Spain by Jaime Bort: it is seductive and inviting, its

emphasis is inwards, it is like a fabulously elaborate accordion that has been stretched to reveal an opening wherethrough its secrets can be explored. Now suppose it were not a church—a secular palace, say; such a perception of it would be inappropriate to say the least, but from a purely sculptural point of view nothing would have changed and the thing would still be as beautiful as it is and just as illustrative of the Baroque's freedom from the tyranny of the right angle and the simple geometry of the circle.

An architecture that is not literal but relies, as does the Baroque, on association and symbol is far more functional in the widest sense of that word than the shed of today which may be private house, sewage works or school for the training of playgroup leaders. The Baroque is an expressive art. A building is first expressive, as we have said, of its author's talent or ability or whatever; next it expresses what it is there for, and in this the Baroque has never been matched. At its best it represents an architectural analogue of the literary ideal of the indissolubility of form and content; this is something that neither copybook classicism nor 20th century international nothingness, both which impose aesthetic handcuffs, could ever achieve. The Baroque was made

Below: The façade of Murcia Cathedral in south-east Spain is splendidly wrought and illustrative of the way that the characteristic motifs of the Baroque were used decoratively.

THE AGE OF CONSTRUCTION

S Ivo della Sapienza

Q Ourla   St Paul's   Monastery of Melk   The Zwinger   San Giovanni

Rome   Rome   London   Melk   The Zwinger   Laterano

Dresden

|1600 |1620 |1640 |1660 |1680 |1700 |1720 |1740 |1760

up as it went along, was more than usually dependent upon the gifts of individual artists, and owed little to precepts or theory—which is no doubt why the French with their schematic stiffness and antipathy towards extemporization never took to it.

The sort of 'development' or 'progression' that can more or less justifiably be discerned in other styles is not applicable here. Or if there is a progression it is, fittingly, not linear and so not reducible to the familiar 'c' follows 'b' follows 'a' formula. In other words, the later masters of the Baroque were no more 'advanced' than the first; this is one of the more evident paradoxes of an art which is unconstrained; it will always contain the contradictions that are to be found in humankind and does not attempt to iron them out. Man's imperfectibility (and, cynics would have it, his vanity) are implicity displayed in the Baroque which is catholic, in the sense of all embracing, and profoundly anti-utopian.

Small is Beautiful

For a style that is, properly, associated with grandiosity, many of the best works in it are physically small even if in conception and effect they are grand. Francesco Borromini's S. Carlo alle Quattro Fontane is of this kind. It is like an assault course for the eye: its parts *do* make a whole but they demand that the beholder make an effort to thus resolve them.

Left: An assault course for the eye—the component elements of the façade of Borromini's S. Carlo alle Quattro Fontane seem to deny or oppose each other. **Above:** A bay of Borromini's design for the Collegio di Propaganda Fide in Rome shows him at his most playful and at his most restless.

119

Catholicism and Illusion

Above: Borromini's S.Ivo della Sapienza is built to an unusual ground plan which is more than matched by its bizarre, asymmetrical spire.

Right: Bernini's incomparable Chapel of St Teresa shows him at his most accomplished – the master of a rich trickery.

Despite the symmetry of the larger part of the façade its elements deny or undermine each other. Whereas in a Classic Renaissance building, elements are differentiated and clear now they begin to run into each other; classical forms are used only to be turned upside down. Here a moulded string course turns into part of a pediment, there a figure in a niche turns into part of that niche. These games do not need to be understood to work — the Catholic Church, and more particularly the Jesuits, appreciated this realizing that the Baroque was a genuinely popular art which appealed to and toyed with the senses as much as to the intellect — it did not captivate only the learned. It is perhaps even an anti-intellectual art in that it derives its greatest power from its ability to dislocate the senses and to disorientate; one does not need to be acquainted with the works of Vitruvius or Palladio to know that one's eyes are being tricked, that the 'natural order' is being tampered with, that one is feeling a bit giddy. It may be an instance of retrospective wisdom, but the spire of Borromini's S. Ivo della Sapienza, perched upon a lantern, suggests a helter-skelter. That this fun fair attraction was known in 17th century Rome seems improbable since it did not make its appearance in England till the 19th century. But for even those born too early to warm their bottoms on such slides the curious corkscrew must have come under the spire's spell; the thing looks askew, as if it is an unrectified mistake, a serpentine bandage that has slipped. Borromini com-

mitted suicide in 1667 not long after his only peer, Gianlorenzo Bernini, had returned to Rome after suffering the major snub of his career in Paris whither he had been summoned by Louis XIV to work on the Louvre. His plans were rejected and so that city was deprived of something that would unquestionably have been more inspired than Perrault's east façade; the world too is deprived of a major secular building by the great sculptor. Neither of his large Roman palazzi, the Odescalchi and the Montecitorio, survives in its original state.

However Rome does have a vast complement of creations by Bernini, the most celebrated of which is the structure of colonnades round the piazza of St. Peter's. In comparison with his earlier baldacchino beneath the dome of the cathedral, the piazza is a rather selfless design. This might appear an odd claim for so colossal a project but its purpose is partly to focus our attention upon Michelangelo's dome and to rectify the harm done by Maderna's elongation of the nave which has the effect of making the façade dwarf the dome. The

effect of the piazza is to *narrow* the façade rather than to diminish its height and thus to concentrate the eye, especially the eye lounging in the via della Conciliazione, upon the centre of the cathedral. Now Bernini achieved his trompe l'oeil by resort to the simplest form of the classical orders; the columns about the piazza are Tuscan, ie undecorated and, so one might think, atypical of the Baroque. In fact their conjunction with Maderna's gigantic façade is marvellously appropriate; where Maderna is flashy, Bernini is humble, the piazza for all its size is like an usher, a footman whose livery may be magnificent but does not match his master's splendour. It is all a form of theatricality, where the lessons of counterpoint are much in evidence. He used similarly straightforward props to create another of his grand effects: the Scala

Left: A lavish pediment, characteristic of the Baroque in central Europe is this one which was formerly atop the proscenium arch of the opera house in Munich.

Left: The Zwinger, Dresden by Mattaeus Popplemann was, despite its somewhat deathly air, conceived and built as a pleasure palace.

Above: One of the last of the great monuments of Roman Baroque. S. Giovanni in Laterano achieves its effect by sheer massiveness.

Regia which links St. Peter's and the Vatican Palace where natural perspective is heightened and parodied by having the stairs narrow as they reach the top

Illusion or Reality?

Bernini's Chapel of St. Teresa in Maderna's S. Maria della Vittoria is more obviously sumptuous, and it parades its devices rather than dissimulating them. Teresa of Avila had only been canonized a quarter of a century before this chapel, in celebration of her ecstacy, was begun, and her writings were widely known. In them she refers to her heart being pierced by a spear of divine love; Bernini makes this literal and portrays her assailed by a young angel with an arrow in his hand. Ecstacy is represented as orgasm. The two figures are frozen beneath an entablature which is also the

Below: The soaring spire of St Paul's in London is evidence of the renewed vigour and confidence in architecture which infected the age of the Baroque.

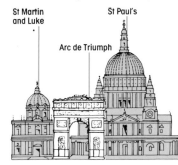

St Martin and Luke

Arc de Triumph

St Paul's

top of a swirling frame, the sense of delirium is heightened by the use of a most gaudy and poly-chromatic marble, and the sense of theatre is emphasized by having the scene witnessed not only by some particularly well fed putti but by (equally well fed) members

of the family which endowed the chapel. This flatters both them and Bernini—it is as if he is having them bear witness to his extreme virtuosity, and, of course, part of that virtuosity comprises his carving of them.

This sort of game about what is illusion and what is not anticipates Pirandello by almost 300 years and is a deal more entertaining. It is incidentally hardly surprising that a far more accomplished writer than Pirandello, Alain Robbe-Grillet should have set *his* schematic jest about illusion, reality and memory, *Last Year at Marienbad*, in a Baroque palace, that of Nymphenberg in Munich. Hardly surprising, too, that the Baroque should have been considered an ideal style of building for theatres at the turn of the 20th century.

While none of the Roman architects who came after Bernini and Borromini were perhaps so original, many of them were very good indeed, and no one who visits that city can fail to be impressed by the sheer *quantity* of Baroque works. Of the late—i.e. 18th century—churches one of the finest is St. Giovanni in Laterano which impresses by the bigness of its columns and pilasters; it possesses a freakish quality, a bit like a boy who has shot up in height but is still wearing short trousers. The designer of this façade was Alessandro Galilei and his example was much copied in, of all places, late 19th century Glasgow. In fact it was not till that revival of the style that Roman Baroque spread abroad. What did spread was the style of two Turin architects, Guarino

Guarini and Filippo Juvarra who bear the same sort of relationship to each other as do Borromini and Bernini. Guarini's work is very complicated and some of it, notably the St. Sindone Chapel of Turin Cathedral, suggests an acquaintance with the Buddhist stupas of Burma. This is by no means the only instance of the Baroque's affinity with the art of the East—whether there was an influence from the Orient is moot, but it must be borne in mind that by the end of the 18th century there was growing a taste for what the English called the 'Hindoo' style. It is beyond dispute that Spanish Baroque owes a debt to Aztec and Inca carving. Both Guarini and Juvarra worked in the Iberian peninsula, the former, in Lisbon and the latter, at the Palace of La Granja near Segovia whose skyline again suggests an Oriental influence. Though it is more elaborate than his work in Turin (e.g. the hunting lodge at Stupinigi or the exquisite Superega) La Granja is positively restrained by Spanish standards.

Icing-Sugar

Juvarra was an almost exact contemporary of Jose de Churriguera who gave his name to the sculptural style which is seen at its most extreme in the Cartuja at Granada and the Transparante in Toledo Cathedral. The sort of spatial and volumetric games that were so dear to the Italians were ignored in Spain, whose Baroque is essentially decorative. But what decoration! The sacristy of the Cartuja is breathtakingly elaborate and no simile—icing sugar is the most obvious—can express its singularity. It is rather more angular than most Spanish carving which looks as if it is melting like wax under a hot sun. This is certainly the impression given by the façade of the Cathedral of Santiago de Compostella; this air of decomposition recurs in the work of the Spanish Art Nouveau architects, and it is very exciting. The affinity between Baroque and Art Nouveau is most evident in southern Germany.

The work of the architects of this period in Germany is far more delicate than that of their Spanish or Italian counterparts. At least it aspires to delicacy, and much of it is reminiscent of something made from china. The influence of the Gothic is frequently apparent, and the sort of massiveness which was so common in Italy is rare. Even in such huge piles as Jakob Prandtauer's monastery at Melk on the Danube there is a feeling of lightness and even the rather morbid Zwinger in Dresden (of which du Cerceau would have been proud, so perverse a design is it) is airy in its way. These places and countless others are bright and colourful and beautiful, but for all that they lack the *gravity* that Bernini brought to his sublime creations—there is nothing so serious as play.

Changing Face of Europe
Emergence of the Town-Planner

Architectural Importance:
A high rate of population increase and a renewed interest in the antiquities provoked a revival of large-scale town-planning during the 18th century. Architects became more conscious of the potential of urban landscape, fitting repetitive units (ie houses) together within a strong overall pattern. In England, there was an emphasis on the romantic and picturesque; in France, town planning provided an opportunity to practise social engineering. Many of the ideas and forms can be traced to Roman origins.

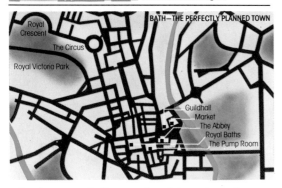

BATH—THE PERFECTLY PLANNED TOWN

Royal Crescent
The Circus
Royal Victoria Park
Guildhall
Market
The Abbey
Royal Baths
The Pump Room

Architects of all periods, although perhaps not all architects, have been concerned with the way their buildings relate to one another and form part of the landscape or townscape, as well as being well-designed in themselves. The beauty of a remote Mediterranean village derives partly from the simplicity of the individual dwellings, but mainly from the rhythms set up by repetition of the unit in a pattern which responds to the natural landscape. Likewise, architects of modern housing estates employ repetition of units and a conscious ordering of the spaces between buildings to give harmony to the complex requirements of many inhabitants. Only the most gifted architects seem to be able to combine visual order with the needs of the individual as in traditional building. Although the idea of the architect as planner dates back to Roman times and received new impetus in the 16th and 17th centuries, it was

18th century town-planning which substantially changed the face of European towns and forms the basis of modern planning.

In the 18th century several new features and ideas were introduced into town and landscape planning. Urban improvements in most European cities meant extensive replanning, both for visual effect and in the interests of cleanliness and hygiene. At the same time the layout of streets took on some new variations, based on a renewed appreciation of classical art. Based on revived Roman principles, the ideas of the circus and the crescent gave new currency to architect-planners. Regular curves were brought into play, and subtly linked to one another. Towns in England and France rapidly adopted the new ideas. One, Bath in England, soon gained an ascendancy. Here is grand architecture indeed, but made up of moderate sized individual dwellings whose architectural meaning depends on the whole ensemble.

At Bath, the crescent represents another new and potent idea in urban design, the incorporation of nature in the form of the open space which faces the houses as an essential foil. The inclusion of nature in town planning, which gave rise to the many beautiful urban squares and parks in Europe, wsa originally an English notion, and has its counterpart in the English planning of country mansions and parks. In the true 'picturesque' garden of 18th century England, not only does landscape design enhance the buildings but architecture also is employed to order and spice the landscape—a delicious and piquant balance between the artifice of man and the forces of nature.

The third ingredient of 18th century town planning to be discussed here came particularly from France. This was the idea of urban design as social reform. Order was imposed on buildings not primarily for visual effect, but as a means of creating new social relationships between classes and more satisfactory conditions for the ordinary people. This was extensively worked as theory and, although little was built at the time those theories lie behind much of 19th and 20th century town and city planning.

Renaissance to Baroque

The first real architect-planner whose ideas for cities have survived was the Roman Vitruvius. His design for an octagonal town with a central piazza and eight radial roads dividing the town into segments was geometrically simple, easily fortified, and offered possibilities of grand vistas. Many of the Renaissance artists and theorists, who looked back to Roman models for their ideas, attempted to design ideal towns based on the Vitruvian form. Their plans became more complex in their abstract geometry and they began to venture into social organization, but none of them progressed beyond patterns on paper. The Dutch town of Naarden, built in the early 17th century, is a good example of Renaissance principles in practice; regularity, symmetry and clarity being the most important characteristics. Generally, most Renaissance build-

Left: A design for an ideal city, by the Roman architect Vitruvius. The plan minimizes the length of perimeter fortifications needed and provides an opportunity for the inclusion of long, broad avenues.

ings were intended to be seen one at a time, as individual self-contained masterpieces.

The 17th century marks a major change in the conception of architecture, and three characteristics of Baroque architecture point towards grand town planning. Baroque architecture demonstrates firstly a new interest in scale and grandeur of effect, secondly an interest in illusion, and thirdly an interest in movement, the changing experience of architecture as the spectator moves through and around buildings. All these three are seen at Bernini's grand forecourt to St. Peter's, Rome of 1656. The triple rows of columns are monumental in scale and awe-inspiring in their intensity of effect. The swelling out of this great oval space forms a rallying place for the devout who approach the heart of the Catholic Church and the seat of Papal power. Then one is compelled onward by the rhythm of the colonnade whose tapering lines give an illusion of even greater length. Religion in Baroque Rome was closely linked with political power, and these buildings are monuments to the dominance of the Papacy.

The Baroque period saw the beginnings of monumental planning which was to be developed in the 18th century; squares, avenues of trees, and vistas, sometimes terminating in fountains or sculptural monuments. The tendency towards centralized planning with converging radial lines, as in the Piazza del Popolo in Rome, reflects the centralization of money and power at this time. The Champs Elysees in Paris was first laid out by Louis XIV outside the city confines, as part of this drive towards self-agrandisement. Later it became incorporated into even grander cityscape as the Place L'Etoile and Arc de Triumph were built.

In existing Medieval cities the development of new squares and vistas could only be achieved by ruthlessly cutting through the dense tangle of narrow streets, an expensive and disruptive process. However, where new country estates and palaces were being planned the same ideas could be given free rein with magnificent effect. Versailles, the palace of Louis XIV, was designed on urban lines. The town, which was mainly devoted to servicing and supporting the palace, contains three radial roads which converge on the palace gate. The palace itself evolves in a sequence of squares, while the landscape beyond is ordered along the same axial lines, with grand vistas, regularity and symmetry everywhere. Power was absolute, and could be seen to extend to a domination over nature as well as the populace.

England too had her Baroque movement, and Wren's naval

Left: The Champs Elysee, for two centuries the model for countless ceremonial boulevards built in the world's capitals to symbolize the grandeur and power of endurance of the state.

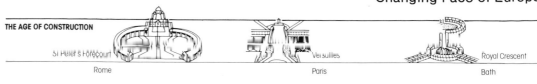
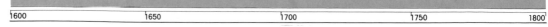

THE AGE OF CONSTRUCTION

St Peter's Forecourt
Rome

Versailles
Paris

Royal Crescent
Bath

| 1600 | 1650 | 1700 | 1750 | 1800 |

college at Greenwich was laid out in the late 17th century to incorporate the best European ideas, a symmetrical plan of great virtuosity. However, the real English contributions lie firstly in urban planning of less drama, and secondly, in the layout of country estates. Both these reflect the patterns of the English nobility. Wealth was still concentrated in the country seats, but increasingly country landowners and their families sought urban entertainments and society and would move for 'the season' to a rented or owned terrace house in London, or in the fashionable city of Bath.

Vanbrugh's early 18 century design for Castle Howard and the surrounding Yorkshire landscape is still Baroque in its grandeur, but unlike Versailles it abandons symmetry to the winds. The drama of the lawns and rides, vistas and prominences, temples and statues depends for its effect on working with the natural hilly landscape, rather than imposing on it. An 18th century writer, Horace Walpole, helps us to appreciate how this relates to urban design, and also the new note of picturesque sublimity it introduces. He wrote: 'Nobody had informed me that I should at one view see a palace, a town, a fortified city, temples on high places, woods worthy of being each a metropolis of the Druids, the noblest lawn in the world fenced by half the horizon, and a mausoleum that would tempt one to be buried alive; in short, I have seen gigantic places before, but never a sublime one.' Increasingly, conceptions of the ideal garden were derived from landscape painting, particularly the idyllic landscapes of Claude Lorraine, and the distant view

Below: The park façade of the Palais de Versailles. The palace itself formed the focal point of the royal city and was laid out with powerful axial symmetry. It was an expression of absolute power.

became an essential part of the total design. It is significant that William Kent, the most important landscape gardener of the mid 18th century, was both an architect and a painter.

The gardens at Stourhead represent an ideal of garden design, a landscape painting with every necessary ingredient, through which one can stroll for pure pleasure. Tamed nature and architecture naturalized continued to be complementary features. Garden buildings were often in Neo-Classical styles, reflecting the

underlying order, while the landscape became ever more 'natural' by increasingly artificial means. Notions of the picturesque demanded ruins, grottoes, waterfalls, meandering paths and rustic bridges but the final effect was to be Nature and not the hand of Man—a conscious rejection of the formality of French gardens, but equally carefully designed. Later in the century Launcelot 'Capability' Brown further changed the face of England by his extensive 'natural' gardens involving prodigious earth movement, water-

Above: The 18th century gardens at Stourhead, in Wiltshire, an artificially created landscape, carefully engineered to seem entirely spontaneous – yet combined with formal Neo-Classical pavilions.

coursing and tree planting. Whole villages were moved and replanned for picturesque effect. With skill any moderate sized estate could indeed appear to extend to a spot beyond the horizon.

Trend towards Uniformity

There are close parallels between developments in landscape design and urban design in this period. Ideas of formality and symmetry had never been as strong in England as in Baroque Europe, and gave way to a balance between restrained regularity and the inclusion of Nature and accidental effect.

Regularity and order in the town square are seen in English towns from the 14th century onwards when the Oxford colleges introduced this feature. In London, greater standardization of houses following the 18th century building regulations meant more uniformity and regularity, often wholly unconsciously arrived at by builders, and this pattern is also seen in provincial towns. One of the more consciously designed squares of London is Bedford Square, laid out in 1775 as new speculative development. Here each side of the square is designed as a whole, built up of slight modifications in the façades of individual houses. However, there is a natural harmony and proportion even in the very humblest terrace of this period.

Changing Face of Europe

At Bath, John Wood the elder had a more comprehensive idea, and turned specifically to Greek and Roman prototypes for the unified elevations commensurate, he felt, with the high point of civilization. He began with Queen's Square in 1728 and then became more ambitious. He intended the Circus, of 1754, to act as an arena for sports displays and he based the design on the Colosseum of Rome, turned inside out. John Wood the Younger continued the scheme with even more regard for linking the sections and for the existing landscape. His Royal Crescent of 1775 takes for its theme a larger version of a demi-Colosseum, the open side falling away towards the town in a pleasure park of gentle open spaces and trees. Gentility meant not merely a civilized urban architecture but also a sympathetic outlook on landscape.

The new planning vocabulary explored at Bath was repeated everywhere in England, most monumentally at Edinburgh New Town, where the breadth of conception and grandeur are again heightened by the natural contours of the site. Humbler and now faded Mornington Crescent and the Crescents of Notting Hill Gate in London all derive from this same model.

The romantic picturesque movement already seen in landscape gardening originated in England and affected towns as well as country estates. Despite the fact that it was essentially concerned with Nature, paradoxically the most complete picturesque town planning can be seen in London. Indeed, Nash's replanning of Lon-don was the most concerted attempt ever made to change the essential form of the city. Nash was an architect of country houses and picturesque cottages, and his Blaise Hamlet, near Bristol, is the quintessential romantic model village, idealizing a simple life of rustic quaintness.

His contribution to the planning of London of 1811-25 extends from one park to another across the heart of the West End: St. James Park to Regents Park, via his new axis, Waterloo Place, Regent Street, Oxford Circus and Portland Place. Symmetry was avoided and the route takes several pleasant turns, marked by the features of Piccadilly and All Souls, Langham Place. He laid out Regents Park to cater for pleasure activities, surrounded it with grand terraces (the concern for theatrical effect being stronger than the design of the buildings), sited two 'villages' of quaint villas, convenient for mistresses and maiden aunts, with grander villas dotted around the park. Nothing is overwhelmingly formal and the casual frivolity of the Regency period still remains today. Regent's Park cannot be described as a

forerunner to the Garden City, since it was soley designed for the privileged classes, but it is almost unique of its period in its blend of housing and parkland, so close to a city centre.

Planning in Europe

The 18th century saw considerable changes to most European cities, sparked off both by the new inspiration for classical principles in planning and architecture, and by a new sense of civic responsibility for urban improvements. Travelling became an important pastime, and travellers in the mid-18th century complained bitterly of the poor conditions of towns, with their crowded, airless streets, dirt, lack of pavements, lighting and sewerage, and their inadequate public spaces, heightened by recent population in-

Above: Bedford Square, London, a fine example of the Georgian square. The individuality of each house is subtly revealed, without in any way disturbing the overall harmony of the design.

creases. Towns and cities reflect growth and evolution and there is no one whole Neo-Classical ensemble of this date, although Lisbon and St. Petersburg come close to that ideal. Nevertheless between, say 1750 and 1830 a new coherence in townscape substantially changed the face of many cities.

The Vitruvian radial plan continued to be occasionally followed in the 18th century, as at Karlsruhe, a new capital laid out in 1715 for Carl Wilhelm of Baden, and at Washington D.C. as late as 1791, but generally European cities followed a grid plan, perhaps relieved of its regularity by a polygonal or circular central

Below: Architecture during the 18th century acquired an appearance alto-gether more impressive than that which characterized the 17th.

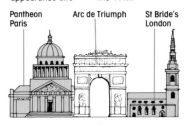

Pantheon Paris   Arc de Triumph   St Bride's London

feature. Simple rectilinear regularity was the essence of the plans seen from Glasgow to Dublin, Munich to Helsinki, and Trieste to Nancy. Gone was the desire for Baroque effect and high drama and in its place was harmonious restraint and a respect for domestic life. The central streets of many towns are impressively broad and long, but nowhere overwhelming.

Lisbon provides a good example of Neo-Classical town planning at its most perfect, since an earthquake had entirely destroyed the city in 1755. Numerous designs were proposed for the rebuilding and opportunity was taken by the ruling classes to totally rationalize the plan. The chosen scheme consists of a regular grid of streets between two squares linked by a central axis, and it also stipulated three different façades for different categories of house, resulting in a pleasant uniformity. The speed of rebuilding under the very competent administration of the wealthy classes meant that buildings were virtually mass-produced, and the initial coherence was not lost. In comparison with other town plans of its date Lisbon was enlightened in its social organization and the services and facilities it provided.

English examples affected the introduction in European towns of more open squares and parks, and, indeed, by the late 18th century less rigid, more picturesque features became fashionable. The

Below: Perhaps the most famous example of Regency townplanning is the Royal Crescent in Bath which apparently received its inspiration from the Colosseum in Rome.

Above: Blaise Hamlet, near Bristol; designed by John Nash. It was conceived as an archetypal rustic village, a romantic haven of rural peace, but without the ugliness of rural poverty.

informal English park can be seen to have entered the European vocabulary at Munich's Englische Garten of 1789, with its informally placed temples and meandering streams. All Europe was jealous of the generous parks of London and cities did their best to emulate.

Most of the town planning discussed above was intended to create visual order although, increasingly, rationalization was seen as an aid to more efficient urban life. Planning went hand in hand with urban improvements, but these only marginally affected the lives of the underprivileged. The seeds of a more modern attitude to urban design were, however, laid in the 18th century, in France, where the crisis of the rising power of the bourgeoisie and working classes was accompanied by new freedom of theoretical thought. The 'Age of Enlighten-

ment brought not only new city forms, but a new, more functional, approach to planning, applied to the buildings of all classes. Both public and official concern for town planning strengthened after the 1789 Revolution.

Ledoux was one of the few architectural theorists of the time who succeeded in realizing plans for a new town laid out on visionary and radical lines. The Town of Chaux at Arc-et-Senans in S.E. France was designed in 1775 as an industrial garden city based on a salt factory and providing accommodation for workers, community buildings and allotments. Perhaps its most modern features were the flexibility of planning, the separate traffic lanes leaving the residential quarters undisturbed, the green belt, and the generous open space in the centre, an openness compatible with the new liberal post-Revolutionary thought. Nevertheless, despite the modern ideas of social reform and Ledoux's desire for architectural simplicity, the style remains unequivocally Classical with a plan based on Vitruvian tradition. utopian vision is sacrificed to pure geometry and this proposition of an ideal solution has a harsh authoritarian ring in the context of a far from ideal social climate.

The importance of the French theorists like Ledoux is due less to their completed works, than to the widening of theoretical debate on the role of the architect-planner in social reform.

Revolution in Ideas

Town planning had moved a long way from the Baroque by 1800 and in ways which closely reflect social and political changes. Centralized wealth and power were less evident, and new plans were more often a response to the need for urban improvements. High drama gave way to visual order and clarity, and increasingly plans were based on defined social requirements, if only for the wealthy classes. Planning vocabulary became more varied and often juxtaposed architecture and nature, seeing nature as evidence

of the natural harmony and proportion to which architecture aspired. It is to this period above all that we owe our conception of urbanity; the individual building as but a minor part of the whole city, and the whole being far more than the sum of the parts.

Only hints of a more socially conscious mode of planning are seen in 18th century French architectural theory, and perhaps also in English estate villages, but seeds were sown for important developments as the industrial revolution advanced. New industrial towns, population increases and a changing pattern of wealth brought greater social deprivation and a greater need for workers' housing. From the utopian solutions of Ledoux sprang Robert Owen's plans for industrial towns and villages of 1820, where special emphasis was placed on education and social betterment, and Fourier's plans for communal living. Other model towns followed, incorporating more sophisticated social understanding, and led directly to the garden cities of the end of the century. More recently architects like Le Corbusier, much influenced by Fourier, and Frank Lloyd Wright have played major roles in shaping attitudes to planning in cities and non-urban communities. Only very recently has it become apparent that the architect still has lessons to learn from 18th century towns, in his search for appropriate urban forms.

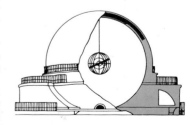

Above: A bizarre idea for a gigantic cenotaph for Sir Isaac Newton, designed by the architectural idealist, Etienne-Louis Boullee. It was never built, but it caused great controversy.

Iron Frames–Glass Cages
The Victorian Revolution

Architectural Importance:
The industrial revolution was primarily about the mass production of iron and then steel – in quantities that would make it feasible to use these as primary building materials. The first iron-frame buildings were the early textile mills in England which, by way of continual improvement and evolution, developed into the steel-frame skyscrapers of the 20th century. Iron and steel also made possible the construction of longer bridges with a much lighter structure. The pioneers of the new era were engineers, not architects.

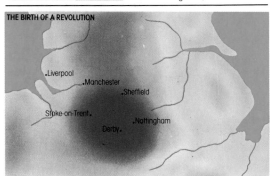

THE BIRTH OF A REVOLUTION

To the artists and architects of the 19th century, the industrial revolution appeared as a loathsome nightmare disturbing man's inner peace and harmony. To the engineer and inventor, though, the new technology created exciting opportunities beyond the wildest dreams of previous generations. Just as we struggle today to cope with the cataclysmic challenge of the microchip, so the people of the Victorian era wrestled with the far-reaching implications of unlimited mass production. The architectural establishments of 19th century France, England and America looked to past civilizations for inspiration and the rapid development of archaeology and a deep-rooted contempt for the machine age were responsible for the historical posturing of Gothic, Greek and Egyptian revivals. Thus the design challenge of new building forms such as factories, docks, railway stations and exhibition halls

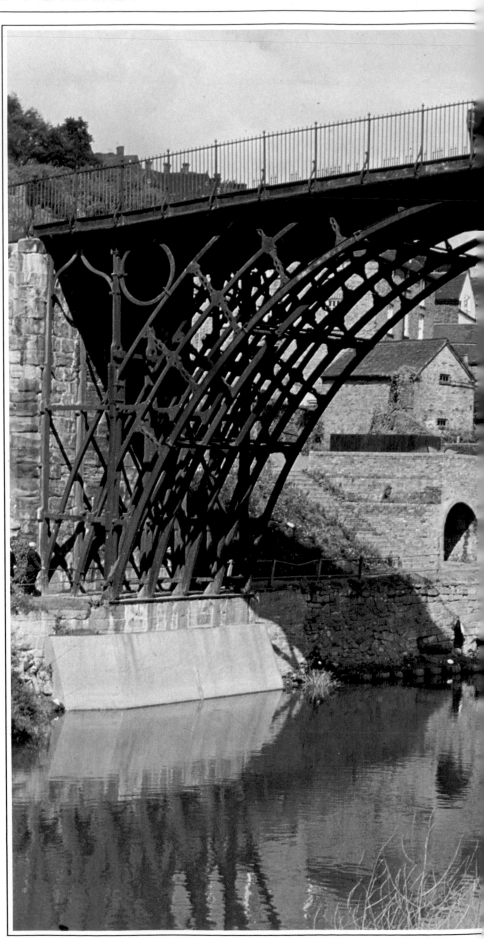

Below: The Iron Bridge over the River Severn, the first successful cast iron bridge in the world. A momentous event in the history of technology, the bridge was assembled in 1770 from prefabricated components. The parts were joined using dowels and dovetail joints, a technique reminiscent of carpentry.

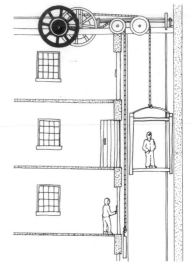

Stylistic Essentials: The first factories were textile mills, built several storeys high in order to facilitate the best distribution of power (via pulleys and gears) from water wheels to each piece of machinery. Iron and streel were used in the construction of factories to achieve greater strength of structure and better fire-proofing. The solid, functional and digni-fied design of early Victorian dock and factory buildings can be extremely pleasing for its own sake—a quality more appreciated today than it was in the time when they were being designed and constructed.

Primary Building Materials: Walls of the early factories were still built of masonry and windows were made large in order to maximize the quantity of light entering the building. Iron was first pro-duced in quantity in the 18th century, but its inherent dis-advantages preven-ted Victorian engineers from draw-ing the full benefit from the revolution they had created.

frame, used at first to reduce fire risk and create wider open spaces for machinery, ultimately de-veloped into the steel frame of early American skyscrapers. Les-sons learned in bridge building were applied to the vast iron, cathedrals of the railway age.

In the second half of the 19th century, iron and steel gradually gained public acceptance, and were applied to many building types: the Bibliotheque National and Bon Marché department store in Paris, department stores in New York and offices, shopping arcades, libraries and even churches in Philadelphia. These buildings were usually clothed with exterior façades of masonry, and when visible the cast iron itself was used with elaborate ornament. The repetitive nature of the casting process allowed economical mass production of richly decorated features, and highly ornamental cast iron columns available 'off the shelf' were advertized in foundry catalogues. It was left to the architectural pioneers of America to rationalize decorative design and to achieve a stylistic language that expressed the true qualities of metal architecture at the turn of the century.

Above: Textile mills were built several storeys high in order to facilitate the dis-tribution of power from a central source such as a water wheel. The first elevators used the same power source.

First Factories

The Romans built factories for processing olive oil, using water power to drive millstones for extraction. Nearly 1,000 years later some 6,000 mills are recorded as being in use in the English Domesday book of William the Conquerer. But the first true factories, in which a substantial number of workers were assembled in one building to fully capitalize on economies of scale and the productivity of machinery, date from the end of the 17th century. These were invariably located near a good water supply—the only viable source of power until the advent of steam engines.

The English (and later the European) industrial revolution was founded on the textile industry, where the mechanization intro-duced by Hargreave's 'spinning jenny', Arkwright's water frame and Cartwright's loom brought about a rapid expansion in pro-duction. The first factories were textile mills, brick-built with heavy wooden floors and beams. Spin-ning machinery, needing large free areas, was located on the top floor, where timber trusses could provide a wide span without inter-mediate column support. The floors below were used for smaller machines and storage. One of the earliest examples was built bet-ween 1718 and 1722 by John Lumbe: a Derby silk factory that was the world's first large-scale

was seized and exploited by engineers, not architects. Iron, the building material that led to the birth of modern architecture, was initially used only for in-dustrial applications, except where it could entertain with novel effect, such as with the frivolous 'palm tree' columns of the Brighton Pavilion by John Nash.

The philosophical battle bet-ween science and art was one of the bitterest controversies of the 19th century and architecture, a discipline which evolved as a result of the fusion of both aesthetic and engineering skills, attracted much of the fighting. The two greatest academic insti-tutions of France, the Ecole des Beaux Arts and the Ecole Poly-technique, hurled insults at each other across the dinner tables of Paris. The engineer Gustav Eiffel, creator of the famous tower, was called a vulgar philistine by the academic establishment, and hailed a hero of the new machine age by his acolytes. A brilliant Beaux Arts student, Henri Labrovste, who tried to preach the gospel of engineering, so shocked his col-leagues that he was denied the opportunity to build until he was 40 years old.

In England the controversy surrounding the use of iron archi-tecture reached a climax in 1851 with the opening of the Great Exhibition, housed in one of the most revolutionary buildings of all time. The Crystal Palace (as it was nicknamed by Punch magazine at the time) was the first example of sophisticated pre-fabricated building, assembled from machine-made parts with the same care and precision that had earlier been lavished on steam engines and spinning machines. Here was a building that fully exploited the aesthetic potential of iron and glass; a monument

that captured the imagination of its millions of visitors, few of whom had seen anything remotely like it before. Yet most of the exhibits on display within this futuristic building—products of the craftsmanship and ingenuity of nations all over the world—were grossly sentimental, obsessed with the past and dripping with extravagant ornament, a complete contrast to the elegant purity and monumental simplicity of the Crystal Palace itself.

Few, if any, of the landmarks of progressive architecture in the late 18th and early 19th centuries were instigated by architects: it was left to millwrights and civil engineers to use iron in a bold and adventurous manner. Solid, functional yet dignified, the early textile mills and warehouses of England contain the seeds of modern architecture. The iron

Right: Fancy ironwork such as this could be cast in large quantities of repeti-tive units, resulting in the mass pro-duction of orna-ment. This example comes from Mel-bourne, Victoria.

THE AGE OF CONSTRUCTION

Iron Bridge Coalbrokedale
Britain

St Katharine's Dock London
Britain

Crystal Palace London
Britain

Eiffel Tower Paris
France

|1750 |1775 |1800 |1825 |1850 |1875 |1900

textile mill. Five storeys high, it housed generous windows and accommodated 300 workers.

Wood and charcoal were already becoming scarce by the beginning of the 17th century, and coal was rapidly replacing wood as the main domestic and industrial fuel. Early iron production used prodigious quantities of charcoal, prompting Abraham Derby to employ coke for his experiments with iron-smelting in 1709. His success, and that of his sons in converting the process to use coal in 1750 led to the development of the mass production of cast and wrought iron, metals that were to change the course of world history.

The iron bridge across the River Severn was the first successful use of cast iron in bridge building (a French attempt across the Rhone 20 years earlier had failed). Abraham Derby III, together with John Wilkinson and Thomas Pritchard, conceived the idea in 1773, and the bridge was erected between 1775 and 1779, using constructional principles derived directly from carpentry. The parts were cast in Derby's Coalbrokedale works, the only plant capable of casting members large enough. Despite its humble size, the construction of the iron bridge was an epic event in the history of technology, the first of a series of developments that led to the steel-frame skyscrapers of Manhattan.

Wood used for floors, columns and beams of the early factories constituted a major fire hazard, especially when oil lamps were used for lighting the night shift. Early attempts at introducing cast-iron into the building structure were largely prompted by this fire risk and the resultant heavy insurance premiums, although the possibility of gaining additional space for machinery was a strong incentive. The Claver mill in Derbyshire was the first to include cast-iron columns in 1785; these were used in conjunction with timber beams and load-bearing masonry walls. In 1793, Richard Arkwright erected a mill with iron columns, plaster-encased wood beams and brick arched floors, described at the time as fireproof. The first totally iron-framed mill was built in 1796, using flat brick arches supported by iron beams. A prototype that was to be copied throughout England and Europe in the 19th century was a mill in Salford designed by Boulton and Watt in 1801. It had seven storeys and used hollow, round, cast-iron

Below: St. Katherine's Dock, London, started in 1827. Several enclosed basins were incorporated in the design to reduce the influence of the tide during loading and unloading operations.

Above: The Albert Dock, Liverpool, designed by Hartley and opened in 1845 by Prince Albert. The severe handling of the windows and the stark cast-iron doric columns impart an air of solid grandeur.

columns that supported 'I' section beams spanned by brick arches.

By this time, power could be provided by steam engine, and there was less need to locate the mill near running water (apart from the advantage of being able to transport coal by river). The Salford mill was designed to use steam power. Its bold, innovatory design was a key event in the evolution of modern steel-frame architecture, for iron-skeleton frames sheathed with stout outer masonry walls became the standard method of construction for warehouses and multi-storey factories for the latter part of the 19th century.

Often the dimensions of the machinery dictated the structural layout, since the frame also supported the drive shafts and pulleys that transmitted power from the central steam engine or water wheel, and some cast-iron pillars even incorporated special brackets for this purpose.

During the 1830s, wrought iron, because of its higher tensile strength, had begun to replace cast-iron for joists and beams. At the Saltaire factory, built in 1858, rolled iron angles were used to fabricate trussed girders to span the attic space in one leap. At the time it was the longest room in Europe (168 metres, 550 feet). Titus Salt, the factory owner, was a reformer who tried to provide better conditions for his workers. Saltaire was a 'model' factory, built on a green field site, with its own village for living accommodation. He put the weaving machinery in a single storey shed, with 'north light' trusses (used here for the first time) to provide better day lighting and the machinery drive shafts were concealed under the floor in pits; an arrangement that anticipated modern factory design.

Building an Empire

Growth in the volume of international trade in Medieval times prompted the erection of primitive multi-storey warehousing at im-portant docks, partly because of the lack of space on the quay. The expansion of commercial traffic to the colonies of the British Empire brought a rapid increase in such building, and in 1800 the London docks began to be rationalized around enclosed basins. Dock buildings in the early 19th century were modelled on textile mills, many of them using cast-iron columns and beams with brick arches to reduce the fire risk. Goods were loaded by hoists outside the building and raised to the required floor level. Some early hoists were powered by water mill, but by the 19th century steam had become the main source of power.

The Albert Dock in Liverpool was designed by the architect Jesse Hartley, who had earlier built the West India Dock in London (started in 1800). While employed as Liverpool's dock surveyor he put up many fine warehouses— solid, massive, functional buildings with a severe style and monumental scale. Hartley constructed the Albert Dock warehouses directly over the quay, with an open colonnaded loggia at ground level for unloading. The building's cast-iron framework is sheathed in masonry; heavy, supporting, cast-iron Doric columns are the sole concession to ornament. Once thought an eyesore, the Albert Docks are today considered among the finest buildings in Liverpool.

St. Katherine's Dock in London was built in 1827, designed by Philip Hardwick. Only a few of the original buildings have survived redevelopment, but those that are left illustrate the simplicity and solidity of Victorian functional architecture at its best. Although we may nowadays appreciate their aesthetic qualities, these buildings were considered by the Victorians dull and plain, and when money was available, later Victorian industrialists did not hesitate to embellish their premises with ornate and romantic façades. In 1840, John Marshall had the architect Joseph Bonomi supply Neo-Egyptian elevation for the main façade, complete with papyrus leaf capitals, for his Temple mills in Leeds, in the Midlands.

The first factories and warehouses had been built by millwrights and engineers. By mid-Victorian times, architects had taken over: their job now was to apply a decorative veneer to the exteriors of functional buildings, as though to disguise the essentially rude practicalities of their utilitarian reality.

The Great Exhibitions

In the first part of the 19th century, cast-iron was still a new and exotic building material. The English architect John Nash used slender iron columns in the Brighton Pavilion, probably the first use of cast-iron in a prominent interior design. The kitchen has extraordinary branching palm-leaf

Above: Gustav Eiffel's famous creation and the focal point of the Paris Exhibition of 1889. The Eiffel Tower is a masterpiece of daring design that had a profound effect on architects around the world.

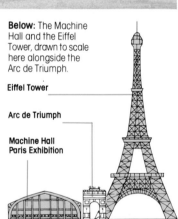

Below: The Machine Hall and the Eiffel Tower, drawn to scale here alongside the Arc de Triumph.

Eiffel Tower

Arc de Triumph

Machine Hall
Paris Exhibition

capitals at the top of its four thin columns. Cast-iron opened up a whole range of aesthetic possibilities because it could be used with far thinner proportions than any other material then available. One of the first non-industrial building types to exploit this potential was the conservatory.

Joseph Paxton was first employed by the Duke of Devonshire as a gardener at Chatsworth, the Duke's palatial country home. He had already built a number of small conservatories for the Duke when he constructed the Great Store, a vast greenhouse that was 69 metres (227 feet) long, 37 metres (123 feet) wide and 20 metres (67 feet) high. Its central

The Age of Railways

Parallel with the industrial revolution of machine technology, came the revolution in communications and transport. The canal network in England was dramatically expanded towards the end of the 18th century. In order to connect and service the new industries, the famous engineer Thomas Telford built a number of aqueducts, tunnels and bridges and, together with McAdam, made great advances in road building as well. Robert Stephenson and Isambard Brunel were the heroes of the railway age, connecting the cities of England with shining new iron highways. Railways in England were built with huge forces of manual labour and the contracting firms involved operated on an international scale, at one time employing more 'navvies' building railway lines than there were soldiers in the British army.

Railway stations and termini required halls with large spans and thus provided a suitable challenge for iron construction. The first large railway halls in England date from the 1850s, and include Paddington, Newcastle and Kings' Cross. At Newcastle, a dramatic iron frame was used to support an arched roof covered with glass. Soon railway stations were providing office accommodation, hotels and improved passenger amenities. The Gare de l'Est in Paris (1847-1852) was designed with a large concourse in front of the tracks to improve pedestrian circulation. It also boasted an all-iron structure and many of its features were adopted by later stations.

Paddington station was designed by Brunel (he had engineered the railway itself between London and Bristol) with a great arched cast-iron vault, sheathed in glass. The decorative details on the columns and arches were supplied by his architect friend Digby Wyatt, and a colour scheme by Owen Jones (who had designed the colour scheme for the Crystal Palace). It still retains much of its original grandeur to this day. The most spectacular station was St Pancras (1865) with a span of 74 metres (243 feet), the largest in the world until the Paris Exhibition of 1889. It served as a model for Grand Central Station, New York, built 1869-71.

Astonishing though these sheds were, brutal structural gymnastics and vast scale alone was not considered aesthetically suitable to express the spirit of the railway age. Hence all the great London termini were provided with façades commissioned from famous architects. Gilbert Scott's St Pancras hotel, the hotel at Paddington and the extraordinary triumphal arch at Euston, both designed by Hardwick, or the mock Tudor of Bristol Temple Meads, show the stylistic confusion of Victorian architects confronted with a completely new building type.

span, 21 metres (70 feet) was daringly wide for its time (1840). The royal palm houses at Kew (London), Dublin and Belfast were constructed during the 1840s. These great glass 'bubbles' were among the most exotic constructions of their day, and so it is not surprising that Paxton was given the commission of providing the building for the most celebrated event in the Victorian era, the Great Exhibition of 1851.

A masterpiece of cast-iron design, the Crystal Palace brought to a head the raging controversy between modern engineering and its use of iron, and the architectural establishment, still looking over its shoulder at the monumental masonry of historic styles. Paxton's design was made up from pre-fabricated components that were manufactured all over England and brought to the site for assembly, a phenomenal feat of organization and coordination. A critical factor in the dimensioning of the system was the limited size of glass window pane available at the time (the furnace used to make the glass is still in use today). The detailed design of the small prefabricated components and their linking system was far ahead of its time: it represented an entirely new conception of

building technology that symbolized the potential of industrial civilization, the architectural equivalent of Hargreaves' spinning Jenny, James Watts' steam engine, or the striking paintings of John Turner.

The astonishing success of the 1851 Exhibition spawned many following exhibitions in Paris, Vienna, New York and Philadelphia, and each was used as a testing ground for structural innovation. Architecturally, the most important was the Paris Exhibition of 1889 which included two remarkable structures—the Machine Hall (now destroyed) and the Eiffel Tower. The Machine Hall had a span of 115 metres (380 feet), the widest attempted until this moment, made up from 20 enormous steel lattice trusses hinged both at the apex of the arch and where they met the

Above: The middle of the 19th century was the heyday of the great train sheds—the vast steel and iron cathedrals of the age of steam power. Shown here is the main hall of Paddington Station, London.

ground. This was an entirely novel conception—there being no distinction between load and support, column and beam or arch, as in all previous styles of architecture. The last vestiges of the antique column (still present in the Crystal Palace) had finally disappeared.

The use of steel lightened the structure beyond that what had been possible with cast-iron—the whole framework with its light glass skin seemed to float effortlessly above its foundations. At last, nearly 100 years after the appearance of the first metal structures, a vaulting system that truly matched the material had been discovered.

Right: The Machine Hall which featured in the Paris Exhibition. This remarkable building marked the final elimination of styles. Steel and glass were the sole materials used. Sadly, this masterpiece of structural design was destroyed.

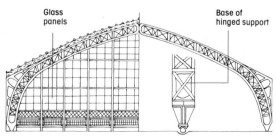

Glass panels

Base of hinged support

A Style without Roots
The Early American Experience

Architectural Importance:
Only in recent years have Americans themselves come to fully respect their architectural heritage. The world's largest capitalist economy has progressed through continual renewal and replacement; many fine monuments in American architectural history are recorded only in dusty photographs, having fallen victim to the bulldozers. American 17th and 18th century architecture is derivative yet unique: English Georgian architecture provided a set of rules which were interpreted according to the inclination and skill of the builder.

The relationship between American man and American land is crucial to the understanding of American architecture. European colonists emigrated to North America to conquer nature, not to admire it or be subdued by it. In spite of great hardship, and against all odds the early settlers fought to tame that wild and spectacular landscape in order to make an honest living for themselves and to build comfortable homes for their families. It was a search for universal freedom and self-realization through tireless struggle and constant hard work.

Before the Revolution, there were no trained professional architects. The first 'colonial' architecture was the work of enthusiastic amateur designers and carpenters, who borrowed designs either from architectural handbooks written by European masters such as Palladio and James Gibbs, or from popular building manuals containing detailed drawings

Stylistic Essentials:
Early colonial: according to the native origin of immigrants, the English built in half timber Elizabethan or Jacobean style. The Dutch brought over their picturesque curved gables. The Swedes perfected the log cabin. The French brought intricate wrought iron work, and a method of house building using closely spaced vertical studs filled in with stucco.

American Georgian: contrasting red brickwork with white trimmings. Rectangular boxlike forms regularly punched with window openings, usually five per storey: elaborately modelled doorways.

Primary Building Materials:
Timber was the first building material and it continued to be used throughout America. Dull jointed or morticed frames were erected from hand sawn hardwood clad with timber boarding using shingles on the roof. Later, when lime was manufactured, it became possible to build in brick, the preferred material for the more prosperous houses.

of windows, doorways, fireplaces or carved staircases.

English architecture was the dominant aesthetic influence during the 18th century, not merely because of English rule but also because the 'Georgian' style suited the needs and aspirations of the time. English Georgian was evolved from the designs of the Italian architect Palladio by Sir Christopher Wren, Sir John Vanbrugh, Nicholas Hawksmoor and James Gibbs. Translated from the stone Georgian façades of London to the naive but enthusiastic carpentry of New England, it produced a sober, restrained, modest yet comfortable and functional architecture. 'American Georgian' was the domestic style in Virginia, Philadelphia, Carolina, Massachusetts and New Hampshire—as the frontier moved West, the style went with it, adapting (though not always satisfactorily) as necessary to the wide variations in landscape and climate on the way.

Today the most famous and spectacular examples of colonial Georgian have been meticulously restored in the historic town of Williamsburg, although some might say that this popularization of history itself has obscured the original scale and way of life.

When the Revolution arrived, the young nation needed an architecture that matched the new spirit of independence. In this 'Age of Reason', Roman and Greek philosophy and democracy provided the inspiration: Neo-Classical styles were enthusiastically studied by gentlemen architects such as Jefferson and Bulfinch, and imported from Europe by a new generation of immigrant professional architects. Although a 'Revivalist' style Neo-Classical architecture was not necessarily backward or romantically escapist, since the past was considered to offer solutions to the problems of the present and future. Despite the aesthetic references to historical analogues, Neo-Classical

Above: A timber-clad house at Sturbridge, Massachusetts. It is an example of the restrained, modest styling of the early American Georgian of the 18th century.

architects built new buildings for a modern world—the first banks, prisons, factories and railroad stations. They often experimented with modern materials and used all their ingenuity to solve practical problems of sanitation services and environmental comfort.

The Virtue of Simplicity

In the early days, European settlers in North America erected unpretentious, functional buildings—there was no conquered culture to impress with the architecture of victory or religious supremacy, nor were there any extravagant emperors or kings requiring imperial palaces. The settlers were simple, hardworking folk who had emigrated in order to build a new life in a new world. Some craved for freedom to practice the religion of their choice, some longed to escape the poverty and repression of their class-ridden motherland.

Jamestown, Virginia, was the first English settlement, founded in 1607. The pilgrim fathers arrived in their ship the 'Mayflower' some

13 years later, and founded Plymouth, Massachusetts. Manhattan Island was taken by the Dutch in 1626 who called it New Amsterdam until 1664, when the English renamed it New York. A Swedish colony was built on the Delaware River during the 1640s and the English Quaker William Penn founded Pennsylvania in 1682. The French explored the Mississippi Valley in the South, founding cities such as Mobil (1702), New Orleans (1718) and St. Louis (1764).

As many of the colonists were craftsmen, each national group brought over from Europe its own architectural styles. English settlers built timber-frame houses in the Elizabethan and Jacobean manner. The Swedes built log cabins, the Dutch copied the picturesque gables of Amsterdam, using wood or brick if available.

At the beginning of the 18th century, the frontier of colonization was moving inexorably Westwards, taking the more adventurous and less prosperous with it. The economy of the Eastern seaboard expanded rapidly, and by 1700 Philadelphia could boast it was the largest city in the British Empire, excluding London. Surplus wealth was now

Above: The House of the Seven Gables, in Salem; an early timber-boarded house in the Tudor-Jacobean style, with typical projecting upper storey.

available for the purchase of arts, crafts and architecture. The style reflecting this was 'American Georgian', a direct acknowledgement of its English parentage.

The first shots of the War of Independence were fired in 1775. It lasted until 1783, and the resultant political euphoria of the peace was accompanied by rapid economic expansion, the great drive westward, and increased immigration which followed the mounting unrest then breaking out in Europe. Now everything had to be 'American' to celebrate the birth of this new nation and establish its own culture. For their architecture, American leaders chose Neo-Classicism, inspired by the city-states of Ancient Greece and the Republic of Rome. The ideals enshrined in the Declaration of Independence, representative government, enlightened self-interest, and liberty itself were symbolized by the adoption of the architectural language and styles of antiquity.

Rude beginnings

In New England, the first form of shelter used by the early settlers was called the 'cellar', a pit cut into a suitable earth bank, lined with stakes or rubble and roofed with logs or thatch. Once established, the colonists built more permanent cottages using timber, the most abundantly available building material. These dwellings were derived from the Yeoman homes of England—in particular those of East Anglia, the origin of many of the settlers.

One of the earliest surviving farmhouses in North America is the Wipple House, Ipswich, Massachusetts, built in 1639. The construction follows the Medieval European tradition of carpentry, with heavy beams intricately

THE AGE OF CONSTRUCTION

Smith-Painter House

Governor's Palace Williamsburg

Monticello Virginia

Philadelphia Merchants' Exchange

Morrill 'Redwood' House

|1600 |1650 |1700 |1750 |1800 |1850   1900|

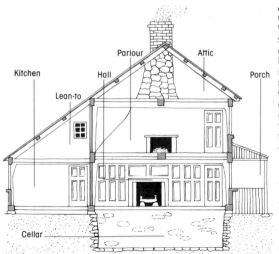

Above: Duke of Gloucester Street, in Williamsburg, the showpiece town of colonial America. Most of the buildings have been meticulously restored, with each house constructed on the actual plot designated for it in the original town plan of the early 1690s.

Left A cut-away illustration of the timber house built by Thomas Painter in 1659. Though not particularly spacious, it was nevertheless very comfortable.

joined to make a rigid frame, clad with 'clapboarding' and roofed with timber shingle. The upper storeys overhang slightly, and the windows are glazed with small diamond panes of glass fixed in lead. (Glass was expensive because it had to be imported.) A large open hearth and brick chimney was the central feature of these houses, and a blazing log fire was the focus of family life. Most early houses were subsequently enlarged, modified or replaced as

the need arose; being made of perishable materials few have survived intact. Brick and stone were used more rarely because of the shortage of lime for mortar.

Further south, in Virginia and Maryland, the more well-to-do settlers built their 'plantation' houses on a grander scale. 'Bacon's Castle', Surrey County, Virginia is a brick manor house that was made famous by its use as the insurgents' headquarters during Bacon's rebellion. Built during

the 1650s, it is the largest of the 17th century plantation houses to survive and one of the landmarks of colonial architecture. The high brick chimneys and curved Flemish gables have a distinctly Jacobean character, an exuberant expression of their owners' new-found confidence and prosperity.

American Georgian

With an economy growing stronger year by year, those with surplus wealth felt a powerful need to display their prosperity. It seemed natural to choose architecture. Likewise, the new institutions of government, religion, justice and education needed buildings of suitable pomp and grandeur. The style chosen was taken from books, originally published in London, but later adapted by Americans into practical builders' manuals and used by carpenters up and down the colonies. Palladio's *Four Books on Architecture* and William Kent's *Palladio Londinensis* provided inspiration for the amateur 'gentlemen architects' who set the pace, while the detailed practical problems of building in the Georgian style were explained to craftsmen in

such popular handbooks as James Gibb's *A Book of Architecture*. Gibb's book was essentially a pattern book: local carpenters would take a detail or two and apply them as it took their fancy. These free and often naive interpretations of the restrained Baroque style evolved by such English architects as Wren, Vanbrugh and Hawksmoor contribute to the great charm and character of American Georgian.

The first American Georgian buildings were public institutions, such as the College of William and Mary, the Capitol and the Governor's Palace in Williamsburg. All were destroyed, but have been carefully rebuilt this century as authentic reconstructions. Williamsburg was the planters' capital, the metropolitan focus of a society whose political and economic prestige depended primarily on the cultivation of tobacco. In 1699 Williamsburg replaced Jamestown as the capital of Virginia. The population remained small, for it was essentially a market town that only came to life twice a year when the legislature met and people from all over Virginia packed out the town for a crowded calendar of varied social events.

A Style without Roots

William and Mary College was founded in 1693, 57 years after Harvard. The site was determined by Governor Francis Nicholson who conceived the first town plan. A wide esplanade was terminated at one end by the college, and the other by the capitol. The width of this boulevard was 27 metres (90 feet), the same width as the streets in Sir Christopher Wren's proposals for the rebuilding of London after the Great Fire. Tradition has it that Wren himself had a hand in the design of the college, in his capacity as Surveyor of the King's Works, but nowadays this curious theory is largely discounted. The college and the Capitol are formal and dignified with a noticeable restraint in applied decoration. Built of brick, the windows and doorways are larger and more numerous than would be the case in England, perhaps made necessary because of the heat of Virginian summers.

Domestic houses in Williamsburg were built on fixed plots laid out in the original town plan. The architecture was modest, practical and above all comfortable: it also lacked ornament or external extravagance. Timber frame was used for most of the houses, clad with white painted boarding. Large, prominent brick chimneys provided wide open hearths for the principal rooms.

Influential landowners who grew rich from the profits of large plantations worked by slaves built themselves generous mansions in the Georgian style. Inspiration came from the plates of villas found in architectural manuals. The designs were rigorously symmetrical, with a strongly-emphasized central doorway richly decorated with pilasters, scrolls and pediments. Formal rooms had elaborate wood panelling and stairways were adorned with intricately turned bannisters. Brick and stone had indeed become symbols of affluence.

A fine example of this type of building is Westover, in Charles County, Virginia. A three-storeyed central block is flanked by two-storey wings containing servants' quarters and the plantation office, beautifully sited in a magnificent park. The central roof is steeply pitched, with tall pronounced chimney. Red brick contrasts with the white decorative trimmings in the classic Georgian manner. Westover was built for William Byrd III, a wealthy plantation owner who had been educated in London and was an influential figure in the public affairs of Virginia. He employed a self-taught and gifted amateur designer named Richard Taliaferro, who is perhaps North America's first named architect. The house is entirely English in both conception and detail—several items such as the wrought iron and ceiling mouldings are thought to have been imported from across the Atlantic.

Georgian styling appealed to 18th century Americans because it was dignified and restrained and yet flexible in application. The system could be applied in a wide range of climates to large, medium or small scale buildings, be they private houses, churches or public institutions. Legendary buildings such as Independence Hall, Philadelphia, derive their well-proportioned, balanced composition from the innate harmony and repose of the Georgian style.

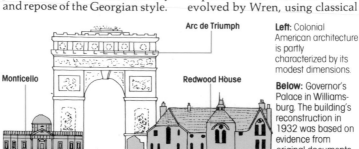

Monticello | Arc de Triumph | Redwood House

Religious persecution was a major reason for the emigration of many of the early settlers, and so church building was an important part of colonial architecture. Most of the Protestant denominations in the 18th century used the Anglican church form with a long narrow nave, a tower or spire at the front end rising above a porch. This was the model evolved by Wren, using classical orders in columns and pilasters, ornate cornices and carved balustrades. All roofs were made of timber, since there were no craftsmen capable of complex stone vaulting. In order to give the illusion of a vaulted roof, the builders used a false ceiling formed with plaster to imitate stone. Carpentry allows more slender and lighter detailing than stone masonry, thus much of the ornament that inspired by Wren's stone churches in England appears in America in a more spidery and delicate form when imitated and executed in wood.

The first American Georgian church was Bruton Parish Church, Williamsburg supposed to have been designed by the English governor, Alexander Spotswood in 1711-1715. A simple brick structure with a cruciform plan,

Left: Colonial American architecture is partly characterized by its modest dimensions.

Below: Governor's Palace in Williamsburg. The building's reconstruction in 1932 was based on evidence from original documents.

its square tower was added later in 1769. A more spectacular church is St. Michael's, Charleston, South Carolina, built in 1752-61. The finest Georgian church of the Southern states, it has a classical columned entrance portico and a four-tiered tower made of diminishing octagons, very much like the church of St. Martin's-in-the-Fields, London, by James Gibbs. The tower is wooden but the rest of the church is made of stucco covered brickwork. The most elaborate Georgian church is St. Paul's Chapel, New York, built out of Manhattan stone by an architect who had studied in England. The full richness of Baroque splendour is realized both inside and out, with all its subtle transitions and graduated geometrical complexity.

Post Revolutionary

The War of Independence and the subsequent political uncertainty interrupted building activity for over a decade. When construction resumed, a new sense of destiny was promoted by political leaders, artists and architects. A need was sensed for an architecture which would reflect the utopian aims of the Declaration of Independence. Although taste in New England was English orientated, elsewhere designers looked to Europe, searching for the root sources of classicism via Palladio right back to Roman and then finally to Greek architecture.

The Adam brothers, Robert and James, dominated architectural taste in late 18th century England. The decorative themes in vogue were popularized by the rediscovery of Pompeii and Herculaneum. Robert Adam took the delicate, small-scale decorative motifs of late Roman art and applied them to basic Georgian

forms, producing a clean-out, hard edged, purist style with low relief modelling and sparce decoration. The Adam style came to New England via handbooks, as an extension of Georgian architecture. The main exponents were Samuel McIntyre and Charles Bulfinch, the former a wood carver, the latter a 'gentleman architect' of considerable talent. Bulfinch came to be the leading character in New England architecture: he was a prolific builder who was responsible for much of the development of Old Boston and was later appointed architect for the final stage of the Capitol in Washington.

Adamesque houses were often less rigidly planned than Georgian, with circular, octagonal or elliptical rooms, with curvy ceilings or even a dome. Bulfinch built many houses in the new style, but he is remembered more for his public buildings, such as the First Church of Christ, Lancaster, Massachusetts, or State House,

Above: Drayton Hall, Charleston, built in 1738 and a fine example of a large Southern plantation house; solidly built of red brick and with a classical portico.

Boston. The Church is a brilliant combination of delicate detail and bold, simple forms. Built in 1816, it has been remarkably well preserved.

Thomas Jefferson was the most important champion of Neo-Classical architecture in the late 17th century and early 18th century. Born in Virginia, Jefferson is often called a product of the Age of Reason; he was a gentleman painter, statesman, classical scholar, architect and inventor. He admired Palladio as a rational, practical architect, and found in classical architecture a symbolic expression of liberty, freedom and the other virtues promoted by the leaders of the newly independent America. Monticello, the house that he built for himself on his Virginian estate is a clear departure from the Georgian style, a study in austere classicism deeply

indebted to Palladio. All the houses he had a hand in designing have a combination of stately restraint and rational utility: the state capital of Virginia, in Richmond, and the University of Virginia at Charlottesville are his most famous designs, the Capitol being directly inspired by the Roman Temple Maison Carrée, at Nimes, France. The University has a uniquely idealistic and formal layout—ten faculties, each with its own facilities linked by dormitory blocks, arranged either side of a green 'campus' or open space with communal buildings at either end. The inspiration came first hand from Roman sources such as the Pantheon.

Washington DC, the capital of the newly formed United States, was laid out in grandiose style by the emigrant Frenchman, Pierre Charles L'Enfant. He created the first 'American' order, combining Greek Doric details with symbolic American themes such as the stars and stripes, the eagle and the olive branch. The plan of Washington was partly borrowed from that of Versailles. Jefferson supervised a national competition for the two principal buildings, the Capitol and the President's House. The original design for the Capitol belonged to William Thornton, another passionate amateur architect. A similar design was produced by Stephen Hallet. Both were appointed to build the monument, but when squabbling broke out Jefferson called in Benjamin Latrobe, a skillful and professional architect to supervise construction. In 1812 the building was fire damaged by the British, and Latrobe was commissioned to remodel and extend the original. The present form of the Capitol is dominated by the great central dome, added by Thomas Walters in 1851.

The North American continent has every conceivable raw material used for the building industry, but it took some time to exploit many of them to the full. The unlimited supplies of both hard and soft wood available everywhere on the Eastern seaboard provided the primary building material for the first settlers. Later, the use of machinery to mass produce nails and standardized sawn timber sections contributed to the invention of the 'balloon frame', a system of lightweight, nailed timber framing that was responsible for much of the rapid urban growth of housing in the 19th century. It took time for the establishment of brick production and lime manufacture, but when available, brick building became a symbol of prosperity and permanence. With the coming of railways and canal transport, the excellent building stone available was more widely exploited.

Left: The Capitol, Washington DC, the result of the collaboration of several architects. Thomas Jefferson supervised the competition for the original design, which was won by William Thornton.

Toying with Old Ideas
Architectural Revivalism

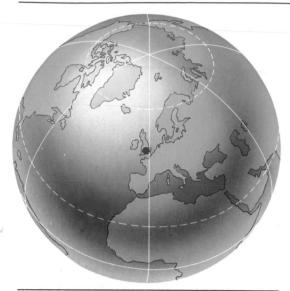

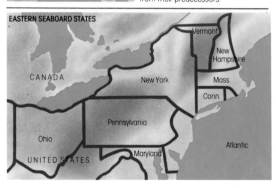

Architectural Importance:
While the classical revival and Palladianism began with archaeologically correct norms that were to be followed, the Gothic (and the chinois, hindoo and Egyptian) was initially playful, later earnest. Either way revivalism is indicative of a desire or need to return to fundamentals as age after age demonstrates. And it may be regarded as a sort of humility — the periods when architecture has been at its worst are those when architects have arrogantly declined to learn from their predecessors.

James Stuart was born in 1713; Alexander Thomson in 1815. Both men were Scots, Stuart was known as 'Athenian' and Thomson as 'Greek'—which should impart some idea of the sort of architects they were. They were chronologically at either end of one branch of the movement which dominated European architecture from the mid-18th century till the late 19th. This movement—the word implies a common purpose which was quite obviously lacking—had its roots in the academic reaction to the Baroque and its relations. Indeed, despite Versailles, the Baroque was almost stillborn in France, and in England, fashion, in the person of Lord Burlington, decreed that Palladio was to be strenuously followed; Paris, under Louis XIV, having become the most artistically influential city in Europe, its example was soon felt in Italy, too.

The history of architecture since the Renaissance can be represented as a series of

the skeletal framing for buildings, thus enabling walls to be something other than load bearing. Industrialization also hastened the advent of prefabricated components which in turn put paid to distinct regional styles.

Stylistic Essentials:
The split is between those buildings which seek to be correct (an impossibility) and those which use archetypes as springboards to something novel. In the 19th century a dubious equation between theological rectitude and Gothic architecture was made; and 'the battle of the styles' was as much about belief in this equation as about sheer form.

Primary Building Materials:
During the 19th century huge leaps in building technology were made. Iron, previously employed for architectural engineering purposes, was used as

Spread of Influence:
Such a salad of styles was current during the period that it is often difficult to say what started where.

recurrent cycles—each of which comprises a period of whimsy or playfulness, a period when there is fairly diligent adherence to some ideal or theoretically determined norm, followed by a period during which the tenets of the ideal are questioned but not discounted, followed by another during which the initial style is but a springboard for individual expression. The last of these periods is potentially the most interesting, but how well the springboard is used depends on the acumen of the diver. Such cycles overlap, are of varying duration from country to country and invariably run in tandem with others. Only in the initial period is a style 'pure', i.e. unafflicted by its begetter's knowledge of a world that contains buildings of countless different sorts.

What is remarkable about the period spanned by the careers of Stuart and Thomson is not the sheer number of former styles that were exhumed, nor the 'correctness' of their realization, but the improvisational exuberance of the greater artists. What this means is that many of the more remarkable achievements are not those which usually attract the attention of the authors of books of this sort. It is especially tempting to point to so and so as the first to discover such and such a detail in, say, Albi Cathedral and to use it in 1855 before what's-his-name; such an approach tends to turn the business of architecture into a practical branch of archaeology or, worse, into a rather recondite competition—this competition is actually a figment of the historian mentality which ascribes to long dead architects its own qualities; all probably very harmless and understandable. For did not these long dead architects themselves ascribe to their predecessors qualities which, had they thought on it, no human could ever possess? Not the least interesting facet of the Age of Revivals is the implicit conviction

that once, long ago, and in Greece or maybe Rome and if not Rome then Flanders during the Middle Ages or Florence during the early Renaissance, there had existed a 'golden age.' That the site of this nostalgically inspired mirage should have moved so often is tantamount to an admission on the part of those who could see it that, yes, it was just a mirage, an ephemera—which is no doubt a sign that retrospective utopianism is healthier than that which posits the ideal world just around the next corner.

This looking backwards was, of course, not only expressed in architecture but also in literature and painting, and it must be understood that even the classical buildings of the time were romantically conceived. Athenian Stuart's famous Doric pavilion at Hagley, in Worcestershire, and his works at Shugborough in Staffordshire were elegant follies. And Leopold von Klenze's marvellous Walhalla on a knoll above the Danube near Regensburg, while as true to its Greek model as Stuart's structures, is conceived of as being a perfect object in a 'natural' setting. These buildings were at least archaeologically accurate even if their sites, their functions and the way they are thus stripped of the associations for which they were, paradoxically, valued render them peculiarly un-Greek. The other styles fashionable in the late 18th century were revived with a cavalier disregard for accuracy and, naturally, for 'suitability' or fitness for purpose. The gothick, hindoo and chinois styles were props of the picturesque and so were the pseudo-rustic whimsies of which the late Marie Antoinette was so peculiarly fond.

Gothic Revival

Gothic had never entirely disappeared in England and enjoyed a minor revival with Hawksmoor at All Soul's, Oxford and at Westminster Abbey, and with Vanbrugh at Greenwich, where

he built for himself a house of a stagey, Medieval character. Even Vanbrugh's palaces, for all their classical components, look a bit like fortresses. But gothick as such did not, however, gain wide acceptance till 50 or so years after Vanbrugh's death and by then, although it was allied to ideas of the picturesque derived from him, it had become an altogether lighter, more frivolous affair. It gained a following among aesthetes and wasters and was an ideal style for eye-catchers and pieces of scenery and lodges, such as that which John Carter built outside Bath and which goes under the grand name of Midford Castle. These buildings are among the most delightful in Britain; it has been rather solemnly suggested that they owe their existence to the inability of their authors to accurately reproduce 'genuine' Gothic. Such opinions are wide of the mark—if men could copy Greek temples, which being Greek were not readily available in England, they could surely have copied Medieval churches, of which there were more than a few. It is, on the contrary, their freedom from precedent and the patent invention they display that marks them as so special.

The same might be said for the

Below: Von Klenze's Walhalla, built to commemorate Germany's heroes is modelled on the Parthenon. However its dramatic romanticism lend it qualities which are singularly un-Greek.

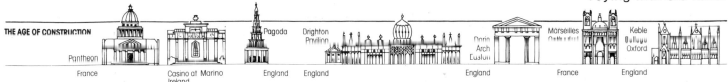

THE AGE OF CONSTRUCTION

Pantheon
France

Casino at Marino
Ireland

Pagoda
England

Brighton
Pavilion
England

Doric
Arch
Euston
England

Marseilles
Cathedral
France

Keble
College
Oxford
England

1725　1750　1775　1800　1825　1850　1875

comparatively few chinois and hindoo buildings of the period, though the best known example of the former, Sir William Chambers's pagoda in Kew Gardens, is as heavy as his Somerset House on the Strand. What is called hindoo is not hindoo, is not even modelled at second or fifth hand on such a thing; it does owe something to the Mogul architecture of the 16th and 17th centuries, though it owes far more to the invention of the few who worked on it—Samuel Cockerell and John Nash were the best and the shock of coming upon Nash's Brighton Pavilion or, less easily achieved, Cockerell's Sezincote in the Cotswolds is a most pleasurable one.

It might be said that these geographically-dislocated borrowed styles are not strictly revivals even though they were roughly based on the example of a foreign *past*. They were interpretations, versions, variations

Below: Brighton Pavilion is perhaps the most famous 'Oriental' building in Europe. John Nash did not, though, attempt to reproduce one particular building and shunned consistency.

and, in the hands of artists of a 'visionary' nature, the original object of inspiration all but disappears. C-N Ledoux's work (mostly in Paris and eastern France, mostly destroyed) became increasingly austere and monolithic, ever less reliant on Greek precedent till his later projects (which were never built) resemble nothing so much as the tough expressionism of the early 20th century. One of these projects, a Memorial to the Honour of Women, is a rare instance of a French borrowing from the Orient—at each corner is a lanterned column of a vaguely Mogul sort. This rarity of essays in styles other than classical outside England is explicable more in terms of the picturesque's lack of wide popularity on mainland Europe till the 19th century, rather than, by crudely pointing with a socio-cultural finger, to Britain's growing empire and her subjects' consequent knowledge of exotic piles. It is worth noting though that, even after the fall from favour of the picturesque in Britain, architects in that country continued to seek inspiration in foreign models whereas elsewhere, with

the understandable exception of the United States, earnest revivalism tended to be nationalistic, i.e. France rummaged through the cupboard of its own past styles and Germany did likewise.

Designing Buildings from Books

The spread of the picturesque in Britain was partly achieved by

Left: Sanderson Miller's Lacock Abbey, Wiltshire, was an influential work in the Gothic manner. This window shows that theatrical effect was what counted – not historical accuracy.

pattern books. Architecture and landscape gardening were at this period fashionable pursuits and these books with their illustrated suggestions for improvements, their plans for cottages ornés, their lodges in the Nile style and so on were as often the work of gentlemen such as Sir Uvedale Price and the famous pornographer, Richard Payne Knight, as they were of architects and gardeners like J.B. Papworth (one of the creators of Cheltenham) and Humphrey Repton who was a sometime partner of John Nash.

Nash was *the* architect of the Regency and the pretty, white, stucco villas and terraces that grace countless spas and seaside resorts gained a sort of airy perfection in his hands. Nash's genius was for the creation of a harmony between buildings and the parks in which they were sited; in this way he rivalled Vanbrugh though his buildings were by no means so original. He

Toying with Old Ideas

would turn his hand to any style that was required, was devoted to his master, the Regent, and was interestingly unorthodox in his business dealings. He was London's greatest architect since Wren and it is to the eternal shame of that city that his Regent Street was torn down—though what replaced it is by no means as awful as its detractors would have you believe.

From about the turn of the 19th century the revived Gothic style in Britain began to show a greater wealth of detail, if not precisely a greater accuracy, and by the 1830s, the prototypical Victorian Gothic had been born. It was a harsh style which was wilfully assymetric in its application—a hangover from the picturesque rather than a feature of archaeological authenticity for symmetry abounds in the buildings of the Middle Ages. Witness the façades of most of Europe's great cathedrals. England was at the van of the trend towards 'correct' Gothic though France, the United States and parts of Germany lagged not far behind. (In fact one of the very few neo-Gothic churches which might be taken for the master blueprint is in Paris, Gau's St. Clotilde.)

Nearly all 19th century work in any of the revived Gothic styles is unmistakably of that century though it must be said that many genuine works of Gothic appear to be, unmistakably, of the 19th century. In what might be fancifully interpreted as an act of collective revenge numerous Victorian architects unable to bring off precise reproductions of the Gothic decided to amend it to look like a reproduction of itself. The reaction to this mania for enthusiastic 'restoration' prompted the foundation of the Society for the Protection of Ancient Buildings; the restorers have for too long been handy whipping boys. Much of their work was unexceptionable, some of it excellent if not entirely sympathetic to the original structures. It should be remembered that all buildings past a certain age are in a way copies of themselves in that their fabric has been replaced down the years, and that to be too hasty in condemnation of the Victorian restorers is to refuse to recognize that buildings are not finite objects, but ones which are bound to undergo perpetual repair and sometimes drastic alteration.

Gothic Revival Spreads to Europe

In Europe and America the use of Gothic was almost entirely confined to the building of churches. In England it became the style of schools, asyla, railway stations, municipal offices, museums etc. It is seen at its best in country houses of a sort which, needless to say, had no precedent in the Middle Ages. Of all the architects in Britain who practised during the middle of the 19th century none perhaps created with the zest and perverse exuberance of

Below: Marseilles Cathedral, the Euston Arch and Trinity Church, New York, drawn to scale with the Arc de Triumph.

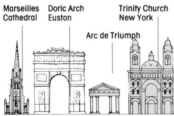

Marseilles Cathedral | Doric Arch Euston | Trinity Church New York

Arc de Triumph

Below: The High Victorian fondness for French detail is clearly shown in Clutton's Minley Manor, Hampshire, where the lessons of Blois and countless other chateaux are (mis) applied.

S.S. Teulon, a gentleman of French extraction whose Elvetham Hall in Hampshire is at once nightmarish and funny and singularly impressive—it is nowadays a conference centre, a use of a kind (others are schools and borstals) to which these great piles have proved most adaptable. Only a short distance from Elvetham is another great house of the late 1850s, Minley Manor (now owned by the army) which is also illustrative of the wild invention of those architects who, if you like, took the law into their own hands. Both show a marked French influence and we must return here to another man of French extraction, A W N Pugin.

He was a Catholic convert, a prodigy and a fanatic. His hatred of classical architecture erred on the far side of pathological; he considered Nash's buildings 'a national disgrace', he hoped to see St. Peter's 'rebuilt in a better style', and so on and on. Gothic he reckoned—and considering the origins of that style it is a dubious assumption—was the only true Christian architecture; buildings of any other sort were pagan, immoral. Henceforth architecture was to be judged not only by aesthetic standards but by moral ones too—the criteria of beauty and elegance were no longer

Below: Alexander Thomson was among the last great architects of the classical revival. St Vincent's, Glasgow was one of several churches which he built in that city in the mid-19th century. It remains a classic example of its style.

enough. In this way Pugin was the first modern architect, the first to justify his work by extra-architectural standards. He died fairly young and quite mad; his buildings however were nowhere near as straightlaced as his theories.

John Ruskin also died mad. He was the most influential writer on art and architecture of the mid-19th century and many of his ideas are rather dubious though seductive. Like Pugin he loathed classical forms: 'it is the moral nature of it which is corrupt'. Both of these men seemed to think that good architecture, indeed good art of any sort, could only be achieved by good men!

In England Pugin's followers evolved a bullying polychromatic style which is especially notable for its inability to age gracefully. Had this sort of building been more widely taken up England would be almost entirely striped; as it was numerous architects gave nothing for such affectation and various sorts of classicism were prevalent well on into Victoria's reign. Greek Thomson's churches and tenements and warehouses in Glasgow are especially notable and were to have an

Left: Viollet-le-Duc's Château of Pierrefonds is a 'restoration' which turned into virtually a new building – a fantasy of the Middle Ages, which gives little indication of its original qualities.

influence on Charles Rennie Mackintosh at the end of the century. Thomson was far freer in his use of Greek, and sometimes Egyptian, motifs than had been Athenian Stuart. Scotland as a whole was, like most of Europe, fairly resistant to Gothic—indeed the further north one gets in England the more apparent is such resistance. As late as 1858 Leeds got a magnificent town hall by Cuthbert

Brodrick (who was to give up architecture and migrate to Paris to become a painter and be forgotten) in a monumental Baroque style. Perhaps one should say as early as 1858, since 30 or so years on the Baroque's turn as flavour of the era was to come.

Wild Fantasies

A quality which is perhaps best called Disneyesque is discernible in some of the more grandiose fantasies of the second half of the 19th century. E-E Viollet-le-Duc was, like Pugin, a writer and scholar of some distinction. He was also the man who restored such Medieval French walled towns as Avignon and Carcassonne, and succeeded in making them look as if they had been built of cardboard. There is no deliberate theatricality here; quite the contrary, it is rather akin to a very bad naturalistic performance by an actor than a self-consciously hammy one. His original buildings too have a charmless quality: the Chateau de Pierrefonds doesn't

take one in for a moment which wouldn't matter save for the fact that one knows that it is intended to. Mad Ludwig's Bavarian castles do at least have an authentic inauthenticity about them as do the creations of William Burges for the Marquess of Bute, Cardiff Castle and Castell Coch, Glamorganshire—the latter being one of the most romantic manifestations of Victorian medievalism.

By the 1870s even in England the Gothic had become slightly jaded. France, besides never having been much interested in it, was working its way forward from its own early Renaissance and, by the 1870s, was doing a fussy neo Baroque whose ultimate example was Charles Girault's Petit Palais for the Paris International Exhibition of 1900. What happened in England during the last quarter of the 19th century does not really parallel the rest of Europe, though there is some kinship with the United States. There was nothing very remarkable in the 1870s in England about pseudo Elizabethan houses—they might have been thought to have had their day about 20 years earlier but they were not unknown. However, at St. Alban's Court, Nonington, in Kent, an architect called George Devey constructed a house that looked as if it had been patched up, added on to—just like countless genuine Elizabethan palaces. He had done the same elsewhere in the same county, notably at Betteshanger, but here the fakery is more extreme. The house is intended to look as if it has been rebuilt to the original plan of a ruin—round the bottom of it is stone, above there is brick and the join is ragged. The effect is cosy, suggestive of continuity and antithetical to the conventional sensation fostered by buildings in a revived style which look as though they have been uprooted in time. Building in a grander manner naturally continued but in the work of Devey and his more celebrated and prolific contemporary Norman Shaw were the roots of the sort of building that was to dominate English domestic architecture till the Second World War.

Of the British revivals which continued well on into the 20th century that which produced the flashiest if not the most accomplished stuff was that of the Baroque. In Britain this also went under the name Wrenaissance and among its most typical achievements was A. Brumwell Thomas's Belfast City Hall. To the avant garde of the time it must have appeared a terrible folly—it is now however clear that when architects abandoned the idea of searching the past for models they imposed upon themselves a most grievous handicap.

Left: Cuthbert Brodrick's Leeds Town Hall was a self-conscious exercise in might and pomp, designed to demonstrate the growing self-esteem and confidence of the newly-rich Yorkshire burgh.

Above: Typical of those architects who attempted 'archaeological' accuracy was William Butterfield. This window at Keble College Chapel, Oxford is a close reproduction of an 'early decorated' Gothic window.

Free Form
Inspiration Triumphs

ENGLAND
GERMANY
FRANCE
SPAIN
ITALY

Architectural Importance:
Considerable if often misinterpreted. The best architects of this epoch – as of any other – were great individualists who tended to see themselves working within a 19th century revivalist tradition though obviously preferring to make versions rather than copies. And their best work is among the most extraordinary architecture of all time. It is also perhaps the last architecture that is widely appreciated – for aesthetic rather than utilitarian reasons – by non architects, which is a sure criterion of its worth.

NORTH-EASTERN SPAIN

Lerida

Catalonia

Barcelona.

Mediterranean

Tarragona.

The criterion by which architects of the late 19th and early 20th centuries have been adjudged fit to lodge in the pantheons of numerous recent historians and critics has too often been that of whether they can in some way or another be seen as precursive of the modern movement. Talent has thus been equated with a spare and austere style; architects of the period who lived long enough to see the works of the modernists in the 20s and 30s and to dislike them have, nevertheless, been granted the questionably complimentary title of 'pioneer'; those who eschewed novelty have been ignored or mocked; those who practised what has been called the 'free style' then turned to some more formal kind of design have been treated like blacklegs and with about as much justification. In other words, we have for many years been shown the period in question through the eyes of modern movement propagandists: there is

Below: Gaudi's Casa Battlo in Barcelona is the first work of this remarkable architect's mature style. Though vestiges of Baroque and, oddly, Belgian art nouveau can be discerned the building exhibits the plasticity and waywardness that he was to develop even further at Casa Mila and Sagrada Familia.

however, Art Nouveau exploited the machine and revelled in the decorative possibilities of tiles and wrought iron.

Stylistic Essentials:
Art Nouveau in Belgium, France and Austria drew on the Baroque; the Arts and Crafts in England and the Stick Style in the USA drew on local building traditions and idealized them; Modernismo in Spain drew on Gothic and Moorish traditions. But all of them were catholic, unbound by rules and only concerned with the creation of good building.

Primary Building Materials:
A reaction against industrialization came to a head in England in the late 19th century and a fierce revival of craftwork took place. In France and Belgium,

Spread of Influence:
The Arts and Crafts never got far beyond being an admirable style for domestic architecture. Art Nouveau was also largely confined to houses, though it also found expression in ie furniture.

some irony here, for the modernists after the First World War proclaimed that architecture was to start anew with a clean slate, but at the same time they were desperately searching for precedents. They found some in 19th century utilitarian building and feats of engineering. This is understandable; but they also demeaned the achievement of numerous revivalists whose story we are obliged to take up here.

Such English architects as George Devey and Norman Shaw, Charles Voysey, Edward Prior and Ernest Gimson were artists of some ability, and they can be seen as precursors of a particular tradition of architecture. But this tradition has nothing to do with international modernism; in fact the heirs to this tradition were despised by progressive modernists. Out of the work of these late Victorian and Edwardian architects came the British suburban villa of the first half of the 20th century. Where these architects differ from their immediate predecessors—or at least do so in part of their work—is in the sources of their designs. One can imagine an awful moment in the life of a young domestic architect bent on making his mark in the 1880s when he realized that there was just about nothing left in the cupboard of grand period styles; it must be recalled that certain styles were linked with particular sorts of building. The Byzantine and the Baroque had yet to be rediscovered in a big way, and anyway they would be used but rarely for domestic projects. What numerous architects turned to at this point was the so-called 'vernacular' manner.

A New Influence Is Felt

Vernacular, in this context, means indigenous, peculiar to a particular locality. It was first used to qualify a type of building in the late 1850s and refers to the manner that is, typically, handed down from father to son. It has little to do with 'architect's architecture' and obviously changed very slowly through the years. Elements of it began to enter the architect's repertoire in the late 18th century when it exerted some influence on the picturesque movement—but like the Gothic of those years it was fancifully reproduced. The 19th century had seen a diminution of genuinely vernacular building; with the inception of industrialized building methods and the growing ease of communications it began to disappear. Devon cob, Kentish tiling, the half-timbering of the West Midlands—these and all the countless other types of cottages and small houses had made virtues of necessity; their forms were to some extent governed by available material and by the fact that the men who built them were unfamiliar with other kinds of building, but not totally unfamiliar. Features espied in this or that grand house of the neighbourhood would creep in. The term vernacular revival is an oxymoron; it is self-contradictory—to revive such a thing one would have to

Below: C.F.A. Voysey's tiny studio cottage at Baron's Court, London is already typical of its architect's pervasive and much copied manner—chimney like a buttress, roughcast, small but muscular.

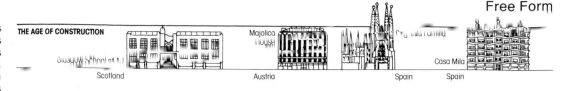

THE AGE OF CONSTRUCTION

Glasgow School of Art
Scotland

Majolica House
Austria

Spain

Casa Mila
Spain

'1890   '1895   '1900   1905'

have as narrow horizons as its original begetter and such horizons cannot be achieved if one has ever seen beyond them. Not that some people didn't try to attain this unattainable state; numerous members of the small self-consciously Medievalist guilds and brotherhoods which comprised the Arts and Crafts movement took themselves off to the country to lead a life and create in conditions appropriate to what they wanted to create—which is, you might think, putting the cart before the horse.

So we have a situation where sophisticated and educated architects (and designers), brought up in socially mobile and scientifically curious Victorian England, are seeking to ape the essentially primitive methods of artisan peasants. It is hardly astonishing then that much of the domestic architecture of the period born out of a variety of beliefs in the virtues of workmen, the virtues of manual endeavour, the virtues of local materials and so on should appear so affected. It is all rather like a musical comedy in which chorus boys are expected to impersonate rude sons of the soil.

The architect who produced the most pretentious houses was undoubtedly Charles Voysey; he was a small man, and there is something dinky rather than delicate about his creations which do, indeed, aspire to a sort of muscularity with their general squatness and 'tough' sloping buttresses—they are extremely *homely*. This sort of coziness is supposed to be the sort of thing that is admired in Germany—*gemutlich*—and among certain English it is a matter of retrospective pride that from 1896-1903 the German embassy in London had an attaché who studied and produced a book on this new domestic architecture. Voysey considered himself a Gothic architect and so did Edward Prior who was less prolific but also less formula ridden—Voysey's houses are only 'vernacular' in their self-effecting humility; they look the same wherever they are and make

Above: Heathcote, Ilkley, Yorkshire was among the earliest of Sir Edwin Lutyens's classical buildings and is, despite its modest size, splendidly massive in a way that recalls Hawksmoor.

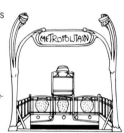

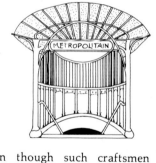

Right: Guimard's celebrated Paris metro entrances, sinuous and decorative.

no attempt to use local materials or methods. Prior's Home Place at Holt in north Norfolk uses an astonishing variety of materials as if in parody of the local tradition of brick and coursed flint—of course it looks nothing like the products of Norfolk craftsmen,

even though such craftsmen actually worked on it as they did on the nearby Happisburgh House by Detmar Blow, who is chiefly remembered for his restorations. Both of these places are built on plans which resemble an X or—if your fancy is so inclined—a butterfly. The Arts and Crafts architects excelled in rural purlieus (to use the fey sort of word they went in for) and the idea of 'country in town' of which Nash and other architects of the picturesque had been fond was one which came naturally to them (as we shall see when we turn to Town Planning.) Only a few of them did much work in cities, and what they did tends to be in a style amended to fit the setting. British cities at the turn of the century must often have looked like vast building sites, so copious was the amount of work then being undertaken. As well as neo-Baroque, which was known as Renaissance for no very good reason, there was neo-

Left: Among Lutyen's most consummate works was Marsh Court, where he combined formality and fancy and a bewildering array of styles in what he chose to call 'the high game'.

Flemish Renaissance (deemed especially suitable for mansion blocks of flats though it was past its prime), neo-Georgian (which was yet to have its day—more on this later), and Beaux Arts classicism. The last was, evidently, French influenced and was rather less grandiose than the frequently coarse Baroque. It was all however rather splendid and fitted well alongside its surroundings. Britain has not seen so much building of fine quality since—Glasgow and the City of London among other places bore witness to this till they were ruined in the 1960s.

Original Style

There remains one British architect who must be noticed here although he will be discussed later, and that is Edwin Lutyens whose work during this period was domestic and wonderfully inspired and unlike anything that was being done then or has been done at any other time. Most of the houses he built were in the south. They are varied in style and their only common quality is that of originality—he mixed elements of all sorts of former periods and in a rather less schematic manner than George Devey, who often made houses that look as if they had been added on to by successive inhabitants. They are though not 'patchy'; in fact the manner in which he succeeded in incorporating self-cancelling elements into one design is often a cause for wonder—sometimes this looks like carelessness, but it is the carelessness of someone with supreme confidence that things

will turn out all right, which they usually do. Of his many houses, perhaps the most startling is a place just south of Stockbridge in Hampshire, called Marsh Court. It is approached by a long and twisting drive from the Test Valley and is sited atop the Downs, from whose chalk it is built; its character changes as one walks round it—here it recalls a Germanic barracks, there the setting for an immensely convoluted detective story of the 'golden age'. It is one of the few places that actually does appear to grow from the ground, and green springy turf stretches to the bottom of its walls. Lutyens's houses of this period have been described as 'dream houses'. This is not to suggest anything so vulgar as the 'Ideal Home' dream house, which is a way of saying that such and such a place is one which people aspire to, wish to possess. What the phrase is intended to connote is, I am sure, that such houses as Marsh Court, Tigbourne Court in Surrey, Folly Farm in Berkshire, look as though they have been conceived in dreams. They have a lucidity and strangeness which borders on the hallucinatory—their appeal is more than aesthetic; like the greatest artists of the

Baroque, Lutyens had the ability to cause those who look at his marvellous creations to feel the jolt of passing through the looking glass. Lutyens has been accused of all sorts of things, from being 'out of touch with his times', whatever that means, to being 'popular,' an apparent contradiction. He was indeed popular, he was indeed out of step with the architecture that began to get a foothold during the second half of his long career; he pursued, and this is a terrible failing in the eyes of modernist critics—an absolutely individualistic course.

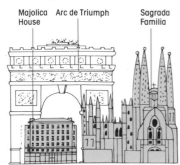

Above: The architectural interest of art nouveau lay in its preoccupation with its bizarre appear- ance. In dimension, it wished to dominate, yet it refrained from taking itself too seriously.

Though he was never seduced by ideas of the 'new man' he was in his energy, variety and richness of invention rather akin to his near contemporary, H.G. Wells— his sleight of hand, limpidity and jolliness are to be found in the author of *Mr. Polly*, *Love and Mr. Lewisham* and *Tono Bungay*; all of which were written during this period. Wells (who actually chose Voysey as his architect when he built a house for himself) bears further comparison with Lutyens in that his reputation is only now beginning to be reconsidered after years of complete neglect by the modernist literary critic industry.

Spanish Inspiration

The other great European architect of the late 19th and early 20th century was the Catalan, Antonio Gaudi, who is sometimes described as an Art Nouveau architect, sometimes as Expressionist— which only goes to show how meaningless such labels can be. Here and there he is undoubtedly indebted to both schools, or at least has affinities with them. The sources of Gaudi's work are—so far as such things can ever be pinned down—peculiarly

Above: Lutyens built Folly Farm, Berkshire in several stages in collaboration with the gardener Gertrude Jekyll who was as much responsible for the renaissance of the English garden as was Lutyens for that of its domestic architecture.

Catalan. He was born at Reus and lived in Barcelona for the greater part of his life. Catalonia was then, as now, seeking independence from the rest of Spain, and there was a strong nationalism abroad. The city was—and again still is—richer than Madrid and was the centre of various mercantile empires, and Gaudi was patronized almost exclusively by nouveau rich textile tycoons.

The sort of archaeologically correct neo-Gothic that had reigned in England and had made some headway in France and Germany was virtually unknown in 19th century Catalonia where neo-Classicism was more prevalent than in the northern countries; the Catalan variant was, typically, fancifully and frequently decorated by painted swags. There was to be sure a Gothic revival of a sort, but it was essentially inventive, and the few churches that are characteristic of it are very spiky indeed; they are also very colourful, encrusted in tiles. The other sources which are (just)

apparent in Gaudi's early work are the Moorish tradition, which again is colourful and that of overwrought ironwork which is tortuous and rather frightening when used to depict Calvaries. It was Gaudi's triumph that he was able to achieve a synthesis of these contrasting elements. His work as a young man was rather ugly: such houses as El Capricho at Comillas or the Archbishop's Palace at Astorga or the Casa Vicens in Barcelona exhibit nothing of the plasticity and fluidity of his later and more justly famous creations. El Capricho has the harshness and fussiness of a Victorian public bath in the Arab style and the poor Archbishop—consigned to live out his term in a pile which looks as if it derives from Viollet le-Duc by way of a lunatic asylum. At about the turn of the century Gaudi's style, which had always been in a state of metamorphosis, made a jolting change which is nowhere better illustrated than in his greatest work, the expiatory temple (*not* cathedral) of the Sagrada Familia in Barcelona. The portals, completed early on, are in a harsh and unattractive Gothic which recalls the Astorga Palace, the pinnacles came later, and they

Above: The spires of Gaudi's Sagrada Familia dominate Barcelona. Even by the standards of that city they are bizarre and are more reminiscent of forms found in nature than of anything 'usually' connected with architecture.

are in a fluid manner that defies description.

Here, and at the Casa Mila and Casa Battlo which are about contemporary with this stage of the temple's construction, can be seen the fruits of Gaudi's study of rocks, trees and any other natural phenomena which caught his eye. Outside Barcelona is a vast dolomitic formation rising from a plain. It is called Montserrat and the beautiful rounded forms of its multitudinous peaks are endlessly reproduced in Gaudi's later work. In the east façade of the Sagrada Familia (the temple is still unfinished and may perhaps forever remain so) one can detect all sorts of organic imagery: leaves, birds, animals, babies (which were cast from bodies in the children's mortuary). And many of the abstract images look like adaptations of vertebrae and pigs' trotters. There are also conches, swags, cornucopias, reptiles, invented beetles, references to Hindu and Mexican carving, and lots of cherubim perched on knobs like

vizored helmets. It is rather like a parody of all other churches, though Gaudi, an obsessively religious man, certainly did not have this in mind. The design might have been achieved by constructing a model in icing sugar and submitting it to both a blow torch and the attentions of a pack of sweet toothed rats. Gaudi who died when he was run over by a trolley bus is buried in his marvellous temple. All Barcelona turned out to mourn him.

The Sagrada Familia is perhaps the single most interesting building of the last 100 years. The products

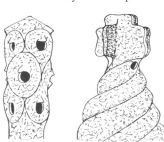

Above: The chimney stacks atop the Casa Mila are typical of Gaudi's preoccupation with anthropomorphic and zoomorphic and geomorphic forms. The heads of birds, even bird masks like those exploited by surrealists – even wind-eaten rocks are all alluded to.

Above: Gaudi's Casa Mila is his most celebrated secular building, an apartment block whose rooms are irregularly shaped and whose appearance again recalls a variety of, strange, non-architectural phenomena.

of French and Belgian Art Nouveau, which are similarly sinuous but terribly limp-wristed beside the work of this master, and of German expressionism and Italian futurism were all however much more interesting than what was to follow them. Gaudi like Lutyens was an artist of genius and his work evokes responses which have nothing to do with a conventional appreciation of architecture—the columns of his church at the Colonia Guell outside Barcelona made one shudder, they are like the bones of a beast from which the flesh had been picked; the chimneys and ventilation stacks on top of the Casa Mila are sculpted in the forms of sinister masked heads and hooded birds.

These sorts of effects were achieved nowhere else in the world. Northern Art Nouveau derived from Rococo decorative devices, among other sources, and its history, despite a few architect-designers who worked at it, unquestionably belongs to that of the applied arts.

International Modernism
Breaking with the Past

Architectural Importance:
Out of all proportion to its achievement. Its leading architects possessed an evangelical zeal and spread the word far and wide, equating their architecture with health, efficiency, progress, the 'new age', technology etc. It became a course as much as a style and was thus taken up by the easily led of all nations. Architects became increasingly concerned with non-architectural matters such as land use upon which they tended to profess an expertize which, largely, they did not readily possess.

A NEW ERA ARRIVES

In a century which has witnessed the regimes and genocidal zeal of Stalin, Mao, Hitler and Pol Pot it would perhaps be hyperbolic to refer to the modern movement in architecture as a tragedy or a disaster. Suffice to say that its consequences have been socially distressing and aesthetically regrettable. The modern movement represented a triumph of propaganda over good sense and was, like the above tyrannies, totalitarian. So many of the claims made for the new architecture were patently spurious that, wise after the event, one can only marvel at its worldwide appeal. One can only marvel, too, at the sheer vacuity of premises upon which these claims were based: chief among them was that man in the 20th century was somehow going to be a fundamentally different creature to his 19th century predecessor. This new man was to be keen on hygiene, physical fitness, nature, etcetera — ideally he would be a vegetarian nudist robot

Spread of Influence: Modernism had its roots in industrial architecture and was developed in Germany and Austria before the 1st World War. It flourished in Germany till its proponents fled Hitler. Numerous refugees found shelter in England and by the end of the 30s that was the only country which had not witnessed a reaction formally to it.

Stylistic Essentials: Decoration was frowned upon. Cubistic shapes were the order of the day, just as white was the colour, irrespective of climate. Horizontally emphasized windows turning round corners were favoured. A puritanical asceticism was evident within. By the late 30s nautical touches and streamlining had become common so that the edifice could make a swift getaway.

Primary Building Materials: Reinforced concrete, steel frames and unprecedented use of prefabricated parts were characteristic as was the use of cantilevered construction.

with a mind as blank as the walls of his undecorated 'advanced' apartment. That such persons were and are few is no doubt the source of modernism's expensive failure, a failure that was compounded by the tiresome unwillingness of old-style mankind to become new style mankind when provided with the appropriate conditions. Modernism was essentially deterministic; it required that architects become social engineers concerned with creating 'new ways to live'—the legacy of this arrogance comprises the systematically vandalized cities of the world which have been reduced to a meagre homogeneity 'reflecting' the machine age, the electric age, the microchip age or whatever. The paradox is all too evident: modernist architects were (and some still are) quite content to dictate to millions of people but were, at the same time, quite willing to be dictated to by machines; rather than master successive technologies they became slaves to them—these technologies were to be allowed to 'express themselves' as if they were people. One of the great catch-phrases of the modern movement was Mies van der Rohe's 'less is more'. The truth of the matter is that, as has been pointed out in recent years, architects in this century have achieved *less with more*. With the most copious and sophisticated technologies the world has known they have created what is possibly some of the worst architecture the world has known.

The Myth of Modernism

The emphasis on allowing technologies (which should merely be means) and materials to reveal themselves in a sort of raw state is irreconcilable with another crucial modernist tenet, that a building should 'express its function'. Function is one of many words (another is rational) which have been appropriated and stripped of their meaning. No building can truly achieve this dubious end. Perhaps a library which looked like a book, or a dairy shaped like a cow (which was designed but not built by the French 18th century architect Lequeu), or a garage in the form of a car would be more expressive in a literal way than anything else that man might conceive. By some crude illogic 'functional' has taken on the sense of plain or undecorated, resembling a factory or abattoir. To a modernist a palace, which though its Baroque grandeur is indicative of its inhabitant's position and magnificence (of which it is part), is not a functional building—King Duane and Queen Sharon would ideally live in a two room high rise flat along with the rest of us.

It is of course possible that populist architecture could actually be popular among those on whom it is foisted, but given the sort of forms that modernism embraced such an occurrence was always improbable. It is surely bordering on the absurd that an architecture of 'the people' should be appreciated only by architects who have expressed their appreciation in ever more incomprehensible jargon. It has taken the best part of half a century for 'laymen' to call the bluff of modernism to the extent that it is now in its death throes. *Less is less.*

The rise of modernism is inextricably linked with that of abstraction in painting; it is hardly surprising that the most influential, most imitated, architect and propagandist of this century, Le Corbusier, should have been a Sunday dauber in the Cubist style. Le Corbusier was not the first to preach the new 'faith', though he undoubtedly preached the loudest; the initiator of the new style was a Viennese architect called Adolf Loos, whose hatred of ornament bordered on the pathological: 'The evolution of culture marches with the elimina-

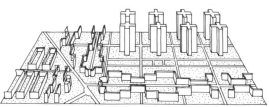

Left: Le Corbusier's inhumane fantasy of a city for 3 million inhabitants was thankfully never realized.

Below: His Villa Savoie at Poissy is raised on stilts: a mannerism aped the world over.

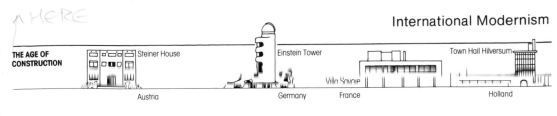
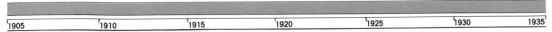

THE AGE OF CONSTRUCTION

Steiner House — Austria
Einstein Tower — Germany
Villa Savoie — France
Town Hall Hilversum — Holland

1905 1910 1915 1920 1925 1930 1935

tion of ornament from useful objects'. Note the use of 'marches' and 'affinisation' Loos's own work was, predictably, plain, cubistic, unadorned and deeply boring; his Steiner House in Vienna, built in 1910, was the model for much 'advanced' domestic stuff of the next 30 years—flat roofed (just the thing for wet northern climes), reliant upon right angles, white. We have shown that houses of this sort are not functional, save in the meaning of that word peculiar to modernists. Nor are they utilitarian: houses are more than warehouses for storing people, nor for that matter are they 'machines for living in'—Le Corbusier's famous dictum is interesting only for what it reveals of its author, who was able to maintain a powerful influence over two generations of sheeplike architects.

Lacking in functional and utilitarian qualities as it was, the new architecture was like all other architecture—simply a style. In their conviction that they had arrived at a perfect form of architecture the modernists deluded themselves and their fellow travellers that they had rendered style irrelevant, a matter not to be considered, since this new perfect form had been 'scientifically' determined and was thus finite, indisputable. This delusion was maintained for a long time despite all visual evidence to the contrary; what happened and has continued to happen is that the extraordinarily rich and complicated 'vocabularies' which had been evolved down the ages were abandoned in favour of a set of very basic building blocks which

Left: Just how badly the 'heroic' buildings of the 30s have aged may be seen in this recent photograph of Lurcat's once celebrated elementary school at Villejuif in a southern district of Paris.

Above: Rietveld's Schroder house at Utrecht is characteristic of his architecture. The architects of the De Stijl group at least attempted some play with their rather unimaginative blank forms.

might be deployed in different combinations. Esperanto—another utopian ideal of this period—was never seriously intended to replace first languages.

Modernism Flees Germany

The spread of the new architecture was unwittingly (or, perhaps, since he loathed it and considered it suitable for nothing but factories, wittingly) accelerated by the rise of Hitler. Among those who fled his hideous regime in the early 30s were Walter Gropius and Erich Mendelsohn. Gropius founded the Bauhaus (literally 'house of building') at Weimar, a sort of polytechnic of applied art, designed its new premises at Dessau (which look like a factory), wrote the sort of fulsome apocalyptic prose that was typical of proselytizers for the new architecture, migrated first to England and then to America where he taught at Harvard and designed buildings for, among other noble institutions, the Playboy Club. One of his chief notions was that the worth

of modernism was proven because it was popular with youth; that this notion was quite widespread was due, perhaps, to the comparative youth of many of the eager participants in the great adventure. Erich Mendelsohn was in his early thirties when he designed his greatest building, the Einstein Tower at Potsdam near Berlin—it is a classic work of architectural expressionism, sculpturally plastic and infected with none of the aesthetic puritanism of his contemporaries' work; its vaguely 'streamlined' form and corner windows were much taken up by the less solemn architects of the 30s who realized that modernism was nothing but a style with a lot of bluff to back it up and played with it. The work of these architects who achieved an agreeable style that was deprecated as 'moderne' represents the characteristic stage of creative divergence from 'theoretically based' (ie dogmatically stated) norms.

Mendelsohn's later work is conventionally international modern; he too fled first to England where he designed, in conjunction with another refugee Serge Chermayeff, a seaside pavilion at Bexhill on Sea. It is perhaps in marine settings that this architecture is at its best, like that of the Regency alongside which it is often to be found. This is no doubt partly because of the use it made of nautical allusion ('portholes', rails like those around a deck and so on), partly because it fits in with plain boat sheds and blockhouses, as well as with the sand and the surf.

The emigrés gathered disciples (young ones who were as near as could be got to the ideal of a mind untrammelled by received ideas, ie ideas other than those of modernism). But even earlier, by the mid-1920s in fact, a prototypical modernism was appearing all over the world. The machine, which could produce the same things anywhere, irrespective of local conditions, was in a state of triumph. Buildings that were virtually indistinguishable from one another began to spring up in Italy, Holland, Morocco, Germany, Finland. . . not places, you might have thought, with common needs nor, certainly, with common climates. Yet young architects in all these countries shared a common 'philosophy'; the strength of the cult of the new in these years cannot be overemphasized.

The Rise of De Stijl

In Holland the two branches of the avant-garde, the purist and the expressionist, are represented on the one hand by the architects of De Stijl group, G.T. Rietveld and J.P. Oud and on the other by Michel de Klerk and W.M. Dudok. The De Stijl group took its name from the magazine in which its members published their manifestos. Here is Oud writing in 1920: 'Life and art have acquired in the present age a different, more abstract accent so that a more intimate contact exists between them than one might superficially be inclined to think.' It only takes a moment's reflection to realize it means absolutely nothing, though one can be pretty sure that Oud believed that mankind had undergone a fundamental change and so required the sort of house that he was keen to build. Oud's best-known work is a large estate in Rotterdam which in photos looks pleasing. In fact it is a staggeringly meagre place, built on the meanest scale and enlivened, like Le Corbusier's similar but smaller estate at Bordeaux, only by the alterations to the houses wrought by their inhabitants.

Another member of the De Stijl group was the painter Piet Mondrian and his work is recalled by that of Rietveld whose exagger-

ately angular houses and furniture are classics of modernist functionalism, ie they are impractical and uncomfortable, liable to cause bruising and are nothing but exercises in *style*. Dudok was the chief architect of the new town of Hilversum; his work, occasionally akin to that of Frank Lloyd Wright, is rather more romantic than that of many of his contemporaries and his Town Hall is notable for its fortress-like quality. Both Dudok and Michel de Klerk tended to work mostly in brick, a less 'progressive' material than concrete, with the result that some of the more fanatically purist modernists disdained them.

One of the most widely perpetuated myths about the new architecture of the two decades between the world wars is that it was both a manifestation and an instrument of social progress, which in this context means socialism of one sort or another. It is of course nonsense to ascribe political labels to forms of architecture; it is, for instance, currently fashionable in certain circles which still adhere to the tenets of 50 years ago to refer to neo-classicism as 'fascist'—that neo-classicism was popular in such different countries as Britain and the U.S.S.R. seems to have escaped them. By this dubious token the Baroque would be called 'catholic'. The fatuity of the equation between progressive architecture and socialism is demonstrated by the case of Italy where modernism was officially endorsed by Mussolini's fascist regime e.g. Giussepe Terragnis's Casa del Fascio at Como. Of course given the emphasis that the movement's propagandists placed on anonymity, collectivism, the unimportance of the individual and so on

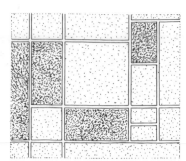

Above: Abstraction in the private art of painting is one thing . . . But for architects to foist the sterile pattern-making of Piet Mondrian on an unwilling public was quite another.

Below: W.M. Dudok was one of the most widely influential designers of the 30s. His Dutch hostel in Paris was among those of his buildings that caused him to be much admired.

it is rather surprising that modernism did not become the officially patronized architecture of all totalitarian states.

It is rather amusing now to witness a modern movement propagandist, J.M. 'Karl Marx' Richards, wriggling out of having to admit that Italian modernism was just like all the rest. In his *Introduction to Modern Architecture*, written on the eve of the Second World War, he pronounces that 'the official architecture of Italian fascism is only superficially modern'. In the same chapter he rues the Russian failure to embrace modernism after an initial flirtation during which a number of European architects were invited to assist 'the great programme of socialist reconstruction'. He describes the neo-

Right: Dudok's Hilversum Town Hall was also much admired and provided the model for much other civic building in Europe. The example of Frank Lloyd Wright is strongly evident in this work.

classicism of the Moscow metro as 'tragic'. Because personalities were assumed to be unimportant, Richards neglected in subsequent, post war, editions of his book to pay any attention to Le Corbusier's collaboration with the Vichy government, to Mies's work for Hitler, to the American Phillip Johnson's attempts to found a National Socialist party.

The frequent references in this chapter to those who wrote on behalf of the modern movement are provoked by the fact that during the inter war years the international style was far from typical in any country. The noise it made and the attention it attracted was in inverse proportion to its achievement. This is partly because many of its younger acolytes received so few commissions that they had plenty of time to write manifestos, form groups, attend seminars et cetera. By the end of the 1930s there was a marked reaction against modern movement buildings and a turn towards older styles provoked, as much as by anything else, as the high rate of failures among modern buildings. Would that this lesson had been heeded after 1945 when all over the world a vast programme of reconstruction was undertaken; speed was of great importance and one of

the advantages claimed for the new architecture was just that. It was also alleged to be cheaper than traditional methods, hence its appeal to commerce and industry. Of course the fact that it is 'disposable' (and frequently self-destructing) is something which added to its appeal: oddly enough, it is modernism's temporary structures which have proved to be among its most enduring—British postwar prefabs, pavilions at countless international exhibitions and so on.

Shadow of the High-Rise

In other words modernism, which between the wars had merely been a tributary, became the mainstream after 1945. Were it not for the awful morass that it

Right: The style of architecture referred to as international modernism presaged the era of the high-rise.

Below: The work of English modernists like Connell and Ward, who designed this house in Middlesex, can hardly be accused of originality, but it does have a certain lightness.

thus presaged, this architecture would be a mere footnote to the history of the 20th century. And it would not be a charmless footnote—there are some individual buildings of those years whose sculptural qualities are undeniable and which, if decently maintained, look fairly fresh today. The sort of monolithic blankness which we have come to associate with modern architecture was not at all common before the war—blankness, certainly, but on a fairly small scale. And, anyway, grand gestures were mostly confined to industrial, institutional and commercial buildings; the unhappy piling of families into 'point blocks' was still rare. Houses such as Le Corbusier's Villa Savoie or Connell and Ward's house at Moor Park are quite quaint in

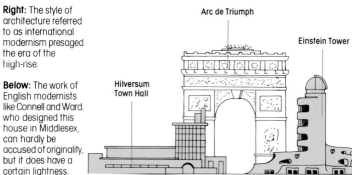

Arc de Triumph

Einstein Tower

Hilversum Town Hall

their predictably futuristic ways. The former, stuck on stilts for no very good reason, is an early example of one of the most disagreeable features of modernism, the tendency to create useless spaces which, when found in cities, invariably become the haunts of vandals or receptacles for rubbish.

It seems improbable that the author of an article in the magazine *Design For Today* had such a seedy future in mind when he wrote in 1934 that 'the modern movement is already ahead of the present' The best laid plans. . . . Perhaps the most curious feature of the rise of modernism and its worldwide acceptance is that those who succumbed to it—architects and their patrons, both private and public—did so in defiance of a recognition of its properties; it was representations that won the day. The persuasiveness of modernistic written propaganda (associating it with youth, progress, a brighter future and all the rest) was matched by the artfulness of those who photographed new buildings for the popular and specialist press where they appeared as objects of pure abstraction—devoid of purpose and never graced by *people* who would, after all, just mess up the whole composition.

Age of the Skyscraper
The Magic of Manhattan

Architectural Importance:
USA, eastern seaboard. One of the five boroughs of New York City – Largest town and capital of New York State. With the development of the elevator and the steel-frame, architects for the first time were able to make their buildings almost as tall as they wished. Consequently, there evolved a rash of high-rise office blocks, each subsequent example a little taller than the one before. The introduction of zoning regulations added a weird, ziggurat effect as buildings were stepped down to occupy the maximum space allowed.

REACHING FOR THE SKY

NEW YORK STATE

Hudson River

New York

Manhattan

The Bronx

STATEN
ISLAND

New York
Harbour

Queens

Brooklyn

Atlantic

LONG ISLAND

Abbots built their monasteries, conquerors their castles, kings their palaces; and now the multinational corporations have built their skyscrapers . . . the prime patrons of 20th century architecture.

Manhattan is the epicentre of Western capitalism and its architecture expresses this with towering monuments to corporate grandeur. Until 1973 the tallest buildings of the 20th century have all been in New York, and the Manhattan skyline still boasts the highest concentration of skyscrapers, dominated by the superstar of high-rise—the Empire State Building.

Only two or three individual buildings in Manhattan have earned the accolade of Great Architecture from the critics. Most of the skyscrapers are considered vulgar and philistine. Even the New York buildings of well-respected architects (for example, the Guggenheim by Frank Lloyd Wright) have

Stylistic Essentials:
A conceptually different form of architecture evolved to serve the needs of a business city through which passes one third of all foreign trade and where the banking community in the mid-70s handled over 100 billion dollars' worth of business. Thus the commercial and financial heart of the city is characterized by variously shaped high-rise buildings – the skyscrapers. The first to really catch the public imagination was the Empire States, until 1971 the world's tallest building.

Primary Building Materials:
The skyscrapers of Manhattan represent the ultimate functionalism of modern life: they are little more than tall, box-like units composed mainly of glass panels fitted between metal strips. The essential services of the building, the lifts, ventilation and garbage disposal systems are all hidden away in the inner core. The tower is little more than a steel skeleton with a light, all-glass skin.

Above: The Flat Iron Building, an example of the near lunatic results of office speculation. The shape of the site (an acute triangle) was simply projected upwards for 20 storeys.

Above: The Woolworth Building. At 60 storeys it was the tallest building in the world for 20 years. The problem of finding a suitable architectural language for skyscrapers was still a burning issue.

been called poor examples of their work. And yet the cityscape of Manhattan *as a whole* has fired the imagination of most pioneers of modern design, including Corbusier.

The physical constraints of an island site and an extraordinary concentration of commercial activity have combined to produce a totally artificial, man-made environment. Of all the world's commercial centres, Manhattan is the truest expression of the fact that, despite the spectacular growth of long-distance communications technology, the best business is still done eyeball to eyeball. Even within Manhattan, specialized commercial activities have concentrated in particular districts:

financial around Wall Street, advertising in Madison Avenue, fashion in Fifth Avenue, artists and galleries in Soho.

Residential apartments have been forced out of the areas of highest land value, but still many New Yorkers can live near their work because of the high density. Here the advantages of city life are maximized, with instant access to the best shops, restaurants and any entertainment desired, from music to theatre, religion to sex. It fosters the feeling (or illusion?) of being at the very centre of

Western society. Here, also, are extreme disadvantages: a high crime rate, traffic congestion, pollution and appalling poverty on the doorstep of unparalleled wealth—all of which have contributed recently to the decision of some corporations to move out in search of a somewhat more amenable climate.

Culturally, New York is a cosmopolitan multi-ethnic jungle, where immigrants from all over the world have established communities. There are more Irish in New York than in Dublin, and

more Jews than in Jerusalem. Little Italy, Little Hungary and Chinatown are all areas where you could almost forget that you are in America.

The street landscape of Manhattan is characterized by long vistas down avenues which form deep canyons between the skyscrapers; and from high up, a dense forest of thrusting towers, with ant-like cars and people swarming the streets below. Arrival by boat or plane is a thrilling experience, as a thousand cathedrals of capitalism loom out from the mist. The skyscraper, though born in Chicago where the technology of steel frame construction was first developed, grew up and matured in New

Above: The Chrysler Building, one of the most popular of all skyscrapers, its architect (Van Alen) borrowed the theme for the building's Art Deco steel motifs from the company's product line.

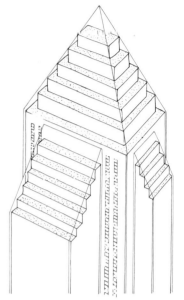

Below: This diagram illustrates the building volumes that were allowed by the New York zoning regulations. Developers sometimes interpreted these diagrams literally.

city-scape ideals, this provided a structure for the rapid growth of the metropolis during the 19th century. The island was almost fully developed by 1880, by which time the metropolitan population exceeded one million.

The First High Buildings

The rapid growth of manufacturing industry and commercial activity brought with it the need for the administrative office, at first adjacent to the plant or warehouse, but later separated and concentrated in 'downtown' areas when communications were improved. Such an office-trading centre was created in Chicago, partly as the result of the Great Fire in 1871 which precipitated radical tightening of building regulations and pushed out residential uses. This generated a real-estate bonanza.

The incentive to build high came from both the need to maximize built floor space per plot/investment and the desire to impress: height equals grandeur. Three technological developments made it possible:

1. More sophisticated understanding of the behaviour of materials in structures led to more accurate prediction of stresses and loads. This was developed from engineering and bridge design.
2. Separation of the basic structure or frame of the building from its outside skin by using steel or iron framing.
3. Introduction of the passenger elevator as a result of Elisha Otis' invention of a safety device.

William Jenny, a military engineer turned architect, built the first steel/iron-framed building, known as the Home Insurance Building in the late 19th century. The change from masonry to steel cut construction time and reduced building weight by two-thirds, thus saving on foundation costs. Lightweight construction allowed bigger windows and generated large, clear internal spaces which gave more freedom for internal planning. The analogy from natural history is the evolution from crustacean (with structural armour) to vertebrate (with skeleton and light skin).

The architectural potential was most fully developed by Louis Sullivan, most famous of the Chicago School. Some consider his Wainwright and Guarantee buildings of the 1890s to be the first true skyscrapers, where the aesthetic problems of bulk and height were first tackled successfully, using strong verticals and delicate ornament that complimented rather than disguised

the structure. The Carson Pirie Scott department store (1899) is considered his finest achievement. New York builders were quick to exploit the new technology: the new Bessemer steels came down in price, and soon replaced cast and wrought iron. Steel erection became a speciality of the Mohawk indians, whose nimble gait and sense of balance enabled them to work at great height.

High-rise Comes to New York

Freed from height limitations by the elevator and the steel-frame, the New York property boom took off anew, fuelled by the city's ever-growing importance as a world trading centre. Higher buildings increased densities, which generated higher real-estate values, which in turn dictated even higher building. The prestige value of height in itself, was such that many buildings were taller than was economically sensible. The designs were, and still are, condemned as philistine by the architectural intelligensia. But there was enormous popular local pride in them at the time, and lately some critics have revived interest in the forgotten names of the architects of these early skyscrapers. The formal grid layout, the space restriction of an island site, and an almost total lack of building regulations, added further incentive to build high. The Flat-Iron (formerly the Fuller) Building is an extreme example: financed by a Colorado gold miner who struck rich and was persuaded to invest in New York by the build-

York. Even if the tallest building is now in Chicago (the Sears Tower) and high-rise building has mushroomed all over the world, Manhattan still reigns as the true home of the skyscraper.

Many of its early skyscrapers may yet achieve recognition as high art, due to a recent revival of interest in their largely forgotten architects, such as Raymond Hood and Cass Gilbert.

Early New York

The first settlement was founded by the Dutch in 1614, and called New Netherland. Manhattan Island was purchased from Indians by Peter Minuit for 60 guilders worth of goods, in 1626 ('the

real-estate bargain of the millenium'). When the small fortified village at the southern tip was captured by the British in 1664 and re-named New York, the population was 1500. It had reached 23,000 by the Declaration of Independence, and 60,000 by the end of the 18th century.

In 1811 the city commissioners planned a uniform grid for the undeveloped land north of Washington Square, with 155 east-west streets and 12 wide north-south avenues. Motivated as much by real-estate revenue as by

ing's Chicago architect Daniel Burnham, it was shaped to fit an acutely triangular site. At the time it was erected, in 1902, it was the tallest building in America.

The aesthetic of elegant simplicity espoused by Louis Sullivan in Chicago was lost and the now simple, cellular, box-framed steel structures were clad in stone, brick, tiles or cast-iron, in a wide variety of styles ranging from High Gothic to New Egyptian, according to current fashion. The 60 storey Woolworth Building (1913) by Cass Gilbert, was sheathed in cosmetic Gothic: a historic veneer that disguised some very advanced engineering and services sophisticated for their time.

In 1916 the City authorities introduced zoning laws in an attempt to control the ever-upward growth. The idea was to define a maximum envelope, or three-dimensional limit, for each site that would protect the light and ventilation of adjacent plots. Formulated by health engineers, the laws were interpreted literally in many buildings to produce a stepped back or ziggurat style that occupied the maximum volume allowed. These buildings helped enhance the vision of New York as a latter-day Babylon.

Plaza Style

The vertical orientation of buildings encouraged layered multi-uses within the same basic frame. The Downtown Athletic Club (1931) had a swimming pool on the 12th floor, golf range on the 7th, health spas and gymnasia below and apartments above. As the scale of projects increased, they progressed to the ultimate in prestige: redevelopment of an entire block to create the 'plaza'. First was the Rockefeller Center, 14 buildings including two skyscrapers, the Metropolitan Opera, a six-storey parking-lot and Radio City Music Hall—an ambitious combination of culture and real-estate speculation, where despite the Wall Street Crash literally no expense was spared.

Below: One of the last works of possibly the greatest of all American architects, Frank Lloyd Wright was the Guggenheim Museum. The plan is based on a continuously descending spiral.

Chief influence in the team of architects involved was Raymond Hood, despised by the architectural intellectual establishment for his commercial attitude: 'Architecture', he said, 'is the business of manufacturing shelter'. He made his name with the McGraw Hill Building (1936), the epitome of early functional skyscraper design—no ornament and a stark façade of glass and glazed tiling.

The Empire State

The tallest building in the world from 1932 to 1971, the Empire State Building has captured the world's imagination as the ultimate skyscraper. 102 storeys high, with a radio mast above, it was designed in only six months by Shreve, Lamb and Harmon, and built in 12 months, a staggering engineering achievement. The rent from the radio mast was supposed to offset the cost of its somewhat uneconomic height, but was redundant before it was even finished.

Built as speculative office space, the Empire State was not entirely

Below: Manhattan, like ancient Egypt, will be remembered architecturally as the focal point of an Age of Gigantism, when the style was for grandiose gesture.

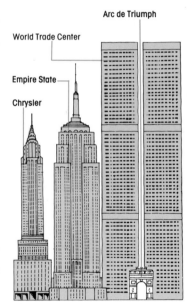

Arc de Triumph
World Trade Center
Empire State
Chrysler

Right: The queen of skyscrapers, the Empire State, for many years the tallest in the world. it contains accommodation for well over 20,000 office workers and an army of service people.

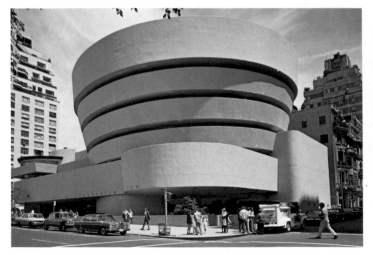

successful as such, some space being unlet to this day. The observation platform at the top sways up to one metre (4 feet) in a brisk wind. Experts today are worried about the implications of structural metal fatigue: should demolition be necessary it would take a fleet of 200 trucks six months, night and day, to remove the rubble.

In 1952 the functional style of the commercial buildings of the '30s was first elevated to high art by the Lever Building, where the last vestiges of masonry were finally cast away to give birth to the metal and glass curtain wall. Influenced by the early work of Mies Van de Rohe, Gordon Bunshaft, chief designer of architects

Skidmore, Ownings and Merrill, produced a prototype that has spawned identikit copies in every commercial centre of the world. Now the tower is reduced to a steel skeleton with a light, all-glass skin, rising 21 storeys above a 2-storey podium set 30 metres (100 feet) back from the street. This was the first application of a potential implicit in high buildings—to make space at ground level. The uniform glass façade conceals all—from ventilation plant to varying internal divisions/uses/tenants within the building. The principle was taken further in the Seagram Building (1958) where tinted bronze glass and bronze vertical glazing fins blend to produce a totally homogeneous

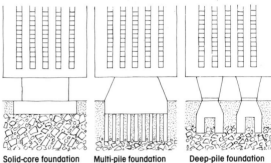

Left: Three types of foundation used for tall buildings: a concrete raft where the soil is well-packed, or piles – columns bored into the earth.

Below: The Lever Building is one of the prototypes of the curtain-wall office towers that now dominate most city skylines.

Solid-core foundation   Multi-pile foundation   Deep-pile foundation

façade which conceals all internal organization. The interior is reduced to a small compressed shuttle space that can be changed, re-organized and re-let to any office tenant, while the exterior presents a cool, dignified and luxurious, if somewhat anonymous, front. Mies was totally opposed to the idea that specific buildings should have 'individual character'; rather, they should have some kind of 'universal character determined by the total problem that architecture must strive to serve.'

The Stress Factor

In connection with the planning and construction of skyscrapers, certain conditions apply which need never concern the designers of low-rise individual units (as opposed to multi-unit complexes). Skyscrapers require intensive and very detailed planning of an order quite different from that for residential or ordinary commercial or industrial properties. The enormous concentration of weight in a relatively small area, the often powerful wind stresses they are subjected to, and the sheer complexity of services contained within their steel and glass

walls are problems that demand special solutions.

Weight and wind stress are probably the most severe headaches. Mathematical tables are available to make general calculations about wind stress for given areas of mass rising to certain heights with certain known wind strengths in the region, but almost invariably for very large or untried shapes a detailed model will be built and carefully tested in a wind tunnel.

Weight is obviously related to the depth of the foundations and the nature of the rock strata the building will stand on. In the case of the Empire State Building, for example, its 365,000 tons were supported on foundations 16 metres (55 feet) deep. The foundations were built on bedrock.

Foundations may take the form of either a solid slab of concrete, where the soil is strong, or sunken concrete piles where the soil is weak. In the case of the very weakest soil, a whole complex of piles might be used, thereby honeycombing the substrata with a dense mass of hardened concrete.

More and more these days, skyscraper builders are making use of ready-made components which can be assembled with a minimum of difficulty. In the case of concrete side panels, these can simply be lifted into place and joined together. In this way whole walls can be constructed in a matter of days or even hours. (It is possibly interesting to note that the Empire State, an 86 storey building, was erected at the astounding rate of over 4 storeys *per week* and that was not far off 50 years ago.)

Equally fast, though possibly more expensive is the so-called jackblock method. This involves the jacking-up of the roof on immensely powerful jacks as concrete blocks are inserted beneath. When enough blocks are in place the whole layer is jacked up and another started beneath. In time, all the 80 or 100 layers are put in and the building is finished.

Below: Close-up of a corner of the World Trade Center, showing the stainless steel window mullions that are the chief feature of this skyscraper. There is no technical reason why skyscrapers should not be five times the height of the Center.

Pre-war Mainstream
Adaptation of Tradition

Architectural Importance:
The last bastion of traditional architectural skills – a concern with good workmanship, fine building and style, which was to disappear from the architectural repertory for some decades. Many buildings can be seen as directly descended from the best pre-World War 1 work – they evolved rather than tried to break with the past. It is to the architects in this chapter than many of today's younger architects are looking as an alternative model to the modernists.

MAINSTREAM DEVELOPMENTS

It was not until after the Second World War that an architecture directly derived from the age of 'heroic' modernism in the 1920s and 30s became a world-wide norm. Before the war and especially in those countries that were resistant to the modern movement much excellent architecture was made, though it has been rather overlooked by historians till recently. This is either because of their antipathy to an architecture which they regarded as 'reactionary', as the instrument of regimes of which they disapproved or because, since it was not backed up by a prolix theoretical literature, it is not possible to have fun pointing out where practice diverges from precept. Either way the sorts of institutional, domestic, ecclesiastical and commercial (if not industrial) buildings that are typical of the years between the wars and which are familiar to those in Europe who have eyes to see have been erased from history's

Below: The stripped classical manner reached its zenith in the Palace of Statues on the E.U.R. site in Rome. Designed by Guerrini, La Padula and Romano it was intended to be one of the showpieces of an international exhibition that was scheduled for 1942, though, for obvious reasons, never held.

POETI DI ARTISTI DI EROI
PENSATORI DI SCIENZIATI
AVIGATORI DI TRASMIGRATORI

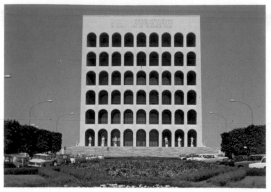

Tendency to low relief decorative sculpture.

Spread of Influence:
A tradition which almost died with the war – though in the USA and in the field of private housing elsewhere it continued with far better results and fewer failures than were incurred by new methods. It became in other words a model for builders rather than for architects.

Stylistic Essentials:
Eclectic. Many identifiable styles, many 'one-offs'. Austere classicism for public buildings; half-timbering, cottage styles and jazz-modern for houses. Very little copyist work but a great deal of free interpretation. Strong sense of attempting to promote individuality. Massive industrial and commercial buildings, most powerfully influenced by USA.

Primary Building Materials:
Steel frames, concrete, brick etc. But no desire to demonstrate the bones of a building – materials were servants, not masters. Dutch brickwork influential.

Above: Art Deco, the familiar mix of Egyptian, Aztec and streamlined mannerisms, takes its name from the Exposition of Arts Decoratives, held in Paris in 1925. Its finest architectural application is to be found in such factories as that designed for Hoover by Wallis Gilbert. **Below:** A detail of the Hoover building, erected in a suburb of west London in the 30s.

Left: The Anzac Memorial in Melbourne, by Sodersteen and Crust, is typical of the late classicism which was quite properly considered fit for the many shrines erected after the Great War.

Right: Art Deco motif over London doorway.

tablet by narrow-minded janitors. It is of course quite possible that the pendulum will swing so far the other way that in 20 or so years one may witness the publication of retrospectives of this century's architecture which omit discussion of the modern movement — they will in their way be just as tiresome as those which have been predominant during the last quarter century.

Now, any building erected in, say, 1930, whether it be a cubistic box or a half-timbered villa is indisputably of 1930; they are both in the proper sense of the word modern — at least they were in that year. So too were examples of a range of indeterminate styles which to lay eyes doubtless looked as 'up to date' as anything by Gropius or Mies but were not, in the quaint phrase of J.M. Richards, 'modern in our specialized sense'. Since the 'silent majority' architecture (to borrow a deprecating epithet to which it is often subjected) that we are talking about often showed the influence of that which was 'modern in our specialized sense' where is the line to be drawn? Along, of course, a necessarily arbitrary boundary sited somewhere this side of total abstraction; the mainstream architecture of the period did not attempt to suppress all the emotional, associational, sensory and other 'non-architectural' properties that a building can, and should, display. It evolved from the practice of centuries and so has a richness which modern movement stuff, the product of a childishly petulant disregard for the past, could never attain. However what really differentiates those whose work is the subject of this chapter from their (mostly younger) modernist contemporaries is their conception of — for want of a more elegant expression — the role of the architect. They were old fashioned enough to believe in the primacy of the creative imagination, to believe that architecture was an art rather than a branch of the social sciences, that an architect's job was to make fine buildings rather than to alter the world or mankind or mankind's attitudes towards its environment.

Buildings of the Reich

The aspirations towards a totalitarian architecture that were pursued by the modern movement were eschewed by the begetters of the two terrible totalitarian societies of the years between the wars. Hitler was, among other things, an architect manqué — had the school of architecture in Vienna granted him admission when he sought it we might never have heard of him. His association of modernism with socialism and Jewry caused him not only to persecute a number of architects, to close the Bauhaus, and promote the spread of modernism by forcing such men as Gropius into exile, but to

Pre-war Mainstream

THE AGE OF CONSTRUCTION | Railway St.
Shrine of Remembrance
Chrysler Building
Hoover Factory
Museum of Modern Art

Italy   Australia   USA   England   France

'1915   '1920   '1925   '1930   '1935   '1940   1945'

pursue a building programme more or less untinged by a style which he abhorred. Now, the excesses and beastliness of a regime should not cause us to deprecate the architecture of that regime—if we succumb to such an easy association it is but a short step to the point where we dismiss a building (or book, or symphony) because its author was an evil man; it is in fact to follow the example of men like Hitler. The truth is that much of the architecture of the Third Reich is good, like its autobahns and its characteristic car, the VW beetle (whose origin is quite rightly of no moment to the millions who use the thing). Millions of ordinary Germans were housed in estates which were determinedly nationalistic in their reliance on traditional 'vernacular' forms—steeply pitched roofs, dormers, small windows etc. Retrospectively one cannot but link these houses with that side of the Reich which promoted hiking, health and heartiness (all of which were, strangely enough, dear to modernists too). Nazi public buildings were altogether different, and it cannot be denied that the idea of fitness for purpose was well understood. A Roman magnificence was sought and achieved under the direction of a number of architects including Albert Speer; the austere and grandiose monuments to itself that the Reich erected probably did as much as anything to discredit neo-classicism in the immediate postwar years and so clear the way for less traditional styles. The disparity between public and domestic architectural forms is one to which the world, after too long a period of 'experiment', is beginning to return.

Hardly surprisingly—though it was a source of chagrin to western fellow travellers in the 30s—Russian public architecture of this period was also vaguely neo-classical and even more indicative of the totalitarian conviction that very big is best, a conviction that is equally well qualified by 'democratic' nowadays, so huge have been many of the West's building projects of the recent past. That the great tyrannies failed to embrace the new architecture is interesting but no more than was to be expected; Hitler, as we have mentioned, abhorred it because of its associations and 'internationalism' and was later to convince Mussolini that it was 'bolshevist'; Stalin rejected it because the immediately post-revolutionary flirtation with it had proved a failure—roofs leaked, walls cracked and stained, and a whole gamut of now familiar failures was presaged. So an archi-

tecture which was regarded by many of its devotees as 'totalitarian' was denied a place in what were, after all, its natural homes. Like a lucky cuckoo it was able to find less eagle eyed hosts elsewhere.

Fascist Facades

The fatuity of matching architecture to political systems has been demonstrated elsewhere in this book by the case of Italy where a fascist critic, P.M. Bardi, devoted a book to the argument that the

new architecture was *the* architecture of fascism; an architect's political persuasions are only of importance in that they may lead him to particular patrons or to specialize in a particular kind of architecture—they are not to be found shown in his work. One of the styles correspondent in Italy at this time to the 'stripped' classicism popular in northern Europe for institutional buildings was derived more or less closely from the Baroque. Armando Brazini's Cuore Immaculata di Maria Santissima in Rome has as

Above: Van Alen's Art Deco lift doors in the Chrysler building, New York. So rich is the Art Deco design of the building's façade that it might easily be called the cathedral of Art Deco.

little in common with neo-Baroque work of the turn of this century as it does with that of any of the Baroque masters of the 17th century. It is a heavyweight composition as is his contribution to the complex of buildings intended, but of course never used, for an international exhibition in Rome in 1942. Brazini also designed a huge neo-Baroque asylum which is probably the last major work in such a style anywhere in the worrld—it too is nothing like a 'genuine' Baroque pile and is the more impressive for that. Aldo Andreani's Palazzo Fidia in Milan is a similarly unorthodox building that mixes elements from a variety of classical idioms in a wild manner with lots of fancy brick-work and pleasantly perverse detailing. Italian neo-classicism of the period reached its zenith at the site, above referred to, for the 1942 exhibition where Arnaldo Foschini's St Peter and St Paul is a building that comprises a hemi-spherical dome perched on a chaste box with the plan of a Greek cross. It does perhaps look like a refugee from a garden city, but it is at the same time un-mistakably a church—which is perhaps not a charge that can be levelled at most of today's liturgy centres and prayer spaces.

A contemporary international exhibition was held in Paris in 1937. The Russian and German pavilions vied to outdo each other and the host nation constructed on a variety of sites some buildings which may like those in Rome be seen as indicative of French insti-tutional architecture of the time— the best known is perhaps the Musee d'Art Moderne; again neo-classical with a deal of statuary and figures in relief and un-adorned columns. Of many other notable Parisian buildings two

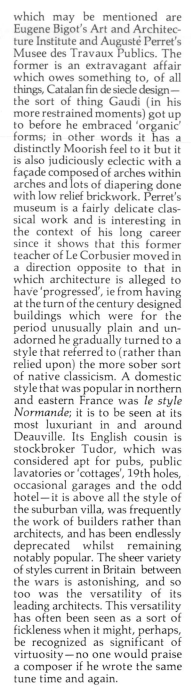

which may be mentioned are Eugene Bigot's Art and Architec-ture Institute and Auguste Perret's Musee des Travaux Publics. The former is an extravagant affair which owes something to, of all things, Catalan fin de siecle design— the sort of thing Gaudi (in his more restrained moments) got up to before he embraced 'organic' forms; in other words it has a distinctly Moorish feel to it but it is also judiciously eclectic with a façade composed of arches within arches and lots of diapering done with low relief brickwork. Perret's museum is a fairly delicate clas-sical work and is interesting in the context of his long career since it shows that this former teacher of Le Corbusier moved in a direction opposite to that in which architecture is alleged to have 'progressed', ie from having at the turn of the century designed buildings which were for the period unusually plain and un-adorned he gradually turned to a style that referred to (rather than relied upon) the more sober sort of native classicism. A domestic style that was popular in northern and eastern France was *le style Normande*; it is to be seen at its most luxuriant in and around Deauville. Its English cousin is stockbroker Tudor, which was considered apt for pubs, public lavatories or 'cottages', 19th holes, occasional garages and the odd hotel—it is above all the style of the suburban villa, was frequently the work of builders rather than architects, and has been endlessly deprecated whilst remaining notably popular. The sheer variety of styles current in Britain between the wars is astonishing, and so too was the versatility of its leading architects. This versatility has often been seen as a sort of fickleness when it might, perhaps, be recognized as significant of virtuosity—no one would praise a composer if he wrote the same tune time and again.

The Influence of Lutyens

After the First World War, the opportunities for building country houses (a form which the vast majority of British architects dur-ing the previous two and a half

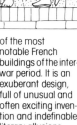

Above: Detail of the fascinating carvings on the exterior stonework of the Institute of Art and Archaeology in Paris.

Below: Designed by Bigot, this is one of the most notable French buildings of the inter-war period. It is an exuberant design, full of unusual and often exciting inven-tion and indefinable literary allusions.

Left: John Joass was among the most original Edwardian designers and his post-war work was very much in the vein he had pioneered – a weighty Baroque, which is lightened by the use of such incongruous details as pantiles. This is the Abbey National HQ.

centuries had at least essayed) declined though, as we shall see, they did not altogether dry up. Consequently architects who had made their names with large houses tended to concentrate upon institutional and mercantile commissions. Chief among them was Edwin Lutyens whose work at this time was, as earlier, like no one else's and once again hugely influential. The greatest influence on Lutyens was always Lutyens. It is not always possible to apply Vladimir Nabokov's dictum that 'there is only one school of writing, the school of talent' to architecture but it is apposite to Lutyens who, more than any other architect of this century, had a sense of the history of his own art. Much of his commercial work during the 20s refers back to his earlier domestic work and, more evidently, to the Viceroy's house at New Delhi, which city's conception was partly his. The Viceroy's house succeeds in the sort of dreaminess that Marsh Court and Folly Farm achieve and further suggests the ghostly deserted courts of the ruined city of Fatehpur Sikri. (No one should leap to the conclusion that Lutyens was thus precognisant of the forthcoming British withdrawal from the subcontinent.) It is grand and plastic

and theatrical as—it is to be presumed—would have been his Liverpool Cathedral.

The elevations of some of Lutyens's commercial buildings are most bizarre, architectural layer cakes if you like. A block in Pall Mall, London begins at the bottom with columns and banded rustication, then comes a two storey layer the second storey of which has windows with segmental tops and bottoms; there sits on this three very plain stages with windows of diminishing sizes; and on top of the lot there is something that looks not unlike a suburban house with inflated sentry boxes at its corners, a pitched and hipped roof and a couple of hefty chimneys. He does the same sort of thing on a bigger scale at the Midland Bank headquarters in the City of London, where it looks as if he has abandoned a motif a bit of the way up the façade only for it to reappear even higher up. Again at the Midland Bank, in Manchester, the building can be seen as at least three diffuse entities.

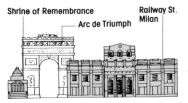

Above: The great revivalist movement was motivated as much by nostalgia for past grandeur as it was by an instinct to preserve a sense of 'fun'.

All of these creations are rather nerveless; they are a bit akin to a work of fiction in which the author has ignored the Flaubertian dogma of 'nothing outside the plot' yet has managed to attain a classical unity. It is perhaps only otherwise in Manhattan that such successful recklessness can be found.

The influence of New York on British architects was hardly widespread, but there is more evidence of an interest in the new world in England than there is elsewhere in Europe—something, no doubt, to do with the admiration of one architecturally isolationist country for another. Charles Holden's London University Senate House and London Transport headquarters are the most obvious examples and are true heavyweights; the big offices of John Joass are much more fun and carry straight on from his prewar work in everything but size.

Straightforward neo-classicism on a grand scale was never as popular in Britain as it was in the rest of Europe, quite probably for the good reason that it was less firmly rooted in national tradition. One of the most emulated exponents of the manner was the Swedish architect Gunnar Asplund whose Stockholm Library may well have been admired by modernists but is equally very close to French and German examples of a century earlier. Asplund's later work is less hefty and distinctive, but his library and the contemporary but much more fanciful Stockholm City

Hall by Ragnar Ostberg gave rise in France and England to a kind of design that you might call 'bus station civic'. In this style were built universities and council offices whose symmetry can never actually be witnessed by anyone on the ground—towers with clocks are essential components of it. Places like Southampton Civic Centre or Swansea Civic Centre suffer because of their well meaning gentility—they lack the quality which is most characteristic of the best interwar architecture, namely fantasy.

Cinemas like the Alhambra, garages like pagodas, factories in a streamlined Nile style, houses like—well, think of it and they existed: Andalusian villas (an architect called J.M. Neaum spread them all over the New Forest in southern England), Cape colonial farms, Regency lodges, Georgian boxes, Alsatian watchtowers, cottages of every ilk, bungalows with stained glass narratives set in their front doors... This I'm afraid is the last we shall hear of such things for the time being: the brave new world constructed after the Second World War may have been many things but it wasn't fun. 'Individualize' became a patronizing word used by architects to describe the attempts of inhabitants to dress up their otherwise dreary houses.

Planning for the Present
New Cities Emerge

Architectural Importance:
The grid patterns of the mid-19th century gave way to equally formal, if more grandoise Beaux Arts exercises, which was in turn succeeded by the 'visionary' totalitarianism of the middle years of this century. The results have been so unhappy that an abandonment of planning has even been advocated.

And, indeed, today's more thoughtful planners, like today's better architects are shamelessly eclectic and are looking again not only at pre-modern patterns but at such formerly despised models as ribbon development.

CONCRETE PLANS

Virtually the only sort of unplanned community of the recent past is the shanty town. Go back a century and the vast, unwieldy mechanism of controls upon building which is now taken for granted was virtually unknown, and so too was the active, instrumental planning of communities. Despite the instances of tied towns and industrial villages (Menier's Noisiel-sur-Marne, Salt's Saltaire, Krupps's Kronenberg etc.) development during the 19th century was, typically, quick and copious and uncontrolled. In the cities of those countries that suffered the industrial revolution the burgeoning population created unprecedented problems. But these were not particularly problems of housing, so much as of hygiene and overcrowding. There was nothing inherently wrong with what in England were called 'byelaw' streets which certainly encouraged sociability and family life to a greater degree than tower blocks and

171

there has also been what proved a socially distressing, artificial division of land use.

Spread of Influence: The garden city derived from the tied town which in turn derived from the estate village. It spawned the dormitory suburb style which was considered wasteful of land but which is now seen to have been a quietly inspired idea.

Stylistic Essentials: The relationship of architecture to planning is always complicated, but since the abandonment of picturesque ambitions it has become even more so. The fusion of planning and architecture into one discipline, seen at its most potent in 'comprehensive' developments, has tended to alienate the public; hence the return to the informal style of recent years.

Primary Building Methods: The primacy of the street was respected till, with a few exceptions, the postwar reconstruction. In many of the postwar communities built from scratch

the stepped and staggered schemes that have been popular in the recent past. Nor was there anything wrong with the great boulevards that were cut through cities during the 19th century; one of their most admirable qualities was that they lacked ambiguity — road, pavements, planting; there did not exist as there do today areas of undefined space, pointless and disquieting which can only be understood by those with a training as planners.

Just as the architecture of the past 30 or so years may be seen as an unforgivable act of treachery on the part of those who should know better, so may the work of planners who have both abetted architects and contrived schemes of the utmost crassness themselves.

The sort of paternalism that is endemic to all planning is particularly explicit at places such as Saltaire and in contemporary (mid-19th century) essays in philanthropic housing in British cities.

The latter was the direct precursor of much subsequent mass housing and we shall return to it. Titus Salt was actually familiar with the Prince Consort's two-storey model flats which were built to design of Henry Roberts. Salt was also familiar with two of Disraeli's novels, Sybil and Coningsby, in which the future prime minister had invented philanthropic employers. Referring in Sybil to the relationship of the manufacturer Trafford to his employees he writes that he 'recognized the baronial principle.' Thus in the case of Saltaire life imitated art and, at second hand, the example of practical estate villages, rather than the idealistic communities of Robert Owen or the Chartists. Salt was a second generation wool dealer whose fortune was founded on the weaving of alpaca at his mills in Bradford, at that time one of the most noxious towns in Britain. Saltaire was built north of the town in the Aire valley where both rail and canal communications were good. The huge mill in the shape of a T (for Titus) and the 800 houses were built during the 1850s in a vaguely Italianate style. There was nothing particularly unusual about that, nor about the straightforward grid on which they were situated. What was remarkable was the extent of Salt's welfarism and paternalism. The place was full of amenities and its inhabitants

were bound by all sorts of rules: there were almshouses, no less than 5 nonconformist churches and chapels, baths, wash houses, meeting hall, school, hospital, literary institute, library, allotments, park, sports facilities, gymnasium, etc. Shops were not allowed to advertize, washing could not be hung out in public, there was no public house and alcohol was forbidden — the legend 'All Beer Abandon Ye That Enter Here' was written across one of the entrances to the town. Workers were allotted houses according to the size of their family rather than their position on the alpaca ladder and they were invited to make representations concerning the sort of facilities they would need. Such concessions were virtually unheard of at that date though of course 'consultation' has become one of the great lies of democratic (another lie) planning.

Garden Suburb

It was evidently as much in the interests of manufacturers as of employees that such colonies should exist. The work force could be overseen and kept in order, the dangers of epidemics of such

Below: Lord Leverhulme's village of Port Sunlight for his workers was copied the world over by enlightened employers who recognized the benefits which could derive from an agreeable environment.

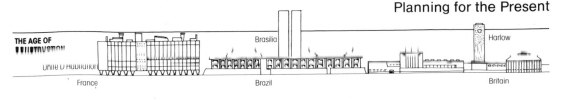

Unite D Habitation

Brasilia

Harlow

France

Brazil

Britain

`1940`   `1945`   `1950`   `1955`   `1960`

diseases as cholera were minimized, the idea of team spirit or community or collective endeavour—call it what you will—could be easily fostered.

A contemporary instance of large-scale planning which does not seek to dissemble its authoritarian ends is to be found in Paris where to this day the city's police are grateful to the Prefect of the Seine, Georges Hausmann whose transformation of the city was at least partly determined and shaped by the need to control mobs. To his eternal credit, however, Hausmann did create one of the prettiest parks in Europe on the site of a former quarry and former gibbet at Buttes-Chaumont. It is the apogee of the picturesque which had by this time in the country of its origin, England, become the norm for many middle class suburbs (e.g. The Park in Nottingham) and, later on, the garden suburb of Bedford Park in west London). The inevitable marriage of paternalism and the picturesque took place at Port Sunlight in Cheshire which was to have a signal influence on the appearance and form of suburbs all over the world during the 50 years after its foundation in 1888.

Port Sunlight was founded by the soap tycoon W.H. Lever whose previous premises at Warrington had grown too small. It was built at what was, as we have seen, a happy time for domestic architecture in England and it does have the appearance of being a catalogue of all the styles fashionable during the period of its construction—half-timbered Gothic and 'French' cottages, tile-hung fantasies and all the rest sit alongside each other in defiant heterogeneity, a near parody of an English village. No village though ever had such a plan which is reliant on boulevard-like avenues and thus evidences the place's 'artificiality', gives the game away; the idea of make-believe is important here as it is in all those places modelled on it, chief among which was Letchworth, the First Garden City. This place owes its peculiar character to the conjunction of the architectural talents of Raymond Unwin and Barry Parker among others and to the initial conception of Ebenezer Howard whose book of 1898 *Tomorrow—A Peaceful Path to Real Reform* (since published as *Garden Cities of Tomorrow*) set out, with much fundamentalist optimism and fury, a vision of half town, half country. Howard's city would be self-sufficient, built on a plan of concentric circles, surrounded by a green belt, populated by 30,000 persons.

As built Letchworth diverges considerably from Howard's plan and is probably all the better for doing so. It is well provided with

public open spaces of a sort which must have seemed curiously informal when the town was being built. Moreover much of its architecture is first class; houses are situated at between 6 and 12 to an acre and the excesses of Edwardian urbanism were sedulously avoided. However it seems today to be all suburb and no centre, and this impression is compounded by the fact that it never became self-sufficient and was so forced to be a rather unusual dormitory town for London workers. In its early years it was made much fun of as the home of cranks, dew bathers, vegetarians, theosophists, anarchists and so on, and was satirized in John Buchan's *Mr. Standfast* as a nest of treacherous weaklings. The second Garden City, Welwyn, is more formal and notable for the toy town neo-Georgian of its buildings. But even though it is patently a more humane place than many of the subsequent planned communities it has been depressingly notorious for the variety and quantity of social problems associated with it—drug addic-

tion, depression and other 'symptoms' of urban ghastliness.

Acceptable Face of Capitalism

The idea of the garden city was taken up with less enthusiasm than the name. Howard had hoped to see his example at Letchworth followed the world over; instead he saw every jerry builder with a couple of acres of suburban villas calling his development 'a garden suburb'. But even in this debased form the worth of the garden city notion is apparent; it promotes cosiness, matiness, individuality, the home as castle and so on. The

Right: The town-planner's worst nightmare, the exponential growth of a capital city. This is a stylized representation of the growth in population of metropolitan Tokyo over the past 170-odd years. Several times the total population doubled and today, despite Japan's overall success with its zero-growth population advocacy, Tokyo remains one of the world's most densely populated cities. In this situation it can seem as though the problem

debased form has actually more to recommend it than Howard's exercises in starting anew for that very reason—speculative builders work for their profits and their clients' pockets and convenience, they do not seek to change the way people live: market capitalism implicitly acknowledges our imperfections, evangelical socialism of the kind that Howard typified seeks to iron them out. Garden cities of which there were few and garden suburbs of which there were many probably bear out the rightness of Aldous Huxley's dictum that 'even the silliest experiment has value if only as

of finding adequate and acceptable living space is beyond the planners' ability.

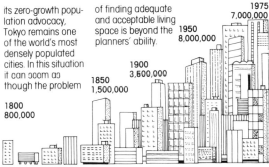

1800
800,000

1850
1,500,000

1900
3,500,000

1950
8,000,000

1975
7,000,000

Right: The conjunction of humane planning and congenial design occurred at Letchworth where the primacy of the street was respected and provision was made for attractive amenities such as the Mrs Howard Memorial Hall.

demonstrating what ought not to be done.' Such a claim cannot be made for certain other traditions of large-scale planning which have enjoyed vogues during this century. Even while garden suburbs were springing up all over northern Europe (especially in Holland and Belgium where they were championed by the planner Louis Van der Swaelmen) they were being attacked for their conspicuous consumption of land and for being a cause of urban sprawl. The reaction had its roots in plans which were more or less contemporary with Howard's. Arturo Soria y Mata had in the 1880s conceived of a 'linear city'; in 1904 the French architect Tony Garnier drew up plans for Une Cite Industrielle; just before the First World War Antonio Sant' Elia published his futuristic drawings of a metropolis. Parts of a city according to Soria y Mata's design were actually built on the edge of Madrid.

Delusions

With the projects of Garnier and Sant' Elia and those who aped them we come to what was to prove to be, regrettably, one of the most powerful weapons of the 20th century megalomaniac planner. Namely the seductiveness of fine draughtsmanship; there is no earthly reason why a talent for perspective drawings should go hand in hand with a talent for town planning and most usually it does not. Garnier's city went

Below: Le Corbusier's Unité d'Habitation on the edge of Marseilles is the most celebrated of all 'vertical cities' – it is an attempt to make a self-contained world with all services, shops on the premises.

Right: Nowhere has the fatuity of starting from scratch been more amply illustrated than in Brasilia which is a compendium of the cliches of 20th century town-planning.

Arc de Triumph

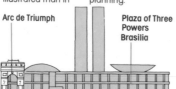
Plaza of Three Powers Brasilia

Above: To Brazilians, however, the Palace of the National Congress is a powerful symbol of their national aspirations.

unbuilt and he ended up as city architect in Lyons where he is remembered for his abattoir; his city of prefabricated, orderly concrete houses owes something to Howard and also to a Beaux Arts classicism disguised as technological necessity.

Sant 'Elia's drawings helped to create and predicted what turned out to be an infelicitous future; a massive flat block, delicately lined on paper, is a gross misrepresentation. Never has the question of scale been of greater moment than in schemes for modern cities, never has it been more carefully exploited. The gulf between the draughtsman's version of schemes (clean, neat) and their reality (tawdry, sordid, monolithic) is huge. Were Sant' Elia's drawings intended as projects for sci-fi film sets one might marvel at them, as it is one can only despair and rue the day that his example was followed by Le Corbusier.

Though Le Corbusier's exercises in planning on a large scale were fairly few his pronouncements on the subject were many and influential. During those periods when he had no architectural commission he frequently turned his hand to the design of an ideal city; ideal for whom? Well, that's a question for another day. All of his plans from the 20s to the 60s are in some degree totalitarian; they adhere to grids and mix terraces with tower blocks. They aim to 'liberate space', are mainly rectilinear and are unwittingly programmed for the creation of ghettoes. Quite who is to be the recipient of the space liberated by piling people on top of each other and by standing blocks on stilts is never made clear. The creation of large areas of undefined space, neither wholly public nor private, is one of the most regrettable legacies of modern planning; boxes on the ground may be nothing but boxes but they are at least on the ground and the space around them is, in planning cant, 'defensible'. And the green spaces between blocks do not stay green for very long if no one has an interest in keeping them so. In a way there is nothing strategically innovatory about Le Corbusier's ideal cities—industry, culture, commerce, managers, workers are each given their place. What is novel is the sort of density that the place would be required to achieve, the multilevel transport systems which separate pedestrian and vehicular uses, and the rigorousness that its inhabitants would have to adopt in day to day life. (It is hardly surprising that monasteries, with their ordered and harmonious ways of life, exerted such an appeal over him.)

Inhuman Scale

It is a common enough jibe that photos of modern buildings can be printed upside down and no one but the architect can spot the mistake. The sort of abstraction that has rendered architecture so meagre has had a similar effect on planning. Rectilinear homogeneity of the kind that Le Corbusier advocated and his disciples put into practice has a severely disorienting influence on those whose lives are led amidst it; the sort of *props*—the fortuitous irregularities—that occur in places which have grown up gradually are not to be found. Allied with an inhuman scale and an absence of ornament and a plethora of spaces, which, far from being functional seem to cry out to be granted some use, it is difficult to imagine what can be done with the urban creations of the third quarter of the 20th century save

Above: A widespread reaction to the totalitarian planning of the Modern Movement has manifested itself in deliberately quaint and self-consciously folkloric developments such as Port Grimaud, a town in the south of France.

destory them. By the time such places as Brasilia and Toulouse le Mirail were built in the 50s and 60s the cult of the new had reached such heights that streets, squares, gardens and so on had been eliminated in favour of spaces whose purpose might be anything or nothing. The featureless, pointless, concrete plaza, the concrete ramp, the concrete stairway leading from one void to another, and above all the destruction of the street — these are among the more obvious mistakes made in the recent past. It is all very well for architectural journals to dignify high rise slums with epithets like 'vertical streets', but it does not mitigate their ghastliness. It is interesting that the only people who seem capable of enduring life in Le Corbusier's overblown folly L'Unite d'Habitation at Marseilles are architects, sociologists and such people who find themselves able to appreciate what the man was trying to do. Just as there has been in the recent past a reaction against the architecture of grandiosity (at least when applied domestically) so has there been a violent about turn in the direction of cosiness and homeliness. Such diverse developments as Port Grimaud, a holiday town in the south of France, and South Woodham Ferrers to the east of London are, if you like, Disney villages. They are 'inauthentic', illusory, fake and so on — but they do at least achieve a 'sense of place' and they do have irregularities, even if they are built in. What is abundantly clear is that architects and planners are at last having to swallow their pride and actually pay attention not to that convenient abstraction 'the people', but to people. They are also having to come to term with a rather uncomfortable truth, ie that the most successful domestic building of the past 30 years has been that of speculative operators who rarely use architects and stick to traditional methods unendorsed by theory.

Below: The LCC's Alton Estate in southwest London was one of many created in the utopian wake of Corbusier's Unité.

While an impressive work of sculpture it has proved socially questionable as an environment conducive to a happy existence.

Below: The era of the high-rise apartment block came to an abrupt end with the growing realization that they tend to create more problems and even misery than they were put there to solve.

'Liberated' spaces for vandalism or piles of untended rubbish to collect in

Dampness in ceilings and walls

Loose concrete panels

Constant lift failures

Faulty wiring

Great American Houses
The Architect as Artist

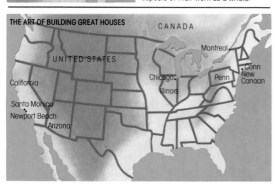

PENNSYLVANIA

Falling Water
.Bear Run
.Pittsburgh Philadelphia.
Scottdale.

UNITED STATES

Architectural Significance:
The demand for distinctive, custom designed houses in North America has provided 20th century architects with a steady source of commission and the opportunity to experiment with different stylistic or technological approaches to making good buildings. Frank Lloyd Wright is undoubtably the greatest architect America has yet produced. His 'prairie houses' are the finest products of the first part of his career. Other great architects of America all built houses that represent vital aspects of their work as a whole.

THE ART OF BUILDING GREAT HOUSES

CANADA

UNITED STATES

Montreal.

Conn
New
Canaan

Chicago.

Penn

California

Illinois

Santa Monica
Newport Beach
Arizona

Earth, fire, water are the most potent symbols of life on this planet: the greatest of American architects, Frank Lloyd Wright, sought to make them the critical elements of his designs. 'Falling Water', his most evocative creation, represents the supreme example of this symbolic content. At the very heart of this spectacular vacation home is the fireplace, kindled upon a great slab of naked rock that juts out of the floor of the living room, which is itself built over a waterfall. All rooms or spaces radiate from this hearth — it is the focus of family life.

'Falling Water' is an entirely 20th century work of architecture: only reinforced concrete could create such dramatic cantilevered balconies that seem to simply hover above the ground. So perfect is the marriage of the sculptural volumes of the house to the spectacular landscape around it that the house evokes an impression of having been

Stylistic Essentials:
Wright's early houses are characterized by their long, low horizontal lines. Wright believed that the horizontal was more sympathetic to the landscape than the vertical. Also typical was his interest in the total integration of inside and outside space. Many of Wright's house designs included built-in furniture and fittings, as well as under-floor radiant heating, features very advanced for their time.

Primary Building Materials:
American houses have been built out of every conceivable material, even discarded beer cans or canvas and bamboo. Wright's early houses used brick, stone and concrete as the main materials. The frank expression of the militant qualities of these materials is a key element in his architecture.

there forever. Yet 'Falling Water' is no temple, despite the magnificence of its conception. Inside there is an air of spacious, relaxed comfort, eminently suitable for its purpose as a weekend retreat. It is also a symbol of the relaxed confidence of the newly rich capitalists of the 30s.

The ever-increasing affluence and wide open spaces of the United States provided American architects with some wonderful opportunities for house design. In contrast to European domestic architecture, the house in America is frequently a vehicle for expressing either the owner's or the designer's individuality. Where European society hides behind the rigid conformity and repetition of Georgian or classical architec-ture, the Americans uninhibitedly demonstrate their lifestyles and their fantasies—thus the dream houses of Hollywood and the hippy dugouts of Vermont, the mansions of midwest magnates and the mobile homes of the lower middle classes. The design of private houses provides an interesting way of comparing the work of different American architects, for their plans reveal their particular preoccupations, obsessions and idiosyncracies.

Often, house design has provided the main source of work while an architect establishes himself. Frank Lloyd Wright, Richard Neutra and Bruce Goff all inaugurated their solo careers with private house-design commissions. Wright produced designs for the new self-made industrialists in Chicago, men who were determined to make their mark in mid-west society. Indeed, owning a spectacular house custom-designed by a famous or near-famous architect was one way of achieving this. Philip Johnson and Mies Van der Rohe, on the other hand, used house design as a way of illustrating abstract architectural concepts: the 'Glass House' and the 'Farnsworth House' are academic exercises in theoretical architectural analysis.

Charles Eames used his house to demonstrate some of the possibilities of industrial culture: his design is entirely made up from standard parts available 'off the shelf' from manufacturers' catalogues. Buckminster Fuller's 'Dymaxion' illustrate his preoccupation with prefabrication and mass production technology.

The dwelling house is the most fundamental of architectural types, yet it was not until the 20th century that wealth and affluence were sufficiently widely distributed to enable those other than the ruling elite to build structures that are appreciably more than crude shelters. 'Falling Water' is both a spectacular sculpture and a comfortable home: its generous organic beauty is indicative of the 'good life' that is within the reach of most Americans.

Frantic Beginnings

In the 19th century, the invention of machine-made nails radically affected the evolution of American domestic architecture. Before 1800, wrought-iron nails were largely hand-made, and their cost was sufficient to keep the time-honoured wood jointing skills of the carpenter economic. With the arrival of machines that could stamp out 60,000 tacks a day, however, it soon became far cheaper to nail a joint than to carve a mortice and tenon: banging in a nail was quicker, and it needed less skilled labour.

'Balloon frame' construction was a system which relied entirely on nailed joints and standard sized timber members, mass-produced in mechanized sawmills. A light framework of thin timber verticals or 'studs' nailed to horizontal 'plates' created a light-weight skeleton, which was clad and held rigid with nailed timber boarding. This kind of house-building was entirely American, and it enabled the great cities of the West and Midwest to grow at a frantic pace during the latter half of the 19th century, when the industrialization of America was drawing people away from the land and into the cities.

Architecturally, the 'balloon frame' allowed a new lightness and airiness in domestic styles. Combined with a fashionable interest in Japanese wooden architecture, and the influence of contemporary English rural romanticism, the balloon frame helped to give birth to a new domestic architecture, unostentatious yet quietly luxurious and, above all, comfortable. These houses broke away from the box-like tyranny of American Georgian; living spaces were opened up to flow naturally into each other, and the use of porches, loggias, verandahs or lean-to extensions articulated

Below: The Robie House, a dramatic example of Wright's preoccupation with the horizontal. The roof, walls and floors extend into the garden, thus creating a unified ensemble of spaces.

the exterior and helped marry the building to its landscape.

As the story of the skyscraper starts with the first iron frame buildings in New York and Chicago, so may the inspiration for the first great houses of 20th-century America be traced to those 'shingle' style houses of the 1870s and '80s. The 'Gamble' and 'Blacker' houses designed by the brothers Charles and Henry Greene provide an early example: built in 1907-8, they draw on 'japonaiserie', American Indian and colonial vernacular, interpreted in a fresh and lively manner for their wealthy Californian clients, with careful, elegant timber detailing and wonderfully contrived landscape settings.

The People's Architect

It was in the first decade of the 20th century that the giant of American architecture, Frank

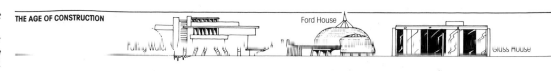

THE AGE OF CONSTRUCTION

Falling Water   Ford House   Glass House

1920   1930   1940   1950   1960

Lloyd Wright, first made his mark. With a series of houses for clients in the suburbs of Chicago he brought the late 19th century timber 'shingle' style into the 20th century.

Wright started his long extraordinary career as an engineering graduate in Chicago, joining the architectural practice of Adler and Sullivan in 1887, and rising to become chief draughtsman within three years. Refusing to go and study academic architectural history at the Ecole des Beaux Arts, Paris, he set up shop instead on his own in 1893, after

being carpeted by Sullivan for secretly designing houses for private clients in his spare time.

Working on his own, and with a large family to support, Wright was often obliged to take commissions he might have preferred to refuse. This was especially true where the client insisted on a 'traditional' design. But when allowed the freedom to do so, Wright began to evolve his own unmistakable architectural signature.

Increasingly, horizontal began to replace vertical as the primary directional emphasis. It seemed to Wright that a horizontal line was more organic—it hugged the ground and was more sympathetic to the landscape, in contrast to the artificial verticality of classical architecture. He was searching for a closer relationship between outdoor and indoor space, and between built form and the ground upon which it stands. He desired interior spaces to flow naturally from room to room; in fact he wanted almost to abolish the very idea of rooms as compartmentalized boxes connected by corridors.

As Wright himself later said: 'I see this extended horizontal line

as the true earthline of human life, indicative of freedom.' This is, essentially, an American theme, an expression of the wide open spaces and epic landscape of the New World. The houses he designed in the first decade of the 20th century are known as the 'prairie' houses, the name referring to the vast grain belt of central North America. Even though many of these houses were built in restricted urban sites, Wright managed to contrive a feeling of open landscape by the clever use of tree planting, landscape modelling and extending interior walls into the garden.

Daring Innovation

The most famous of the prairie houses is the 'Robie' house, built in 1909 for a progressive client willing to give Wright a free hand. It seems to grow from the ground, almost as though it were an outcrop of horizontal rock strata. Hovering above is a slab-like roof, projecting far beyond the actual walls that support it. At the very centre of the house is the fireplace, the core from which all spaces radiate outwards, extending even into the garden

Left: The impact of Japanese architectural influence on American building styles is strongly evident in the Blacker House, built in the first decade of the 20th century by C. and H. Greene.

Below: A 'poem in glass and steel' was how the Farnsworth House was described. Typical of the work of Mies van der Rohe, Farnsworth is a perfect work of skilfully contrived simplicity.

by projecting terraces. The main rooms lead into each other in a series of special surprises; light appears from unexpected sources; ceilings are alternately high or low, and everywhere there is the frank expression of the natural qualities of the materials—fine brickwork, rough stone and polished wood.

The Robie house, and other prairie houses such as the Martin House or the Willits House, contain all the elements of the modern American house. They are remarkable for the inventive spirit and daring innovation of the master who designed them—the first integral garage and the first 'car port'; the first 'utility core'; the use of radiant floor heating; built-in furniture, 'storage walls', tables and lighting. Many of these features are so commonplace today, and the low land-hugging lines of the prairie house style have been so plagiarized, that it is hard to comprehend how outrageously 'modern' the houses were when they were built.

The designs were publicized in Europe, where they were received enthusiastically by an emerging avant-garde, pioneers of what later came to be known as the International Style. These houses alone would have been enough to establish Wright as a major force in American architecture. As it turned out, they were but the first phase of a highly eventful career that spanned nearly a century, and was to involve cycles of disaster, debt, despair and bad publicity alternating with adulation, extravagant spending and a dangerous reputation for arrogant wit. Single-handed, he had created his own philosophy and a style to go with it.

Wright fought off bankruptcy, personal tragedy and the Depression (a hard time for all architects), resurfacing in 1936 with the two most famous designs of his career: 'Falling Water' (a house at Bear Run, Pennsylvania) and the Johnson Wax building at Racine, Wisconsin. Falling Water is undeniably Wright's most spectacular house and, not surprisingly, his most famous. The client was Edgar J. Kaufman, a wealthy department store executive who wanted a house that would give him a view of the waterfall. Wright built it over the rushing water, forcing the owner to move outside to view the falls (the idea being that he would never tire of it that way).

The key to the design is a central stone and concrete core

Above: The Lovell House, designed by Richard Neutra in the 1920s. It was this house that was responsible for bringing to America the sharp, unpretentious lines of the European 'International Style'.

which supports a series of 'shelves' jutting out of the naked rock. These balconies seem to float above the tumbling waterfall; in fact their weight is counterbalanced by the solid stone core on the upper part of the slope. Masonry materials are used throughout, rough-hewn stone contrasting with smooth cast concrete. The composition is timeless, for the building seems to entirely belong to its dramatic site.

'Less is More'

The Farnsworth House is the very opposite of 'Falling Water': it is a steel and glass box whose only relationship to the site in which it stands is via the 12 thin white steel columns that hold it above the ground. This house took the German-born architect Mies van der Rohe five years to design and build; it was finished in 1950. He had arrived in America in 1938 from Hitler's Germany,

Above: A rear view of Goff's Ford House. Goff's work has often been described as being strikingly individualistic, intriguing and even witty. The Ford House was designed and built in 1949.

having closed down the famous German school of architecture, the Bauhaus, of which he was the last director. In America his search for a universal architecture—cool, precise and devoid of emotional content—was rewarded by the unlimited space and technology of the New World.

The Farnsworth House makes not a single concession to the romantic conception of domestic bliss, the picturesque comfort of the American homestead or weekend cottage. It is a 'study in the relationship between supporting and supported elements', a poem of glass and steel with the economy of a Japanese haiku, and a perfect illustration of the architect's famous dictum: 'Less is more'.

The floor of the house is made of polished Italian travertine, supported on a steel deck. The all-glass perimeter wall is lined with raw silk curtains, enclosing a rectangular space that is really

one room, with a 'service core' in the middle. The dwelling is thus reduced to the most naked realization of shelter and services, a roof and running water. The Farnsworth House was an architectural legend before it was built, but is in reality a beautiful art object, not a container for human habitation.

Immigrants and Natives

Richard Neutra was an Austrian-born architect who emigrated to America in 1923, having trained and worked with several key personnel of the 'modern movement' in Europe—in particular with Adolph Loos, Otto Wagner and Eric Mendelsohn. Attracted at an early age by the dynamism

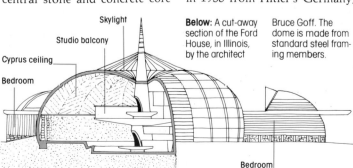

Skylight

Studio balcony

Cyprus ceiling

Bedroom

Below: A cut-away section of the Ford House, in Illinois, by the architect Bruce Goff. The dome is made from standard steel framing members.

Bedroom

Left: The Eames House in Santa Monica, was built by the architect philosopher Charles Eames to demonstrate what can be achieved when 'off the shelf' components are used.

Above: The Glass House a country retreat in New Canaan, Connecticut built by the architect, Philip Johnson for himself. It is the ultimate 'box', a skillfully designed container

Arc de Triumph

Ford House by Bruce Goff

Above: Modern US domestic (residential) architecture has tended to concentrate on the horizontal effect.

and high technology of the New World, he began work as a draughtsman in a huge office of over 1,000 designers, building factories. Having met Wright at Sullivan's funeral, he moved to California and joined up with another Austrian emigre, Rudolph Schindler. These two architects brought the European 'International Style' to California.

Neutra's houses are characterized by his rigorous and analytical attitude to technology, extracting the most from new materials and construction techniques without allowing them to take control of the design process or philosophy. His house of 1929 for Dr Lovell, perched on the side of a deep ravine in Griffith Park, Los Angeles, was one of his earliest and most famous commissions. The open steel skeleton frame was prefabricated in sections and assembled on site in less than 40 hours. Walls were poured from concrete pumped through flexible hoses. Despite this machine age construction, the house itself is married elegantly to the natural landscape around it.

Bruce Goff is a fierce individualist, and as such has been called the most American of U.S. architects. Almost entirely self-taught, his first loyalty has been to his clients, for whom he has created a series of romantic architectural extravaganzas which have disgusted academic critics as much as they have delighted the public at large. Born in 1904, Goff was an early admirer of Frank Lloyd Wright, and his first works showed this influence. Like Wright he searched for an organic architecture, but his sense of ornament and colour, combined with his witty use of 'found' materials, has produced a unique style.

Philip Johnson's Glass House at New Canaan, Connecticut, is his best-known building. Johnson studied classics at Harvard, developing an academic interest in modern architecture during his mid-twenties. He later studied architecture at Harvard under Marcel Breuer, but his most telling influence was Mies van der Rohe, whom he first met in 1930 when he was 24. The Glass House is a steel frame box, punctuated only by a brick cylinder that contains a leather-lined bathroom. Johnson himself has chronicled the sources of his inspiration, chief of which is Mies van der Rohe himself.

Cult of the New
Gimmickry and Waste

Architectural Importance:
Hard learned lesson that social engineering is not the job of architects, whose public reputation sank as a result of the large and featureless schemes they designed to replace traditional cities and houses. Considerable opposition to all new architecture resulted and eventually many architects succumbed and went back to building modest schemes which while not particularly architecturally notable are also not unpopular. This was a magnificent triumph indeed.

In 1966 Le Corbusier died. That year the last school of architecture in the world to oblige its students to be instructed in the classical orders ceased to do so. Whether or not Le Corbusier would have regarded this as a triumph is moot, for he must have realized that reaction to that which is taught is at least as liable to form the student as is acceptance of it. (That, anyway, is conventional wisdom whose application here is questionable.) Architects of that generation which effectively 'invented' modernism had mostly been trained in the Beaux Arts tradition, traces of which they kicked over with outsize boots. Those who came after had been reared on the new dogmas and were thus ill-equipped to do anything but follow them — modernism was the norm to the young men who got the chance to undertake the reconstruction of Europe after the war. Unlike their elders they did not have the zeal of the convert,

Below: The Pompidou Centre for Art and Culture in Paris has excited more controversy since its inception in 1972 than probably any other building in modern times. Part of the reason lies in Piano and Rogers' decision to 'turn the building's service systems inside out'. The result: oil refinery, or glass palace.

Stylistic Essentials:
A reaction against the purity of early modernism brought a variety of quasi-decorative styles which relied on abstraction. There were also crazes for board marked con-crete, tinted glass, and any new material that might come to hand. Rectil-inearity was a norm for most of this period and so was the insistent use of the repetition of motifs.

Primary Building Materials:
Prefabricated, 'systems' building employed synthetic materials. Concrete was predominant for part of the period, as was steel and glass for another. Increas-ingly clever engineer-ing enabled archi-tects to hang the floors of a building from the top and perform other inter-esting structural tricks. During the 70s there was a return to traditional skills.

Spread of Influence:
The international style is just that – international. Al-though it is now out of favour in many western countries it is doing well in the Arab states.

they simply knew nothing else; committed to the ideal of the new they fashioned an architecture in which it was against the rules to refer, save in the most oblique way, to even the recent past. The worship of novelty fostered an architecture which is crass and ugly, which has proved socially unsuccessful, which has been extremely expensive in financial terms; indeed one might opine that the best thing about many modern buildings is that they are unlikely to enjoy a long life and will, with good fortune, be re-placed by something a great deal more congenial. *pleasant*

This commitment to novelty displayed itself in the enthusiastic employment of untried methods of construction, untried materials, untried programmes of housing and planning. And of course the desperate efforts to be different founded on a thoroughly in-adequate body of knowledge re-sulted in more and more of the same. The simple fact is that modernism is a cul de sac, though those who found themselves trapped there were oddly unwil-ling to admit this truism and, instead of turning about, persisted in chipping away at the blank impasse before them. To that curious figure of fiction 'the com-mon man' this was clear from the beginning; it took most members of the architectural profession

nearly a quarter of a century to discover that they were regarded by their fellow men with some-thing less than approbation and during this period (from the end of the war till the early 70s) cities the world over were irreparably damaged by the apparently anomalous conjunction of big business, profligate local govern-ment and architects whose words were more persuasive than their deeds.

A meagre and vague idea that has had some currency during the recent past should be recalled here. It is that 'architecture is a reflection of society' or that 'society gets the architecture it deserves'. Now the lie is surely given to it by the fact that all societies— the newly industralized, the totalitarian, the 'third world' countries, the once mighty, the still rich, and the impoverished— had foisted upon them the same architecture; 'society' in this context means anyway a great collective pudding, and is a fiction that happily ignores the individual. Buildings are a part of the world, not a mirror to it. This notion has been propagated as a sort of excuse: thus, it is not architects and their clients who are culpable but all of us. Not good enough; in this century as in all others build-ings are indicative of nothing but the talent of their authors and, less apparently, the aspirations of those who have commissioned them. These aspirations have often been no nobler than to get the goods delivered quickly and cheaply—which must lift some of the blame from architects as must the fact that big corporations and big public bureaucracies tend

perhaps to be less fastidious and more easily pleased than the smaller private patrons of the past who would take an interest in the details of a design (often to the chagrin of the architect). But nothing said in mitigation will disguise the way that the inter-national profession, which was cockahoop and willing to take the credit when, just after the war, things were going well did a swift aboutturn when its more ambitious schemes were discovered to be faulty and passed the buck to cost-cutting patrons, dilatory builders and anyone else unfor-tunate enough to be involved.

Rejecting the Past

Of course, the unpopularity of contemporary architecture is not peculiar to the third quarter of the 20th century; the Victorians found much to loathe in what went up around them— the Eiffel Tower, for instance, was much derided; John Nash was reviled for years after his death (though as much for his dubious practices and connections with the Regent as for his architecture). What is remarkable about the opposition to new architecture during the past few years is its extent and its concert. These may be indicated by two rather different phenomena. Take the case of the very rich. Only in rare circumstances do they commission new houses from architects: they prefer the old. Of course, it may be argued that the

Below: The soulless, and crass qualities of modern architec-ture are splendidly illustrated by the Aylesbury Estate in south London. No previous society had housed its people in boxes quite so small.

Ronchamp
France

Marina City
USA

Expo Dome
Canada

Sydney Opera House
Australia

Pompidou Centre
France

| 1950 | 1955 | 1960 | 1965 | 1970 | 1975 | 1980 |

very rich of today may not have the gigantic private fortunes of their predecessors but they still have a great deal of wealth and their decisions are, one feels, aesthetically rather than economically determined.

Or take the case of the preservation lobby which has gone from strength to strength and has gained large popular support simply because new buildings are *feared* (better to retain the mediocre old than risk what an architect is going to dump on its site).

It took time for such hostility to reach the point where commerce and public authorities began to seek both economic justification for refurbishing existing buildings and architects who might attempt to design buildings that would not be abhorred by the public. But no one should believe for a moment that modernism is dead—a reaction to it is discernible everywhere but it is still thriving in a multitude of forms which, even the most torpid observer can see, are closely related to the stuff of the 20s and 30s.

The first decade after the war was characterized by the bigness of many of its schemes and by the beginning of the split of modernism into ever more strands, those which gained the widest acceptance were: a hard-edged rec-

tilinearity that derived from Mies van der Rohe and was exemplified in the work of the American firm of Skidmore, Owings and Merrill and the English firm of Gollins, Melvin, Ward. This kind of building is often to be found standing on stilts, is curtain walled in glass with 'aprons' of (usually) opaque

material and is often very high indeed. The design of such things makes them look as if they are inspired by cigarette packs or graph paper or perhaps even a conjunction of the two; it is a point of honour that their structures shall be apparent and the development of extra strong alloys

has meant that ever greater distances between vertical columns can be achieved, thus emphasizing their horizontality.

The Glasshouse

Owings and Merrill's Sears Tower in Chicago is currently the world's tallest building, though Colonel Richard Seifert has recently (1980) pulled out a really big one which he wants to erect at Liverpool and so take the record. It is perhaps curious that those who design such huge structures should pursue a policy of architectural minimalism and one of the most frequent and obviously justified criticisms of their work is that it is simply so boring, the same motifs being repeated over and again with no distraction or relief; moreover it is humorless, though it seems likely that these architects do not regard this as a shortcoming, doubtless preferring to consider themselves engineers rather than artists. This minimalism has been taken a stage further in recent years with the appearance of buildings which are clad in nothing but glass; increasingly the size of panels has grown while that of joints and armatures has decreased—no doubt the day will come when an entire façade is composed of a

Above: Le Corbusier's great gifts as a sculptor are nowhere more apparent than in his pilgrimage chapel at Ronchamp. It is the archetypal non-utilitarian building of the 20th century.

Below: A huge seabird, the hulls of countless sunken ships .... Jorn Utzon's Sydney Opera House, a metaphorical white elephant, has reminded observers of all these things.

Above: The Hayward Gallery in London is typical of the monumental lumpenness achieved by 'brutalist' architects who single-mindedly ruined decent, elegant cities the world over.

Right: Though size alone no longer dominates the thinking of modern architects, it still has an important bearing on decisions about the building's environmental impact.

Pompidou Centre

Arc de Triumph

Sydney Opera House

Left: Night view of the Willis, Faber, Dumas building in Ipswich, on England's east coast, fiercely criticized for having the sleekness of the all-glass tower without also its sense of scale.

single panel. Tinted glass, mirror glass and, of course, tinted-mirror glass has been extensively employed— that the tints have often been of truly hideous hues, that the mirrors often reflect nothing but further ghastly buildings should not concern us here. Mirror glass hides what it covers and so can give a façade a homogeneity (or blankness if you like) which has nothing to do with the revelation of structure; again, some of the more inventive instances of all-glass cladding have been buildings which are by no means rectilinear. During the 60s and 70s John Portman in the USA and Norman Foster in Britain were among the numerous architects whose ostentatious vitreous exercises drew attention to themselves with their curves and fancy. Portman's work in Texas and California is monumental; Foster's Willis, Faber, Dumas building in Ipswich, Suffolk is merely sleek, like a giant's patent leather pump. Its glass panels seem to be bandaged together and at night passersby can see into the building— akin, perhaps, to gaping at an X-ray. Foster's greasemonkey chic is also rather more brashly displayed by his sometime partner, Richard Rogers, whose Pompidou Centre in Paris (designed in conjunction with Renzo Piano) was the most publicized building of the 70s. The jejune idea here is that everything shall be turned inside out; 'services' are shown outside. The whole thing has the spurious frankness of 'open' government and to a great many people is also very ugly, a piece of oil refinery which could as well be seen at Rotterdam or Le Havre. It is, however, atypical of its decade which was more normally one of reaction to this sort of 'structural' building and the other postwar norm, 'the sculptural'.

When one talks about 'the sculptural' one is talking as much about aspiration as about achievement for the two great models for postwar architects were not easily matched: they were the 'functional', allegedly utilitarian buildings erected during the war (blockhouses everywhere, the Citadel in London) and the far more selfconscious work of Le Corbusier in Marseilles and at Ronchamp. The latter is a most bizarre and bulky chunk of sculpture and looks like nothing else on earth. Both these models evidently derived from one kind of early modernism, namely expressionism, which had rather gone underground after its First World War flowering; they also showed the influence of primitive art and megaliths. Le Corbusier was a *sculptor* of great talent, most of his disciples were not and their commonplace yen to recreate Stonehenge, whose aptness as a prototype for mass housing is questionable, was horribly wayward. Brutalism (a fittingly nasty word which comes from béton brut, ie untreated concrete) was more suited to institutional buildings but even here it makes for a disagreeable sort of environment— witness the 'kulchur' ghetto on the South Bank in London, an unhappy site that is a catalogue of postwar architectural styles. The National Theatre is generally accepted to be a ridiculous building; a huge lupus on the already pockmarked face of London. Even so, it is better than the Hayward Gallery next door. Still these places and similar ones the world over have been so derided that even architects have begun to suspect that they are perhaps not all they were cracked up to be, and no one any longer really takes seriously the pretentious drivel of the designers of such things who talk about the 'raw poetry of board marked concrete'. At least one hopes it is not taken seriously. An odd feature of much brutalist architecture— and indeed post-war architecture in general— is its naive 'democratization' of a building's parts; thus in, say, a theatre scenery docks are granted as much prominence as the auditorium— the traditional hierarchy is overturned to what seems absolutely no purpose.

The Art of Architecture

The striving for 'honesty' that has handicapped so many architects did not noticeably afflict those who revived expressionism in the late 50s. The 'ruthless expression of function' (to use a silly term of which architectural journalists are fond) has no part in this architecture which is concerned with dramatic effects and the engagement of those who use and look at it. To compare it with the Baroque is rash, maybe, but not altogether inapposite. In the

Ventilation units

Glazed exterior escalators

Air-conditioning ducts

Above: It has been suggested that it was Piano and Rogers' intention to create in the Pompidou Centre both a beautifully designed 'container' and a servicing mechanism. In essence, the Pompidou Centre has the characteristics of an industrial facility.

Museum areas

Left: This view is reinforced when we see a side elevation of the building.

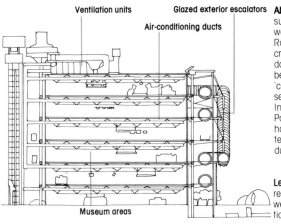

Above: The biggest and arguably the best building of the worldwide 'vernacular' revival of the 70s was Hillingdon Town Hall, built by Robert Matthews, Johnson Marshall partners.

work of such architects as Gottfried Bohm one discerns the same sort of ambition as in that of, say, Bernini; of course the means by which Bohm tricks and disconcerts his—for want of another word—audience are a world away from those of the Italian master. And even those who have gone so far as to borrow Baroque motifs do not use them in 'the old way'. Architectural expressionism is a case of art into life—numerous buildings of the 60s and 70s look as though they have been inspired by such films as Metropolis by Fritz Lang (who was himself an architect). It is rather ironic that these German silent films intended to show a nightmarish world—not perhaps the sort of thing that architects should be attempting to create. The most extreme form of expressionism is rather strangely named 'organic' and buildings of this kind, made with concrete sprayed onto a mesh, tend to recall slugs or monsters or conches—they are great fun and, understandably, pretty rare.

The reaction against modernism which has gained momentum over the past few years has such a complicated genealogy that it can only be faintly sketched here. The dream of internationalism having turned into something of a nightmare there has been a lot of rummaging by architects through the cupboard of their local pre-modern styles. Thus in America the shingle tradition has been hauled out and modified; in England the terrace and speculative builder's suburban villa have at long last been recognized as meritorious; in Catalonia a crop of Gaudiesque building has appeared. In England the new domestic architecture is often aggressively humble and is indicative of both a desire to please and to fit in; the label 'neo vernacular', ie neo indigenous, is hardly accurate for this architecture is not naturally dependent upon the combination of traditional crafts and local materials that characterize vernacular architecture. It is now becoming increasingly sophisticated and is being employed for uses other than domestic. For example, Hillingdon Civic Centre by Robert Matthew, Johnson-Marshall & Partners is situated in an area of London where the typical building is an interwars' semi-detached house; this building looks like the largest ever suburban villa with touches of Victorian detailing and good quality brickwork. Jeremy Dixon's houses in west London are colourful and neo Victorian; they are notable in that they exhibit blatant *façades*, something which is abhorrent to the modernist mentality.

In the USA the influential writer and less influential architect, Robert Venturi, has practised what he preaches, that architecture should not be simplistic and coherent but, rather, ambiguous and inconsistent. His buildings are predictably self-conscious and draw upon a variety of past styles, notably the well mannered and homely shingle style of the late 19th century; in his work and that of his followers all references are, so to speak, in quotes. Architecture is here played as a game of sorts, but it is a fairly healthy, outdoorsy game. Venturi's achievement has been to provoke his contemporaries and juniors to rid themselves of the modernist induced guilt which requires that the tenets of that 50 year old 'philosophy' still be followed. The new eclecticism is still in its infancy and may lead to another period of full blooded revivalism; there are certainly signs of this and two of the world's leading architects, James Stirling and Ricardo Bofill, are currently enjoying a prolonged flirtation with neo classicism. Bofill who works with a team of non architects began as a designer of Gaudiesque flats in Barcelona and is now building entire cities. His magnificent Monument to Catalonia on the border of Spain and France recalls of course the architecture of the Third Reich, which will surely be enough to condemn it in many eyes. However it is undeniably potent and has none of the preciosity of the work of many of today's architects whose efforts to recreate their art involves them in smug and knowing exercises. The best work of the last few years gives some encouragement for the future. There is some cause for concern still, notably in the area of commercial speculation where developer's 'rampant' has given way to developer's 'couchant', a slightly better mannered but no less hideous style than the glass, concrete and steel stuff of the 50s and 60s. But the fact that architects are no longer scared of ornament and that modern is now distinctly old fashioned indicates that all may not yet be lost.

Glossary

Abutment: The masonry slabs that support each side of an arch.

Acanthus: A plant whose leaves are used as an ornamental motif on Corinthian capitals.

Agora: A market place or space used for public meetings in ancient Greek cities.

Aisles: Longitudinal spaces on either side of the nave in a church.

Ambulatory: Aisle around the circumference of a circular building.

Apse: The semicircular or polygonal space at the far end of a church, usually behind the main altar.

Arcade: A series of arches (supported by columns) adjacent to a wall and often forming a covered walkway.

Arch: A curved structure that spans an opening.

Architrave: A moulded frame around a door or window. Also the beam which spans and is immediately above the columns of a Greek temple.

Arris: A sharp edge made by the junction between two surfaces; eg, the fluting of a Greek column.

Ashlar: Masonry walling constructed from smooth, square-cut stone laid in regular courses.

Atrium: The entrance hall or courtyard of a Roman house, often open to the sky in the centre. Also the forecourt of a Byzantine church.

Attic: In Renaissance architecture, the upper storey above the main cornice.

Bailey: A stockaded or walled enclosure surrounding a castle.

Balustrade: An ornamental handrail supported by pillars.

Barbican: Outer defence of a castle or city; in particular, a tower above a gate or drawbridge.

Basilica: A Roman hall used for legal and public meetings. The term is also used to describe early Christian churches that consisted of a high central nave with lower aisles on either side.

Battered Wall: An inward-sloping wall.

Bay: Division of a wall between pillars or buttresses; or compartments into which the nave of a church is divided.

Bouleuterion: A Greek senate house or a council meeting-room.

Brise Soleil: A perforated screen used as a sun shield.

Buttress: A projecting spur of masonry used to stiffen a wall or to resist the thrust of an arch.

Caldarium: Hot water room in a Roman bathhouse.

Campinale: A bell tower.

Cantilever: Part of a beam which projects beyond its support.

Capital: Decorative feature forming the uppermost part of a column or pilaster.

Caryatid: A sculpted female figure used as a support or pillar in Greek architecture.

Caravanserai: An inn or rest house on the main trade routes in the Middle East.

Cella: The inner room of a Greek temple.

Chancel: Part of a church reserved for the clergy, separated by a screen.

Chapterhouse: Meeting room for the officials of a monastery.

Chevet: The apse and its adjacent chapels at the east end of a church.

Choir: Part of the church where services are sung, usually the western end of the chancel.

Clerestory: Upper level of a building with windows looking out above adjacent roofs.

Cloisters: A courtyard surrounded by arcades, forming part of a monastery.

Coffers: Recessed panels formed in ceilings or vaults.

Colonnade: A series of columns.

Column: A vertical support or pillar, usually comprising a base, circular shaft and capital.

Composite: A Roman variation of the Corinthian and Ionic orders.

Concrete: A monolithic building material made from cement mixed with aggregate (crushed brick or stone, coarse sand or rubble).

Corbel: A carved block, projecting from a wall, that supports a beam.

Corinthian: One of the three Greek orders; characterized by a high base, fluted shaft and ornate capital with acanthus leaf ornament.

Cornice: A moulded projecting feature that forms the upper limit of a wall or entablature.

Crocket: In Gothic churches, a repetitive carved projection that decorates the edges of a spire.

Crossing: Point of intersection of the nave and transept of a church.

Cruck: A pair of timbers that forms an arch, creating the main structure of Medieval European houses.

Crypt: Basement of a church.

Cupola: A small dome.

Curtain Wall: The outer fortified wall of a castle. In modern architecture, a non-loadbearing outer cladding, often glass.

Dado: Lower portion of a wall, decorated with a different treatment.

Dome: A concave roof, usually hemispherical or elliptical.

Donjon: The innermost defence of a castle.

Doric: The simplest of the Greek orders, characterized by a stout fluted column without a base, and a capital consisting of a square slab above a plain circular moulding.

Dormer window: A small window projecting from a sloping roof.

Drum: Circular wall supporting a dome.

Eaves: The underside of an overhanging roof.

Engaged column: A column attached to a wall.

Entablature: The upper part of an architectural order, between the columns and the pediment, containing the architrave, frieze and cornice.

Entasis: The deliberate bulging of Greek column shafts to counteract optical illusions.

Façade: the front face or elevation of a building.

Faience: The glazed earthenware used for pottery or decorative tile work.

Fan vault: A variation of medieval rib vaulting in which the ribs 'fan out' from a series of single points.

Finial: The ornament at the very top of a pinnacle or other vertical feature.

Fluting: Shallow vertical channels on the shaft of a column.

Flying buttress: An arch springing across from a wall to a pier, to transfer the thrust of a vault.

Formwork: Temporary framework of wood to contain concrete in the required shape while it sets.

Forum: A central open space surrounded by public buildings in a Roman city.

Frieze: The middle section of an entablature between the architrave and the cornice.

Frigidarium: The cold water room at a Roman bathhouse.

Gable: A triangular-shaped wall enclosed by two sloping roofs.

Gallery: An upper floor with one side opening on to the main part of the building.

Groin: The curved line formed by the intersection of two vaults.

Hammerbeam roof: A Medieval method of timber roof construction that created wide spans without the need for beams across the full width.

Hypocaust: A system of ducts to distribute hot air from underground furnaces in Roman buildings.

Hypostyle: A hall in which the roof is supported only by columns, without vaults or domes.

Insular: A Roman apartment building.

Ionic: One of the Greek orders, characterized by a circular moulded base, a slim fluted shaft and a capital decorated with volutes.

Iwan: A vaulted hall with a large arched opening, a feature of Islamic architecture.

Keep: The inner tower of a castle.

Keystone: The central stone of an arch.

Lancet Arch: A tall pointed window in English Gothic architecture.

Lintel: A horizontal beam that spans an opening such as a door or window.

Loggia: A gallery behind an arcade or open colonnade.

Machicolation: An overhanging parapet with holes in the floor, allowing defenders to drop boiling oil, stones, etc, on to an enemy below.

Mastaba: An ancient Egyptian tomb, rectangulat and flat-topped.

Martyrium: A building erected to commemorate or contain the relics of a martyr.

Medrassa: An Islamic school of theology.

Megaron: The main hall of a Mycenaean palace.

Mezzanine: An intermediate level between ground and first storey.

Mihrab: A niche that faces Mecca—the focus of prayer—in the wall of a mosque.

Minaret: A tall tower, adjacent to a mosque, from which the Muezzin calls the faithful to prayer.

Mosaic: Surface decoration using small squares of glass, tile or stone set in concrete.

Mosque: Muslim place of worship.

Motte: Earth mound upon which a castle is built.

Mudejar: Term applied to Spanish architecture that blends Muslim and Christian styles.

Mullion: Vertical member dividing a window.

Naos: The sanctuary of a Greek temple.

Narthex: An arcaded porch or entrance hall to an early Christian basilican church.

Nave: The central space of a church, west of the crossing.

Necropolis: A burial ground or city of the dead.

Niche: A recess or hollow in a wall, often containing a statue.

Obelisk: A tall, square, tapering pillar with a pyramidical top.

Orders: The design systems of columns and entablature in classical architecture. The five main orders are Doric, Ionic, Corinthian (Greek), Tuscan and Composite (Roman).

Pagoda: Multi-storeyed pavilion in Chinese and Japanese architecture.

Pediment: A triangular wall or gable enclosed by moulded cornices, located above the entablature in classical architecture.

Pendentive: A concave, curved, triangular vault that enables a circular dome to sit upon a rectangular space below.

Piano nobile: The floor that contains the principal apartments of an Italian Renaissance palace, usually raised one floor above ground level.

Piazza: An open public square.

Pier: A massive masonry support for an arch.

Pilaster: A rectangular column attached to a wall.

Pillar: A detached upright support.

Pilotis: Pillars that raise a whole building above ground level.

Podium: A raised mound on which a building is constructed.

Portcullis: An iron grill or gate that is opened by raising vertically.

Portico: An entry porch or vestibule supported by columns.

Propylaeum: The entrance to a Greek religious enclosure.

Pylon: The monumental entrance to an Egyptian temple.

Qibla: The wall of a mosque, facing Mecca.

Rendering: Cement or plaster applied to an outside wall.

Rib: A projecting moulding that forms the boundary between different parts of a ceiling vault.

Ridge: The apex of a sloping or pitched roof.

Rose: A decorative circular window.

Rustication: The stonework with deeply recessed joints and roughened surface used in Renaissance architecture.

Sarcophagus: an ornate coffin.

Shaft: Part of a column between the base and the capital.

Span: Distance between the two supports of a beam, arch or roof.

Squinch arches: Arches built diagonally across the corner of a square hall to support an octagonal spire or dome.

Stucco: Plaster that is moulded to give low relief decoration.

Stupa: A Buddhist burial mound.

Stylobate: The stone platform on which a classical temple is built.

Tepidarium: Warm water room at a Roman bathhouse.

Terracotta: Unglazed, burned clay used for mouldings and decoration.

Tessara: Small cubes of glass or marble used in mosaic.

Thrust: The force exerted by beams against a wall, or the weight of an arch, vault or dome.

Trabeated: Buildings that are made entirely from pillars and horizontal beams.

Transept: The side projecting arms of a cruciform plan church.

Vault: An arched, curved ceiling of brick, stone or concrete.

Volute: A spiral scroll used in Ionic, Corinthian and Composite capitals.

Ziggurat: A pyramidical construction with stepped layers—a feature of ancient Mesopotamian architecture.

Index

Index

Index

Picture Credits

The publishers wish to thank the following photographers and organisations who have supplied photographs for this book. Photographs have been credited by page number and position on the page: B, bottom; C, centre; T, top; BL, bottom left, etc.

Jacket Front Flap: Salmer. Half-title page: Spectrum. Title page: Hornak. Credits and Contents page: Spectrum. Master Time Chart page: Spectrum. 8/9 Ronald Sheridan. 10 TL: Ronald Sheridan; C, B: Salamander/Guedes. 11 Salamander/Guedes. 12 Salamander/Guedes. 13 Salamander/Guedes. 14/15 Spectrum. 16 Ronald Sheridan. 17 Spectrum. 18 B. Peevor. 19 B. Peevor. 20/21 Spectrum. 22 Spectrum. 23 Berman. 24 BL: Spectrum; C: Ronald Sheridan. 25 Architectural Association. 26/27 Spectrum. 28 Zefa. 29 Zefa. 30 T: Spectrum; B: Angelo Hornak. 31 T: Spectrum; B: Angelo Hornak. 32/33 G. Cubitt. 34 G. Cubitt. 35 TL: MacQuitty; TR: G. Cubitt. 36 MacQuitty. 37 C: MacQuitty; B: Zefa. 38/39 Spectrum. 40/41 Spectrum. 41 C, B: Zefa. 42 T: MacQuitty; C: Fawcett. 43 MacQuitty. 44/45 Zefa. 46 Eric Crichton. 47 Eric Crichton. 48 C: Eric Crichton; B: John Woolverton. 49 BL: Zefa; BR: John Woolverton. 50/51 Ronald Sheridan. 52 Brattaner. 53 BL: Ronald Sheridan; BR: Elisabeth. 54 Spectrum. 55 T: Brattaner; B: Zefa. 56/57 Ronald Sheridan. 58 Ronald Sheridan. 59 Spectrum. 60 Ramsay. 61 T: John Woolverton; B: Zefa. 62/63 Spectrum. 64 Ronald Sheridan. 65 Ronald Sheridan. 66 Angelo Hornak. 67 T: Elisabeth; B: Ronald Sheridan. 68/69 Ronald Sheridan. 70 Spectrum. 71 Spectrum. 72 Brent Porter. 73 T: Ferguson; B: Turkish Ministry of Tourism. 74/75 Ronald Sheridan. 76 Spectrum. 77 C: Spectrum; CR: Ronald Sheridan. 78 Spectrum. 79 T: John Donat; BL, R: Spectrum. 80/81 Zefa. 82/83 Ferguson. 83 T: Spectrum; C: Zefa. 84 T: Ferguson; B: Spectrum. 85 T: Ferguson; B: Zefa.

86/87 Zefa. 88 Spectrum. 88/89 Zefa. 89 Elisabeth. 90 T: Douglas Dickens; B: Spectrum. 91 T: Spectrum; B: Ferguson. 92/93 Zefa. 94 Zefa. 95 Zefa. 96 T: Douglas Dickens; B: Zefa. 97 Douglas Dickens. 98/99 Scala. 100 Angelo Hornak. 101 Angelo Hornak. 102 Ferguson. 103 T: Lindstrum; C: Scala; B: Ferguson. 104/105 Ronald Sheridan. 106 Ronald Sheridan. 107 Michael Solant. 108 T: Brattaner; B: Ferguson. 109 T: Spectrum; B: Michael Solant. 110/111 Ramsay. 112 Spectrum. 113 Spectrum. 114 Michael Solant. 115 T: Lindstrum; BL: Ramsay; BR: Eric Crichton. 116/117 Spectrum. 118 Brattaner. 119 Jacobs. 120 TL: Jacobs; TR: Scala. 121 T: Ronald Sheridan; C: Jacobs. 122/123, Spectrum. 124 Spectrum. 125 T: Jacobs; C: Spectrum. 126 T: Ramsay; B: Ronald Sheridan. 127 Eric Crichton. 128/129 Spectrum. 130 Eric Crichton. 131 Ramsay. 132 TL: Lucinda Lambton; TR: Eric Crichton. 133 British Transport Film Library. 134/135 Angelo Hornak. 136 T: Douglas Dickens; C: Sturbridge. 137 Elisabeth. 138 Spectrum. 139 T: Douglas Dickens; B: Ferguson. 140/141 Ramsay. 142 Elisabeth. 143 Zefa. 144 Ramsay. 145 T: Lindstrum; B: Photo Library International. 146/147 Zefa. 148 Ramsay. 149 T: Lindstrum; B: Ramsay. 150 Ramsay. 151 TL: Ann Bolt; TR: Lindstrum. 152/153 Scala. 154 John Donat. 155 T: B. Hofmeester; B: Elisabeth. 156 C: Elisabeth; B: B. Hofmeester. 157 Ramsay. 158/159 Zefa. 160 L: Spectrum; T: Angelo Hornak. 161 Michael Solant. 162 C: Spectrum; B: Ferguson. 163 T: Angelo Hornak; B: Zefa. 164/165 Salmer. 166 Eric Crichton. 167 Angelo Hornak. 168 Angelo Hornak. 169 T: Elisabeth; B: Ramsay. 170/171 Spectrum. 172 Elisabeth. 173 Ramsay. 174 T: Zefa; B: Sheridan. 175 T: Spectrum; B: Clarke. 176/177 Western Pennsylvania Conservancy. 179 Hedrich Blessing. 178 Architectural Association. 180 Architectural Association. 181 Architectural Association and Philip Johnson. 182/183 Elisabeth. 184 Elisabeth. 185 T: Zefa; B: Eric Crichton. 186 John Donat; Willis; Dumas; Faber. 187 TL: Mark Holt; TR: Eric Crichton.